Praise for
Oil, Profits, and Peace

"Jill Shankleman asks whether oil and gas companies can, and should, do more to promote peace and mitigate conflict in the fragile countries where they operate. Her answer is an emphatic "Yes!" Intensely conscious of both the opportunities and the constraints that corporations face in difficult environments, she focuses on three case studies: Azerbaijan, Angola, and Sudan. The result is a balanced, comprehensive, and practical analysis that is thoroughly readable. Shankleman offers concrete recommendations encouraging companies to increase shareholder value while at the same time reducing conflict risk. A must-read for the governments of oil-producing countries, officials from donor countries and multilateral organizations, NGOs, students of conflict resolution, and, most of all, oil industry executives."

> —Pauline H. Baker, President, the Fund for Peace, and founder, the FFP Human Rights and Business Roundtable Fund for Peace

"Oil, Profits, and Peace is a masterly and accessible analysis of the rising social costs of oil production in emerging countries. This well-researched, appealingly written book points up the dangers posed by volatile oil prices, and the links between oil export and conflict. In a compassionate and sincere tone, Shankleman presents compelling suggestions to oil companies on how their activities can promote peace, even in difficult environments. This should be obligatory reading for anyone interested in the politics of oil and global development."

> —Toyin Falola, the Frances Higginbotham Nalle Centennial Professor and University Distinguished Teaching Professor, University of Texas at Austin, and coauthor of *The Politics of the Global Oil Industry*

"A superb nonideological, analytical primer on the oil industry, the 'resource curse,' and the efficacy of corporate social responsibility programs. Essential reading for corporate managers, NGO advocates, and serious students of oil and conflict."

> —David Goldwyn, President of Goldwyn International Strategies, LLC, and former Assistant Secretary, U.S. Department of Energy

"If you read only one book about the international oil industry, this should be it. This advice applies whether you work for an oil company, a government, an NGO, or the media, or are just a member of the general public interested in how the presence of oil companies affects the lives of people and nations. Shankleman's scope is vast, and the data she marshals daunting, but she imposes order effortlessly on what could so easily have been chaos, presenting her arguments and recommendations in lucid, easily read prose. Speaking from some thirty-eight years' exposure to the issues involved, I find her analysis scrupulously fair both to governments and to the oil industry, well founded on practical examples, and clear on the limits to responsibility and freedom of action. Her focus on revenue-associated issues and their potential solutions as the critical concern is wholly correct, yet she also emphasizes the other areas—especially responsible social impact management and employment creation—where more systematic and proactive oil company action than is currently the norm can improve things greatly. Here as in other areas, her suggestions for the path ahead are pragmatic in the extreme. As a long-term oilman, I would find it a matter for regret if Shankleman's book did not become required reading for the in-house courses run by oil companies for their graduate staffs, or if a well-thumbed copy did not have a place on the desk of every oil company executive."

    —Donal O'Neill, Resource Advisors Ltd., retired from Shell
    International, Exploration and Production

"Managing 'resource curse' and its elements of conflict is one of the greatest challenges facing future supplies to world oil markets. Shankleman's book is a balanced, intelligent, and innovative contribution to the growing debate on what the nature of that challenge is and how it might be managed by all players but especially the oil companies. It should be compulsory reading for all involved in investing in upstream oil."

    —Paul Stevens, Professor, the Centre for Energy, Petroleum and
    Mineral Law and Policy, University of Dundee, Scotland

Oil, Profits, and Peace

Does Business Have a Role in Peacemaking?

Jill Shankleman

UNITED STATES INSTITUTE OF PEACE PRESS
Washington, D.C.

The views expressed in this book are those of the author alone. They do not necessarily reflect views of the United States Institute of Peace.

UNITED STATES INSTITUTE OF PEACE
1200 17th Street NW, Suite 200
Washington, DC 20036-3011

First published 2006

Printed in the United States of America

The paper used in this publication meets the minimum requirements of American National Standards for Information Science—Permanence of Paper for Printed Library Materials, ANSI Z39.48-1984.

Library of Congress Cataloging-in-Publication Data

Oil, profits, and peace: does business have a role in peacemaking? / Jill Shankleman.
   p. cm
  Includes bibliographical references and index.
  ISBN-13: 978-1-929223-98-5 (pbk. : alk. paper)
  ISBN-10: 1-929223-98-6 (pbk. : alk. paper)
  ISBN-13: 978-1-929223-99-2 (hardcover : alk. paper)
  ISBN-10: 1-929223-99-4 (hardcover : alk. paper)
  1. Petroleum industry and trade. 2. Petroleum industry and trade—Angola. 3. Petroleum industry and trade—Azerbaijan. 4. Petroleum industry and trade—Sudan. 5. War—Economic aspects. I. Title.
  HD9560.5.S438 2006
  338.2'7282—dc22
                  2006024309

To Hannah and Josh, and other family members and friends, with thanks for putting up with all those dinnertime talks about oil wealth and pipelines.

Contents

Foreword

ENERGY SECURITY—RELIABLE SUPPLY AT REASONABLE COST—has become the subject of front pages and summit meetings. But *governance* of the energy sector, though central to the issue, is not nearly so well understood, and all too often ignored. To understand it, we must decouple the physical exploration, development, production, transportation, and consumption of oil and gas from the funds that these activities generate.

The physical functions are largely technical, and best practices and state-of-the-art technology are well known and recognized. The revenues generated from oil and gas, however, are a different matter altogether. Most of these moneys are controlled by despotic governments accountable to no one but themselves. The fiscal management process is opaque by design, and the result, almost always, is massive corruption.

Oil and gas are exceptional natural resources, controlled by the state and overshadowing all other potential sources of revenue. Very few oil- and gas-producing states have strong institutions of government based on rule of law, transparency, and accountability. Most are in the Middle East, Africa, Latin America, and the former Soviet Union, where democracy and civil society are still only remote concepts, much less functioning institutions.

Oil and gas activities are capital intensive, not labor intensive, requiring huge sums of money based on little labor; thus, only a small number of workers must be paid. Moreover, much of the critical labor is provided by the international oil service companies themselves, using professionals paid by arm's-length contact at established market rates. In general, then, oil production brings scant employment opportunities to local populations.

Since funds from oil and gas investment production dwarf all other government receipts combined, control of those funds becomes an enormous potential prize. It represents control of the government itself. With large oil receipts, the government doesn't need tax revenues. Unfortunately, with no need for taxes, the government has no need to seek the people's permission to levy them. Thus, the people have no leverage for holding officials accountable, and consent of the governed goes out the window.

Corruption and despotism are the predictable results of oil and gas production in all but a few places. High oil prices simply lead to greater misrule, since governments that have more money to steal or squander will cling to power ever more desperately.

Given the current high prices and correspondingly huge revenues, the citizens of oil-producing countries are furious that they have received no benefits from their corrupt governments. And their governments, rather than share the benefits, either repress opposition and disrupt or fix elections, or blame others—often the developed world—for the suffering and indignity wrought by their own greed and incompetence. Because rulers of oil-producing countries will do anything to hold on to power, which equals wealth, their decisions are calculated to centralize power, not diffuse it. Large, inefficient government-controlled enterprises are encouraged, since they provide money and jobs to friends, while small businesses are discouraged because, living by market rules, they challenge the state.

Patronage and corruption, by definition, lead to bad political and economic decisions. One area of massive corruption in the energy sector is the fees and kickbacks surrounding the investments necessary to generate further revenues. Huge bribes are paid to government officials in exchange for inflated contracts in large projects. Platforms, pipelines, refineries, tankers, and other infrastructure investments cost billions, and officials at all levels take their cut.

The result is inefficient, undemocratic governments, which are inherently unstable, controlling the essential commodity of the international economy: energy. And yet, the options for externally imposed reform are seriously limited, since control of natural resources is fundamental to national sovereignty; that is, the oil and gas lying beneath the land belong to that nation alone, as does the money generated by those resources.

The leading international oil companies (IOCs) are frequently and wrongly blamed for this disastrous situation. Their job, as they see it, is to produce efficiently the oil and gas owned by the host countries, and to pay taxes, bonuses, and royalties consistent with their contractual requirements. All the large IOCs are barred by law from paying bribes, and they have enormous reputational risk as well. The populations of energy-producing countries are deeply frustrated and look to the IOCs to meet their aspirations for civil society, sustainable growth, and a clean environment—considerations typically ignored by their own governments. Although IOCs are making efforts to correct these ills through corporate social responsibility, the solution to many of these issues lies beyond both the resources and the responsibilities of the companies.

An added obstacle to corporate social responsibility is the arrival of new IOCs from emerging countries, competing directly with established IOCs. These companies will not scruple to pay bribes and have little interest in international public opinion or corporate responsibility. Free of the constraints governing the established IOCs, they can do great harm.

To the extent that an answer to this destructive situation exists, it lies in transparency. Precisely who is stealing the money or taking the bribes? Where is the money being banked? The World Bank and the International Monetary Fund are pushing for transparency, as are the established oil companies, though their efforts are hindered at every turn by the laws and traditions in many of the producing countries, where stealing money and receiving bribes may not even be illegal.

That said, even in the most blatantly corrupt countries, misappropriation of funds is deeply embarrassing and can threaten the legitimacy of the government, and corruption identified can bring down some of the worst governments. A key to promoting transparency rests with the international banking community, which has been woefully lax about accepting corrupt funds, and diligent in keeping the sources of those funds quiet.

Governance of the petroleum sector is a vital and pressing international problem that must be confronted at the highest levels of authority, and now rather than later. The reasons for this urgency are twofold: one humanitarian, the other pragmatic. Millions of people suffer needlessly under corrupt, unstable governments, while the lifeblood of the world economy, petroleum, is being grossly mismanaged by those in power—a situation that is both untenable and unacceptable in political, economic, and moral terms.

In her timely and perceptive book *Oil, Profits, and Peace,* Jill Shankleman explores in detail how the oil companies can be agents of change in alleviating the "curse of oil," and the limits to their ability to exert influence over the governments that own oil resources. Faced with activist demands for reform and the escalating costs of conflict in oil-producing countries, the industry is now paying more than lip service to the notion of corporate social responsibility, because concern for the people living in production areas, and for where the oil revenues go, is making better business sense than ever before.

Shankleman, a veteran consultant to oil companies, governments, and nongovernmental organizations (NGOs), presents an evenhanded, insightful picture of the incentives and impediments that Western oil companies encounter in the effort to lessen or even prevent conflict in the host countries where they operate. In exploring and analyzing the links between oil and conflict, and the rapidly evolving field of corporate social responsibility, she focuses on Azerbaijan, Angola, and Sudan, three countries whose experiences with conflict and the oil industry vary widely. Shankleman's conclusions and recommendations for industry and government policymakers are uniquely tailored to each situation, and yet they resonate with wider implications for anyone involved in the many political and social issues facing oil-producing countries worldwide. Increasingly, companies are taking the route of enlightened self-interest, seeking collaboration with governments and NGOs to increase transparency, improve local livelihoods, and create a new paradigm for the pursuit of both profits and peace. The strategies discussed in this important book will prove indispensable in bringing this about.

J. Robinson West, Chairman of the Board
United States Institute of Peace

Acknowledgments

WOULD LIKE TO EXPRESS MY GRATITUDE to the United States Institute of Pcace for the wonderful opportunity provided by the Jennings Randolph Fellowship Program, for the support, encouragement, and stimulation provided by the institute's staff, and for its excellent library services. I would also like to thank Hugh Attwater, Ginny Bouvier, Michael Carr, Harriet Hentges, Nigel Quinney, Rachel Siddy, Robin West, and the anonymous reviewers for contributing in no small measure to the insights, arguments, and structure of this book. I take sole responsibility for its weaknesses.

Oil, Profits, and Peace

1

Introduction

THE PRESENCE OF OIL RESOURCES IN DEVELOPING COUNTRIES presents a huge paradox. On the one hand, oil and gas discoveries make the eradication of poverty and the development of strong economies a possibility. This is what happened, for example, in Texas and Alaska in the nineteenth and mid-twentieth centuries. More recently, in 2004, then Prime Minister Mari Alkatiri of East Timor declared that oil discoveries in the Timor Gap could provide "the money to immunize and educate every child"[1] in his country, one of the world's newest and poorest states. Angola, too, sees its burgeoning oil industry as a means of escaping poor economic conditions. Forecast government earnings from oil exports alone will average between $350 and $700 per capita per year between 2002 and 2019. This compares with Angola's entire per capita gross national income of just over $1,000 in 2004.[2]

On the other hand, the "curse of oil" is evident in many oil-rich countries worldwide, with oil-producing states showing a high incidence of corruption and violent conflict, and low scores in education and health services and economic strength. Countries with petroleum resources made up over a quarter of the seventy poor countries potentially eligible for aid under the U.S.-sponsored Millennium Challenge Account (MCA) launched in 2004, but only two (Bolivia and East Timor) were among the twenty-three countries that gained eligibility in

2005 by meeting the required criteria: "ruling justly," promoting "economic freedom," and "investing in people."[3] And whereas oil might be expected to provide the economic means for preventing or resolving conflict or for rebuilding countries that have suffered civil war, the reality is that countries with oil and gas resources, much like those producing diamonds or narcotics, are among the world's most persistent trouble spots. Of the seventy-four countries considered to be in situations of current or potential conflict by the International Crisis Group in February 2006, 35 percent have known oil or gas resources.[4]

This book explores these paradoxes, focusing on the links between oil and gas resources and conflict in producing countries and considering the potential for, and limits to, corporate social responsibility approaches, by which corporations look beyond short-term profits to their wider impacts, as a means of weakening these links. In considering local violent conflict and civil war, I define "peacebuilding" to include, along with the traditional sense of "peacemaking" (i.e., conflict prevention and resolution), the added aspects of postconflict stabilization and reconstruction. I take a close look at the international oil industry—the hundreds of private-sector, state-owned, and hybrid companies that lead the business of exploration and production of oil and gas—and more specifically at the operations of these businesses in Africa and the Caspian region, where most foreign investment goes to the oil and gas sector.[5] The book focuses on oil rather than gas production because, as set out in greater detail in chapter 3, while the links between gas and conflict are broadly similar to those for oil, they are generally less strong because higher production costs reduce the government revenue that is the key factor linking oil and gas production and conflict.

This work builds on the efforts of two developing schools of endeavor: (1) the emerging discussions in business, policy, and academic circles on the extent to which the long-term business interests of corporations create a "business case" for their engagement in conflict prevention and resolution; and (2) the growing interest of those involved in peacebuilding in the role of economic factors and agents.

The first three chapters set out a framework for understanding the two key links between oil and conflict. The first and strongest link derives from the wealth that oil production generates for the governments of producing countries. Control of this wealth can be a powerful stimulus for conflict; resource-based wealth in general is often, paradoxically, an obstacle to economic development and is thus an indirect contributor to conflict. The second link derives from the damaging impact that oil production can have on the stability of oil field areas, in the form of environmental damage, social tension, and incentives for secession. Oil companies are aware of these problems, and corporate social responsibility concepts, reviewed in chapter 4, provide a framework for addressing the role of business in solving them. The specific links between oil and conflict, and the ways in which oil companies have confronted and may confront them in the future, are then examined in three case studies: Angola, Azerbaijan, and Sudan. The final chapter presents overall conclusions addressing three main questions: First, what is the causal relationship between oil production revenues and violent conflict, and what potential actions can oil companies take to improve this relationship? Second, what is the relationship between oil and gas production methods and violent conflict, and how can oil companies effect positive change? Third, what is the potential for oil companies, as major foreign investors, to play a role in conflict prevention and resolution and postconflict stabilization by virtue of their size, resources, and networks?

The issues surrounding business's role in peacebuilding are important to petroleum companies because violent conflict in oil-producing areas jeopardizes investments. Consider that in the mid-1980s an American oil company had to abandon its $2 billion operation in Sudan; production facilities lie unused today in parts of the Niger delta because operations cannot be protected from attack; and corporations risk damage to both their share value and reputation by doing business in conflict zones unless they have convincing arguments that they contribute to peacebuilding.

Governments and the wider international community have their issues, too. Sharp increases in oil prices in mid-2004, with consequences for the world economy, are attributable in part to concerns about the security of supply from strife-torn Nigeria, Iraq, and Venezuela. For the United States in particular, efforts to diversify sources of oil imports away from the Middle East depend on stable access to supplies from emerging oil states in Africa, the former Soviet Union, and Latin

America. It is therefore vital to ensure that economic, political, and social decline does not accompany the growth of oil production.

Meanwhile, the human cost of present-day violent conflict, whether localized or on the scale of civil war, is rarely confined to active combatants. Attacks on, and forced expulsion of, civilians have characterized post–Cold War conflicts, as has the spillover of conflict into neighboring states, adding to demands for international humanitarian assistance and intervention.

This book is aimed at students, researchers, and practitioners in the business and policymaking communities. The analysis of the oil industry, and the oil-and-conflict framework presented, as well as the references to key information sources, is intended to provide a starting point for analyzing oil, conflict, and corporate responses in any producing country. The country case studies should be of interest to researchers and policymakers involved in these countries, in part because they highlight the complexity of the relationships between oil and gas resources, economic development, conflict, and corporations, and the importance of undertaking country-specific assessment before making policy decisions.

I decided to write this book because, as a consultant to the oil industry on the social impacts of investments in developing countries, I have seen gaps in the resources available to industry decision makers, policy makers in oil-rich countries, planners of development programs, and activists in nongovernmental organizations (NGOs).

One gap is in analysis that explores, in a nontechnical way, why oil company investments in developing countries often have the unintended consequence of increasing rather than reducing stability, and why in countries with oil wealth it is particularly difficult to achieve a democratic, market-based economy and a peaceful environment. Though much excellent research has been done by political scientists and economists, little of this has yet percolated through to decision makers in corporations, government departments, and civil agencies. Further, among those who are alert to the risks that oil production may exacerbate conflict, some overestimate the degree to which individual corporations can influence outcomes. The specific trigger for researching this book was the repeated discussions with NGO activists about whether the oil companies investing in Azerbaijan could, or should, contribute to resolving the Nagorno-Karabakh conflict, and, more widely, about whether investor companies have a responsibility for engaging in peacemaking if they invest in conflict zones.

The approach of this work is to draw together the findings of academic research on natural resources and conflict, and information from industry and corporate sources about how the oil industry is structured, where it invests, and how decisions are made, in order to develop a framework for understanding the links between oil and conflict at both the national and the local level. Then, using a mix of document-based research and interviews, I test and refine this model by applying it to three country case studies. I aim throughout to keep the focus on how individual oil companies could influence outcomes, and on the incentives and disincentives for doing so.

Although the Middle East accounts for the largest share of world oil production (31 percent) and proven reserves (62 percent),[6] no countries from this region are included as case studies in this book. This is because, since the nationalizations of the mid-twentieth century, international oil companies have had little involvement in exploration and production in the area. Thus, in Saudi Arabia, where the largest reserves are located and the greatest share of the world's oil is produced, almost all reserves are controlled by the state oil corporation, Saudi Aramco.[7] However, while consideration of the role of the international oil industry in peacebuilding is therefore not directly relevant to the Middle East, the broader questions explored in this book, particularly those relating to the political and economic effects of government revenues from oil, are nevertheless relevant.

Many countries could have been drawn upon to provide insights and evidence for this study. Of these, Azerbaijan, Angola, and Sudan were selected for a mix of practical and analytical reasons. I have worked in both Angola and Azerbaijan as a consultant to oil companies, seeing firsthand how the issues of revenue, local impact, and conflict are being understood and addressed, and discovering how governments, civil society organizations, and businesses outside the oil sector view the actual and potential roles of oil companies. The case of Sudan poses critical questions about the influence, responsibilities, and competitiveness of

Western companies in the context of an increasingly globalized oil industry, and about international leverage to control maverick regimes that thrive on earnings from oil. Sudan is an important focus area for the United States Institute of Peace. During my fellowship tenure at the Institute in 2003–04, I was privileged to attend meetings of the Sudan Peace Forum that the Institute hosts, and to meet many of those from Sudan and elsewhere concerned with the north-south peace negotiations then underway.

The countries profiled in this study share interesting similarities. All have a growing oil industry and increasing government reliance on oil revenues as a source of income; all have high levels of poverty; all have governments with poor human rights records and weak or, in the case of Sudan, nonexistent democratic credentials; and all have embryonic market economies. With these common themes in mind, the three case studies provide an opportunity to explore different business and conflict contexts.

Angola has nearly doubled its oil output in the past decade to become the second largest producer in sub-Saharan Africa (after Nigeria), and many of the largest stock market–listed oil companies, as well as some smaller businesses and state oil companies, do business there. Angola's oil fields are mostly offshore, so the industry was able to expand virtually unimpeded during the thirty years of civil war. This complex war started with competing anticolonial liberation movements and, after independence, became enmeshed with Cold War competition between the superpowers. At the end of the Cold War, Angola's civil war was increasingly financed by oil (and, to a lesser extent, diamonds) until a peace agreement was made in 2002 following the death in battle of the leader of UNITA, one of the two contesting forces. A long-standing intermittent and violent secession conflict remains unresolved, however, in Angola's oil-rich Cabinda Province. This is a barrier to stabilization in Angola and a contributor to tensions in the wider Central African region. In the post–civil war environment, one of the key issues for Angola, and a major factor in its international relations, concerns control and management of the country's extractive industry earnings—whether and how they will be used to build a stable, democratic, peaceful country. This case gives insights into a historic relationship between oil production and conflict, and the challenges faced in changing this relationship in a postconflict environment.

Azerbaijan, in the former Soviet Union, is another country on track to become a major source of oil and gas to world markets, albeit on a smaller scale than Angola. Its economic and political development is circumscribed by the unresolved conflict with neighboring Armenia over the contested territory of Nagorno-Karabakh, which fell under Armenian control after the bitter conflict of the late 1980s and early 1990s, which erupted into full-scale war during 1991–94. Although a cease-fire has been in place in Nagorno-Karabakh since then, sporadic incidents causing fatalities among soldiers and civilians have continued, and there is little popular or political momentum toward peaceful resolution. The border between Armenia and Azerbaijan remains closed. This "frozen conflict" is a barrier to economic development in the South Caucasus region, and a flashpoint that carries the risk of drawing in the neighboring countries of Iran, Russia, and Turkey. Long-standing international diplomacy, in the form of the Minsk Group process, has been ineffective in brokering a solution. Hundreds of thousands of people remain displaced in temporary accommodations and camps. Azerbaijan's rising oil and gas exports will alter the balance of power between Azerbaijan and Armenia by providing large additional financial resources to Azerbaijan's government. International investment in Azerbaijan's oil industry is dominated by one large company that has a strong commitment to corporate social responsibility. This case, therefore, gives insight into the opportunities for, and limits to, business engagement in conflict prevention and resolution.

The third case study, Sudan, like Angola, has suffered a long and complex series of civil wars dating from before its independence in 1956. The principle conflict has been between the Arab north and African south, but there is also conflict within these two regions: in Darfur in western Sudan and, to a lesser extent, in the east. While disputes over the scarcity of some resources (agricultural land and water) have contributed to conflict, so has an abundance of other resources, particularly oil. Oil fields were discovered in Sudan in the 1970s, in the area straddling north and south, during the thirteen-year peace that separated the first and second periods of civil war. Although production stopped shortly after civil war resumed (because of attacks made on oil facilities), in the late 1990s oil exploration and production restarted in some areas amid ongoing civil war. Other oil areas have remained undeveloped because of the war. The initial discovery of oil raised the stakes in the north-south conflict, and export production since 1999 has provided the government of Sudan with sufficient resources to prosecute wars. The sharing of oil wealth between north and south in the future is an integral component of the Sudan north-south peace process, first formalized in the July 2002 Machakos Protocol. In mid-2004 the "Framework Agreement on Wealth Sharing," which includes provisions for sharing oil revenues between north and south, was negotiated as part of the package to end the north-south conflict—a first example of oil revenue management comprising an explicit component of a peace agreement. As well as examining links between oil and conflict, this case illustrates how the distribution of oil wealth can be a key component of peace agreements. It also highlights the limited impact of an individual company's presence or withdrawal on conflict dynamics.

I did much of the research for this book in 2003–04, while a senior fellow at the United States Institute of Peace. The book also draws on my experience as a consultant to international oil companies and nongovernmental organizations on the social impact of international investments. The research has benefited from discussions with many people in the oil industry, governments, NGOs, and academia, as well as with colleagues at the United States Institute of Peace. In several cases, those I spoke with did not want to be identified, because they were critical of the organizations they worked for or were associated with. Consequently, few quotations are included, and interviewees are usually not identified. Nevertheless, every effort has been made to reflect accurately what was said. I acknowledge with gratitude the insights and comments of all those I have spoken to and worked with on these subjects. The study's limitations, however, are wholly my responsibility. In the two years since my tenure at the Institute ended, the doubling of crude oil prices has exacerbated the forces that I discuss. As final edits were being made, in spring 2006, hopes in the New Year for a settlement to the Nagorno-Karabakh dispute have faded, the 2005 north-south peace agreement is threatened by a laggardly transfer of wealth to the autonomous South Sudan created by the agreement, and the government of Angola and the international community have failed to resolve their dispute over transparency about oil revenues, so that hopes of a post-conflict donor conference to support the country's transition to peace are at an end. In the countries discussed to a lesser extent in this book, the bold effort to prevent oil wealth from fueling conflict in Chad is under duel threat: from the government, which is reneging on laws intended to ensure good management of oil wealth, and from rebels challenging the government's hold on power. In the Niger delta, some 40 percent of oil production is "shut in" due to conflict, and conflict over the sharing out of Iraq's oil wealth continues to bedevil a political settlement there as well. This book seeks to explain why such impasses occur and to outline the ways in which corporations can seek to exercise a restraining influence. Ultimately, however, it is the people and the governments of oil-rich countries, not the corporations that invest there, who determine the outcomes.

2

The International Oil Industry

THE OIL INDUSTRY DIFFERS FROM MOST OTHER TYPES of international business because of the level of control exercised by governments, which "sell" the right to find and produce hydrocarbons—often to international companies—in return for a share of the profits. What economists refer to as government "rents" can be huge. One recent British television program estimated, on the basis of information published by the Shell Petroleum Development Company of Nigeria, that the government of Nigeria was in receipt of $2 million per hour in oil revenues from the concessions let to that company in early 2006.[8] This chapter outlines how these arrangements work, where oil and gas companies are investing, the different types of companies in the sector, the regulatory and contractual framework of the industry, and the principal phases of oil project development.

Current and Emerging Production Areas

Most of the world's oil reserves,[9] and the largest volumes of current production, are in the Middle East (see table 2-1). Since the nationalizations of the mid-twentieth century, when the Middle Eastern states took over the companies that had been producing oil there, this region has been largely, though not wholly, closed to international oil companies. State-owned companies, including the world's largest oil company, Saudi Aramco,[10] are responsible for most exploration and production in the region. The international oil industry therefore concentrates its investment outside the Middle East, although the size of Middle Eastern reserves means that this will become a key area for future investment if and when the political barriers to investment by international companies are lifted.[11]

Table 2-1 World Oil Reserves by Region (2005)[12]

	Production %	Proven Reserves %
Middle East	31.0	61.9
Europe & Eurasia	21.7	11.7
North America	16.5	5.0
Africa	12.0	9.5
Asia Pacific	9.8	3.4
South & Central America	9.0	8.6

Outside the Middle East, oil and gas production is distributed very widely. Fifty-four countries each produce 0.1 percent or more of global output.[13] Many countries, including current producers, are inviting oil companies to bid for concessions to explore for oil and gas, onshore and offshore, within their "exclusive economic zones" (EEZs).[14] For example, in mid-2004 half the countries in sub-Saharan Africa had announced tenders.[15]

As oil and gas reserves in North America and Western Europe are depleted, the industry is increasingly investing in developing countries and the former Soviet Union (FSU). Two notable areas of growth are the Caspian states and Africa. In the case of the Caspian states, this growth involves restoring and expanding an industry initially developed under the FSU.

Of the four FSU Caspian littoral states, the international oil industry is investing most heavily—billions of dollars—in Kazakhstan and

Azerbaijan. Production of oil and gas for export from these countries is already increasing and will be substantially higher toward the end of this decade (see table 2-2). Turkmenistan has large gas reserves but has not negotiated contracts with international oil companies to bring its gas to the world market. It currently exports to Russia and elsewhere in the FSU, and output is returning to levels first achieved in the early 1990s. Oil and gas production is also rising fast in the Russian Federation, although expansion is primarily from Siberia and the east, with little development yet of potential Russian resources in the Caspian. This could soon change. In January 2006 the Russian company Lukoil announced that it had discovered a major oil and gas field in the northern Caspian Sea.[16] The fifth Caspian state, Iran, has yet to explore in the Caspian Sea, but tenders to begin drilling were in negotiation in late 2004.[17]

Table 2-2 Caspian Oil and Gas Production[18]

	2000 in millions of tons[a]	2005
Azerbaijan	18.7	27.2
Kazakhstan	39.8	84.1
Turkmenistan	46.7	62.4
Russian Federation	813.8	1,008.2
Iran[b]	233.6	278.7

Notes:
[a] Oil and natural gas (in millions of tons oil equivalent)
[b] Output from areas outside the Caspian region

In Africa, international investment has led to a substantial expansion of oil industries in place since the 1970s, as in Nigeria and Angola, and has fostered new oil developments, in such countries as Equatorial Guinea and São Tomé and Príncipe. With Libya no longer considered a "pariah state," international investment is expected to expand there, too.

Oil and gas production in Africa is distributed across many countries operating at very different levels of output (see table 2-3). In North Africa, the largest proven reserves and production levels are in Algeria, Libya, and Egypt; in sub-Saharan Africa, Nigeria dominates production and has the largest proven reserves, while Angola is becoming a major producer. Among the smaller-scale producing countries, some, including Gabon, have reached peak production and are on a declining trend, while output is rising in others, such as Sudan and Equatorial Guinea. In a few other nations, notably Chad and São Tomé and Príncipe, oil resources are being explored and developed at levels that might be considered small-scale in international terms but that are very significant in the context of these economies. Elsewhere, many areas with possible reserves remain largely unexplored.

Table 2-3 Major African Oil and Gas Producers[19]

	2000	2005
	in millions of tons[a]	
North Africa		
Algeria	142.8	167.5
Egypt	55.3	65.2
Libya	74.1	90.6
Sub-Saharan Africa		
Nigeria	116.7	145.0
Angola	36.9	61.2
Equatorial Guinea	5.8	17.6
Sudan	8.6	18.7
Congo (Brazzaville)	14.2	13.1
Gabon	16.4	11.7

Notes:
[a] Oil and natural gas (in millions of tons oil equivalent)

Table 2-4 Excess of Oil Consumption Over Production (in millions of tons/year)[20]

	1990	1995	2000	2005
USA	353	424	545	635
China	25	11	61	146

The growing demand for oil and gas is the driving force behind the spread of the industry across an increasing number of countries. Between 2000 and 2004, global oil consumption increased by 8 percent, with the most marked increase—36 percent over five years—occurring in China. The United States, the world's biggest consumer, and China are both substantial producers of oil, but each uses more than is produced domestically, and both have shown an increasing gap between annual production and consumption (see table 2-4).

This increase more than offsets the declining trend of consumption in other major industrial countries, such as Germany and Japan. The growing reliance on imported oil is driving investments by Chinese state oil companies in oil exploration and production worldwide, in a pattern mirroring that of U.S. and European companies in the twentieth century (see table 2-5). Of the three Chinese state oil companies, China National Petroleum Corporation (CNPC) has invested most widely internationally and shares in exploration or production operations in Algeria, Azerbaijan, Chad, Ecuador, Indonesia, Kazakhstan, Niger, Peru, Russia, Sudan, and Syria.[21] In mid-2005 China National Overseas Oil Corporation (CNOOC) placed an unsuccessful bid to acquire all assets of America's Unocal Corporation.

Conflict in producing countries is becoming a pertinent issue for the oil industry as it moves into an increasing number of unstable countries. The expansion of the industry in the Caspian region and sub-Saharan Africa includes investment in many countries characterized by conflict, such as Azerbaijan, Chad, Georgia (the transit route of export pipelines for oil and gas from Azerbaijan), Nigeria, and Sudan. Beyond these regions, the international oil industry currently has a substantial presence in several other countries experiencing ongoing conflict or political

Table 2-5 Major Oil Consumers and Domestic Production (in millions of tons/year)[22]

	2000		2005	
	Consumption	Production	Consumption	Production
USA	898	353	965	310
China	224	163	327	181
Japan	256	—	244	—
Germany	130	—	122	—
Russian Federation	124	323	130	470
South Korea	103	—	106	—
India	106	36	116	36
World	3,537	3,614	3,837	3,895

instability, including Bolivia, Colombia, Indonesia, and the Philippines. Looking into the future, there is likely to be increased offshore exploration in the weak, new state of East Timor, and investors are being invited to fund exploratory operations in countries with fragile peace settlements, such as Sierra Leone and Liberia. Political change may also lead to international oil company investment in other unstable countries, including Afghanistan, Iraq, and Uzbekistan, and in the construction of pipelines linking Central Asia and markets in China, India, and Japan via Afghanistan.

Oil accounts for over 60 percent of world consumption of oil and gas. Natural gas is often found in quantities alongside oil in oil fields. This "associated gas" is either flared, reinjected to the oil reservoir, or captured for processing and marketing. Some hydrocarbon reservoirs consist predominantly of natural gas and are exploited only for their gas reserves. The Shah Deniz exploration concession in the Caspian Sea, for example, resulted in significant gas finds. Some countries, such as Russia and the United States, produce more gas than oil.

Table 2-6 Major Producers of Natural Gas[23]

	2005 (in millions of tons of oil equivalent)
Russian Federation	538
United States	473
Canada	167
United Kingdom	79
Algeria	79
Iran	78
Norway	77
Indonesia	68
Netherlands	57

The international trade in gas, and hence exploration for gas resources, is hindered by the complexity and cost of transportation, which is significantly higher than for oil. An analysis published in 2004 by the Oxford Institute for Energy Studies shows transportation costs for oil, consisting of onshore pipelines and crude oil tankering, at below $2.5 per barrel, compared with at least $15 per barrel of oil equivalent for gas.[24] Up until the 1990s, technical and cost restrictions on gas transportation meant that most gas was consumed in the region where it was produced, with producing fields and consumer systems linked by a small number of dedicated pipelines. As late as 2002, only 23 percent of world gas consumption was imported.[25]

A combination of rising oil prices, increased demand for natural gas for electricity generation, and technical developments that enable longer gas pipelines to be constructed and for gas to be traded internationally in liquid form (liquefied natural gas, or LNG), are raising the demand for gas. The International Energy Agency predicts that global consumption of gas is expected to increase more than that of any other primary energy source, almost doubling by 2030.[26] The outcome of these factors is that investment is taking place in gas fields that were heretofore considered "stranded" due to high transport costs, which rendered them uneconomical to develop.

Another aspect of natural gas production, explored in greater detail in chapters 3 and 8, is that development of gas resources in areas of conflict presents a somewhat different set of issues from those of oil. In particular, the higher costs of producing and transporting gas to world markets means that the revenues, or "rents," paid to governments are lower than those for oil.

Types of International Oil Companies

Three types of companies operate in the international oil industry,[27] backed up by a range of service companies and financiers. They are all subject to different business priorities, incentives, and constraints. For the larger shareholder-owned companies, of which ExxonMobil is the largest, the measure of success is the ability to secure access to new exploration areas, discover oil or gas, and sell it profitably over the long term. These companies compete for exploration concessions but also often combine forces to share the costs and risks of major developments, such as those in Azerbaijan and Angola. In contrast, smaller oil companies have a shorter time horizon. They focus on producing oil from the smaller oil fields that are uneconomic for the major companies, or on exploring for oil in high-risk locations, for example, where the probability of success is lower or the political environment is more unstable. Business success for these independents is measured by building up assets or enterprises that can be sold to larger companies. Thus, they typically have less interest than the large companies in the long-term local impacts of their business. Government-owned companies operating outside their own state are a recent and heterogeneous phenomenon. Some, such as Brazil's Petrobras or Norway's Statoil, have ambitions to compete with the major shareholder-owned companies as international investors; others (such as the Chinese and Indian companies) are hybrids pursuing a mix of commercial and government interests and focusing largely on securing access to the oil and gas needed to fund their countries' economic development.

The organization of the oil industry is fluid—frequent mergers and acquisitions, privatizations and partial privatizations of state-run companies, and successes and failures in exploration all change both the structure and size of individual companies, and with them the overall pattern of the industry. For example, the five "super majors" discussed below were all formed in the late 1990s as smaller companies merged, larger companies regularly bought up successful independents, and independents with major exploration successes joined the ranks of the larger companies. The phenomenon of "international" state oil companies is recent and reflects both a trend toward partial privatization, requiring state companies to act in a more commercial way, and the high value that countries with limited oil resources place on securing guaranteed access to supplies.

Super Major and Major Oil Companies

Some twenty large stock exchange–listed multinational corporations, often referred to as the "super majors" and the "majors," have worldwide investments in oil and gas production, and "integrated" operations extending from exploration for new oil and gas fields to sales of gasoline at retail stations. The five super majors (ExxonMobil, BP, Shell, Total, and Chevron) are ranked number two, five, seven, fourteen, and twenty-four respectively in the 2005 listings of the world's largest public companies; each has annual sales amounting to hundreds of billions of dollars.[28]

The key business priorities for these companies are the search for new oil and gas production fields to replace depleting assets, and competition with other oil companies in finding new reserves and bringing them into production profitably. As the chairman of one company (Total) explained at a shareholder presentation in October 2003, "The challenge is to maintain current levels of oil production, combat the natural decline in fields, and increase production to respond to world demand. Emerging countries will account for more than 90 percent of new production of oil and gas." Securing new reserves is a key factor determining these corporations' share prices, as shown by the firing in 2004 of the chairman and other top executives of Shell, following the announcement to shareholders that future oil and gas reserves were lower than previously reported.[29]

As well as satisfying shareholders, these businesses, with global brands and consumer markets, also seek to have a good reputation in the eyes of both governments and customers. Good relations with governments of oil-producing countries are critical to securing the exploration rights that are sold by those governments (referred to as "host governments"). However, relations between companies and governments are complex and have built-in tensions. The large multinational companies are attractive investors to host governments because they provide the technical skills and capital necessary for large-scale developments, especially in the offshore fields where much new oil production is taking place and which are particularly costly to develop. Some governments are also keen to attract the large Western companies because their presence raises the profile of the country in the United States and Western Europe—the companies' "home governments." On the other hand, there are often suspicions within host governments—and the publics—that the large companies are too powerful and thus able to press weak or ill-advised governments into signing unsatisfactory deals, or that the companies and their home governments could interfere with host country politics.

In terms of their reputation with customers, experiences such as the "Boycott Shell" campaigns in the mid-1990s, attacking the company for its activities in Nigeria, have revealed the vulnerability to activist pressure of integrated companies that operate with retail outlets in the West and production fields in developing countries. A broader campaign by environmental, human rights, and development NGOs, arguing that investments in the oil and mining (extractive) industries damage people and the environment, led the World Bank, during 2001–04, to reexamine its financial support for the industry and to require higher standards of environmental protection and information disclosure by companies and governments as a condition of World Bank involvement.[30] These are important factors behind the attention paid by these companies to corporate social responsibility over the past decade.

Independent Oil Companies

A much larger set (hundreds) of smaller companies, often referred to as "independents," invest internationally in exploration and production but, unlike the majors, do not have their own branded retail outlets or refineries. The value of these companies is much less than that of the majors—counted in billions rather than hundreds of billions. Like the majors, the independents are also driven by the need for success in finding new oil and gas reserves and in developing new fields. Unlike the larger companies, the independents rarely need to concern themselves with their public or consumer reputation except where, as in the case of those investing in Sudan in the 1990s, they are targeted by NGOs. The focus of the independents is primarily on developing assets to sell profitably to other companies, or positioning themselves for takeover by the majors. Independents typically have a shorter time horizon—one analyst reports that the average life of an independent oil company is only ten years.[31] In most cases, the independents show little interest in corporate social responsibility initiatives, although there are exceptions, for example, where NGO campaigning has made this a business issue for them, or where small companies explicitly choose to develop approaches similar to those of the majors. Table 2-7 provides a profile of one relatively large UK-based independent company, drawn from the company's Web site. This profile illustrates the fluidity in company name and structure, and the frequent shifts in the location of operations through sale and purchase of exploration and production concessions that are typical of this set of businesses.

International State-Owned Oil Companies

Most countries with oil reserves have a state oil company. Exceptions are Canada, the United States, and, since the 1980s, the United Kingdom. State oil companies range in size from the huge (Middle East) to the small (Sudan's Sudapet, for example). As well as producing some or all of the oil from their own countries, state-owned (or partly state-owned) oil companies are beginning to invest outside their home states, thus forming an emerging sector of the international industry. State oil companies from China, India, Malaysia, and Norway in particular compete internationally with shareholder-owned companies. The investments of this set of international state oil companies reflect a mix of commercial and national strategic objectives. Those from oil-producing countries, such as Brazil and Norway, operate internationally largely like private-sector companies, with a focus on making profitable

Table 2-7 An Industry in Constant Change:
The Example of Premier Oil

Early days

Premier Oil started as the Caribbean Oil Company, which was registered in the UK in 1934 to pursue oil and gas exploration and production activities in Trinidad. Two years later, it was publicly floated as Premier (Trinidad) Oilfields. For the next two decades, the company concentrated its attention on oil production in Trinidad.

UK

Having acquired its first interest in the North Sea in 1971, Premier gradually expanded its presence on the UK continental shelf, merging with the Ball and Collins North Sea Consortium in 1977 to gain significant interests in the North Sea as well as properties in Sudan and West Africa. In 1984, the company took a 12.5% stake in the onshore oilfield at Wytch Farm in Dorset. This acquisition transformed the company's reserve base and cash flow and, even today, continues to make an important contribution to Premier's revenues, thanks to large-scale expansions that have only become technically feasible with modern technology.

Exploration success

In the late 1980s and early 1990s, Premier enjoyed a series of exploration successes, notably the discovery of the Qadirpur gas field in Pakistan in 1990, the Fife and Angus fields in the UKCS and the Yetagun gas field in Myanmar in 1992, as well as the offshore extension to Wytch Farm.

UKCS expansion

In 1995, Premier acquired Pict Petroleum. As a consequence, Amerada Hess which had a substantial stake in Pict came to hold 25% of Premier's enlarged equity. From this point, Premier was participating in numerous North Sea oil and gas fields, including Fife, Fergus, Galahad and Scott.

Looking east

Supported by production revenue from the UKCS, the company turned its attention to the Far East with a view to developing energy resources to serve this region's rapidly expanding economies.

Table 2-7 continued

Pakistan

In 1998, Premier and Shell brought together their exploration and production interests in Pakistan to form a joint venture company, PSP (Premier & Shell Pakistan). In May 2001, Premier announced an asset swap with Shell which dismantled the partnership and, in September 2001, the formation of a new joint venture with KUFPEC.

Indonesia

In 1996, Premier acquired Sumatra Gulf Oil Ltd which gave it a majority interest in the Natuna Sea Block A offshore Indonesia, comprising the Anoa oil field and substantial gas reserves, as well as exploration prospects. It also acquired Discovery Petroleum thereby obtaining an interest in the Kakap license, also in the Natuna Sea, which added oil and gas reserves and provided access to further prospective exploration acreage. In 2002, Premier sold part of its interest in West Natuna.

Myanmar

Premier was the original license of concessions M13 and M14 when they were awarded in 1990. Shortly afterwards Premier farmed out its interests to Texaco, who became operator, and Nippon Oil of Japan; Premier retained a 30% interest. The Yetagun Field was discovered in 1992 and development began in 1996/7. In late 1997, Texaco sold its entire interest and transferred operatorship to Premier, who at the same time introduced Petronas to the project. Construction of the pipeline and facilities continued through 1998 and 1999. The field started production in May 2000. In 2002, Premier sold its entire interest (see Restructuring below).

Strategic alliance

To consolidate its position as a leading independent production company in the southeast Asian energy markets, Premier formed a strategic alliance with the Malaysian oil company Petronas and Amerada Hess in 1999, within which both Petronas and Amerada Hess owned a 25% stake in Premier.

Restructuring

In September 2002, Premier agreed to transfer its entire Myanmar Business to Petronas and part of the Indonesian West Natuna asset to Petronas and Amerada Hess. In consideration for these transfers, Petronas and Amerada Hess cancelled their combined 50% shareholding in Premier and provided $376 million in cash and debt repayment.

Source: Premier Oil[32]

investments and building up technical capacity through international partnerships. Those from countries short of oil focus principally on negotiating exploration and production contracts that will provide an assured flow of future supplies. Chinese and Indian state companies are becoming increasingly prominent given the two countries' rapid economic growth and accelerating demand for oil.

Other state oil companies currently operate only in their home countries. These include companies such as Azerbaijan's SOCAR and Angola's Sonangol. Often these companies are part of the system for managing international investment on behalf of the government; many also hold shares in production fields operated by international companies. Some, including both SOCAR and Sonangol, undertake domestic exploration and production on their own account and could start operating internationally in the future.

Contractors and Financiers

Oil company operations are supported by an array of service companies and financiers. Like the oil sector itself, this category includes very large-scale global businesses (such as Schlumberger, Halliburton, and Baker Hughes), government-owned companies, and smaller-scale specialist businesses involved in drilling, construction, engineering, surveying, and a wide range of other services. The practice of outsourcing in the industry allows companies with limited in-house technical skills to make speculative investments through contracting out some or all of the on-the-ground activity to oil service companies. The incentives to set up speculative companies to explore for oil anywhere the geology looks promising are greatest when, as in the mid-2000s, oil prices are high.

Financing for exploration and production may be provided by the oil companies themselves, from equity capital and banks, or it may be drawn from multilateral finance organizations such as the International Finance Corporation (IFC, the private-sector arm of the World Bank) and the European Bank for Reconstruction and Development (EBRD). Government-supported export credit and risk protection organizations, such as the U.S. Export-Import Bank (Exim Bank) and Overseas Private Investment Corporation (OPIC) also provide finance. Whereas oil companies generally work under contract to the governments of oil-producing countries, contractors and financiers operate under contracts negotiated with the oil companies. Like the majors, financiers and, to a lesser extent, contractors are under pressure from NGOs regarding the social and environmental impacts of their activities.

The Contractual and Legal Framework

The oil industry operates within a legal and contractual framework different from that applying to most other business sectors.[33] States generally own subsoil and subsea oil and gas resources. Companies carry out oil and gas production under contract to host governments and are subject to special arrangements to allocate a share of the returns to those governments. The general structure is the same worldwide, although the details and terminology of the legal and contractual frameworks differ substantially from state to state and sometimes from concession to concession. Governments issue exclusive concessions to companies to explore for oil and gas and to exploit, for a number of years, those resources that they find. In return, the companies make payments to the government in the form of royalties (per unit of output), acreage fees, taxes (on the company's profit from the concession), or a share of production. Companies generally cover the costs of exploration and bear the risk that exploration might be unsuccessful; areas without known reserves have approximately a one-in-six chance of success.[34] When production starts, companies generally recover some or all of their costs before paying royalties or other revenues to the government. Contracts between governments and companies are long-term—anything from seven years (renewable), which is generally the pattern in Alaska, to twenty-five years or more in some developing and transitional[35] countries, such as Azerbaijan. Concessions are usually held by a consortium of companies, and the composition of a consortium may change over its life as shares in oil and gas exploration and production "assets" are bought and sold. Within most consortia, one company, designated as the "operator," is responsible for organizing and managing the development of the resource. For many countries, little information is publicly available about where concessions are located, which companies hold them, and on what terms, although this information may be found in specialist industry newsletters and, to a lesser extent, oil company Web sites and publications. For example, official maps showing the location and ownership of blocks are not available from any of the countries covered in case studies in this book.

A common pattern for exploration and production contracts in developing countries, including those in Africa and the FSU (though not always in Russia), is the "production-sharing agreement" (PSA).[36] The government of Indonesia introduced PSAs in the 1960s as a form of contract designed to empower governments vis-à-vis oil companies. PSAs replaced concessions under which oil companies had sole control of exploration and production and merely paid governments a royalty on the oil produced. The formal legal structure of a PSA is an instrument by which the host government contracts companies to explore for and produce oil on its behalf. Under a PSA, the government shares control with the consortium over when and how production is carried out, and pays the companies a fee, in the form of a share of the oil, to offset exploration and production costs and provide a profit. By defining the government's and companies' shares of revenue as a function of production levels and the price of oil, PSAs enable governments to share in the benefits of oil price booms. They also expose government earnings (revenues) to oil price shocks, since the value of the government's share, like that of the companies, falls as well as rises with the oil price.

As discussed further in chapter 3, the production-sharing contracts for many oil concessions are confidential documents, open only to the government and consortium partners. Table 2-8 shows the principal generic components of a PSA, based on PSAs in the public domain for projects in Azerbaijan. This PSA, however, is unusually farsighted in also specifying the environmental, health, and safety standards to be applied, although practices may be changing elsewhere, too. As discussed in chapter 7, when Total's concession in Sudan was renegotiated in 2004 it reportedly "took account of new international industry standards, particularly in relation to corporate social responsibility," although the agreement's text was not published.[37]

Table 2-8 Key Elements of a Production-Sharing Agreement (PSA)

Specifies the parties to the agreement

Defines the geographical area covered by the PSA, and the activities and resources that it covers

Specifies the time period allowed for exploration and for any subsequent production

Defines the composition and working methods of the joint government/ contractor committee that oversees the contract and the work program

Specifies what costs may be recovered by the contractor

Specifies how profit oil (the balance after costs have been deducted) will be split

Defines what taxes the contractor is responsible for

Specifies what bonus payments are to be made by the concession holder to the government (for example, on signature of contract), and when oil production starts

Defines the environmental, health, and safety standards and procedures to be applied

Defines "force majeure" and conditions that permit the parties to abrogate their commitments temporarily or permanently

Specifies what legal systems govern the contract, and how contractual disputes are to be resolved

Specifies the starting date for the contract

Defines the confidentiality status of the contract

Source: Azerbaijan Shah Deniz PSA[38]

Three aspects of the contractual and legal framework of the international oil industry are of particular relevance in terms of conflict risks and their limitation: (1) the extent to which contracts are openly and transparently tendered; (2) the extent to which contracts allow for public disclosure of contract terms—especially the revenues payable by companies to a government; and (3) the extent to which requirements for the environmental and social protection of producing areas and the communities living there are included in the contract terms. In general there is a marked difference between developing and developed or transitional countries in all three respects. Exploration and production concessions in, for example, Alaska (United States), Alberta (Canada), the UK, and Norway are publicly tendered, and their terms are a matter of public record, as are the revenues that accrue to the state. Companies operating in these countries are required to meet stringent requirements for environmental management, impact assessment, and public consultation in relation to new or expanded operations. Elsewhere, exploration and concession contracts are often settled without an open tendering process; the terms of contracts are confidential; disclosure of information about payments by companies on signature of contracts, and about government revenue shares when production starts, is often protected by confidentiality clauses; and requirements for environmental protection and public consultation are minimal.

Phases of Resource Development

The global oil industry consists of hundreds of thousands of organizations involved in some aspect of the process that locates underground (and undersea) oil and gas reserves, brings them to the surface, then transports and processes them into energy products for consumer and industrial use. Technically and commercially, this process is divided into four stages: exploration (finding resources), production (bringing crude oil and natural gas to market), refining/processing (turning crude fuels into usable products), and marketing and distribution (delivering products to customers). Exploration and production are known as "upstream" activities, refining and marketing as "downstream."

The upstream oil industry, on which this study focuses, itself involves a phased set of processes. This starts with the acquisition of licenses to explore for oil, followed by an increasingly complex series of research, surveying, and drilling investigations to determine what resources can be found. Not all exploration concessions will result in oil or gas finds. If exploration is successful, the next step is to assess the finds and determine whether and how to develop the field. Some oil fields are not commercially viable, because of the amount of oil they contain or the costs of bringing the oil to market. Where finds are commercially viable, decisions are then made about how to develop the field—for example, the number and type of wells to be drilled, the pace of extraction, whether tankers or pipelines will be used to take oil to market, and the route of new pipelines if these are needed. Together, the exploration and development phases can span five to ten years and sometimes longer for projects that are technically or politically complex or where it is difficult to raise financing. Exploration and development involves large-scale capital investment, for example, for drilling rigs, pipelines, and storage terminals. Once production starts in any field it is likely to continue for at least a decade. Developments in technology often extend the planned lifetime of fields, or depleted fields are relicensed to companies that specialize in extracting oil from fields that are no longer commercially viable for the consortia that initially developed them. An example of the time-scale and investment costs of a very large-scale and complex project is the Azeri-Chirag-Guneshli (ACG) production-sharing agreement in the Caspian Sea. It was signed in 1994, and the first finds came into production in 1997, with full-scale production scheduled to start in 2007. BP estimates the total investment required to develop these oil fields (and the nearby Shah Deniz gas field) and to construct the pipelines taking the product to export through Azerbaijan, Georgia, and Turkey at $20 billion.[39] When the PSA expires in 2024, or if production is exhausted sooner, the ownership of all the facilities will transfer to SOCAR, the State Oil Company of Azerbaijan, which may be able to extend their use. In contrast, the smaller-scale development of the Heglig and Unity fields in Sudan, and construction of a 900-kilometer export pipeline, took only three years (1996–99) to complete.

Typically, the oil majors deploy different teams of people for exploration, development, and operations, and control passes from corporate head offices to in-country operations as exploration is successful and the prospect of setting up a development project becomes stronger. In smaller companies with fewer concessions at any one time, the divide between corporate and in-country staff is much less pronounced. As discussed in chapter 4, this sequential transfer of responsibility between exploration, development, and operational teams, and the shift of control away from corporate head offices, often leads to the various projects' managers having a short-term focus. This hinders efforts to apply corporate social responsibility approaches that devote attention to building relationships in the host community and to careful, consultative project planning.

The Oil Industry in Angola, Azerbaijan, and Sudan

The three countries profiled in this book are, on a global scale, small- to medium-scale producers with expanding production levels based largely on investment by international oil companies of all types. In Angola and Azerbaijan almost all current production, particularly from recent PSAs, is from offshore fields, involving relatively expensive operations. Much of the new production from Angola is located in deep offshore waters at the outer reaches of the EEZ, where oil is loaded directly onto tankers from floating production, storage, and offloading vessels (FPSOs). Azerbaijan's new output has to be transported from the landlocked Caspian Sea to tankers on the high seas. Sudan's oil fields are all onshore, with output piped to a refinery near Khartoum and to an export terminal on Sudan's Red Sea coast.

Many of the major oil companies have investments in Angola and Azerbaijan. Total is the only major with a presence in Sudan, and up to July 2005 it had not carried out work since conflict halted all activity in the 1980s.[40] Several independent oil companies are active in Angola and Azerbaijan, mostly as junior partners in concessions operated by the majors, although some are beginning to take on a higher-profile role, particularly in Angola. In Sudan independents and state oil companies lead the active operations. State oil companies have a particularly prominent position in Sudan, both in production from existing fields and in exploring for new resources; they are also growing in importance in Angola. In Sudan the absence of most Western companies follows their withdrawal (temporary or permanent) because of dangers posed by conflict, sanctions (which prevent U.S. companies from investing in Sudan), and pressure to divest brought by NGO campaigns alleging that oil industry investors were complicit in human rights abuses. In

Angola the increasing role of international state oil companies reflects deliberate choices made by the government in the allocation of concessions, with Chinese companies receiving concessions against a backdrop of loans to the government of China.[41] (Table 2-9 lists the principal oil companies with assets in Angola, Azerbaijan, and Sudan as of mid-2005.)

Conclusions

Efforts to find and extract oil are likely to take place in an increasing number of "weak states," including those affected by conflict, unless demand for oil falls and international oil companies become able to secure concessions in the Middle East. An emerging characteristic of the international oil industry is the growth of state oil companies, particularly from Asia, as international investors. In an era of high global demand for oil, reflected in high prices, it is likely that state oil companies and independents will play a significant role in increasing exploration and production activity in pursuit of oil reserves and profits in these weak states. As will be discussed in chapter 4, this is important given the limited development of corporate social responsibility approaches—and the weaker business incentives to develop such approaches—among independents and state oil companies.

A key common element of the international oil industry is that its operations are based on long-term concession agreements with host governments, which set the terms for exploration and production. This structure, particular to the extractive industries, is important in considering the potential influence of business on peacebuilding, for several reasons. First, it makes companies partners of the government, both in legal terms and, in most circumstances, through close, contractually determined collaboration on how exploration and production is carried out. Second, with rising demand for oil generating increasing competition among companies to secure concessions from host governments, the companies need to ensure that they have a reputation as a reliable partner, one that neither criticizes government nor interferes in its politics. And third, within the constraints of this business-government relationship, the precise terms of concession agreements—particularly provisions regarding environmental or social protections, and about making public the terms of contracts—offer untapped opportunities for enabling concession contracts to contribute to conflict prevention.

Table 2-9 Oil and Gas Industry Profile:
         Angola, Azerbaijan, and Sudan[42]

	Angola	**Azerbaijan**	**Sudan**
Oil Reserves and Production, 2005			
Proved reserves[a]	1.2	1.0	0.9
Production – oil[b]	61.2	22.4	18.7
Exploration activity	Much	Little	Some
Oil field locations	Mostly offshore	Mostly offshore	Onshore
Principal oil companies			
Majors	Agip/ENI BP Chevron Conoco Phillips ExxonMobil Hydro Marathon Total	Agip BP Chevron Conoco Phillips ExxonMobil Total	Marathon Total[c]

Table 2-9 continued

	Angola	**Azerbaijan**	**Sudan**
Principal oil companies continued			
Independents	Canadian Natural Resources Devon Energy Galp Kerr McGee Oldebrecht Roc Tullow	Amerada Hess Devon Energy Inpex Itochu	Al-Thani Corporation Arakis Energy Gula Oil Petroleum Lundin Systems International Group White Nile Zafir
National state-owned	Sonangol	SOCAR	Sudapet
International state-owned	Petronas (Malaysia) Petrobrás (Brazil) Sinopec (China) Statoil (Norway)	NICO (Iran) Statoil (Norway) TPAO (Turkey)	China National Petroleum Company (CNPC) Kuwaiti Foreign Petroleum Company ONGC Videsh (India) Petronas (Malaysia)

[a] In billions of tons
[b] In millions of tons per year
[c] Operations suspended since 1980s

3

Links between Oil and Conflict in Producing Areas

O IL AS A TRIGGER FOR GEOPOLITICAL "RESOURCE WARS" has been a theme of international relations analysis since the OPEC oil shocks of the 1970s.[43] Since the end of the Cold War, with the growing incidence of civil wars worldwide, more attention has turned to the relationship between oil and conflict within producing countries. This chapter introduces the current framework for analyzing the causes and incentives for conflict, and the link between natural resources and conflict. Recent research shows a higher incidence of civil war in oil-producing countries, and oil revenues are central to this trend. I analyze the evidence tying the ways in which oil projects are planned and managed with the incidence of violent conflict in the forms of localized violence and secessionist conflict. There is a persuasive argument, supported particularly by research on the Niger delta and Indonesia, that changes triggered by large-scale oil and gas developments can interact with disputes over revenue allocation and thereby intensify preexisting ethnic and political fissures, resulting in intractable violent conflict.

The Political Economy of Civil War in Developing Countries

The World Bank has been conducting research since 1999 on the economics of civil war, crime, and violence. Led by economist Paul Collier, this work has taken an innovative and controversial approach to conflict analysis. First, it asks how far "opportunities" rather than "motive"—"greed" rather than "grievance"—explains the outbreak of civil conflict.[44] Second, it uses econometric techniques on global data sets (covering civil conflicts between 1960 and 1999) to identify risk factors. As well as generating its own results, this research has stimulated a substantial academic and policy literature.[45] In the process, arguments about the importance of economic incentives in starting and maintaining conflict have been largely validated, and the analysis has become more sophisticated. In particular, the current research now considers the interaction of "greed" and "grievance" rather than posing either-or questions; it explores the mechanisms behind the relationship between these two motivators; and it has led to the development of policy recommendations, particularly for the World Bank.[46]

The World Bank research makes four central conclusions: (1) "the key root cause of conflict is the failure of economic development such that many of the world's poorest countries are locked in a tragic vicious circle where poverty causes conflict and conflict causes poverty";[47] (2) countries that have low, stagnant, and unequally distributed per capita incomes, and that have remained dependent on primary commodities for their exports, face dangerously high risks of prolonged conflict;[48] (3) "once a country has had conflict it is in far greater danger of further conflict: commonly the chief legacy of a civil war is another civil war";[49] and (4) ethnicity and religion are much less important than is commonly believed in making countries prone to civil war.[50]

A key implication is that the risk of civil war is concentrated in two sets of countries. The first set comprises stagnating countries with low incomes, dependent on exports of primary commodities—particularly natural resources, including oil, minerals, and timber—and without policies, governance, and institutions that enable development. The second set comprises countries that have experienced civil war within the previous decade.

Collier argues that concerted international action—going beyond providing stimuli for economic growth—could "more than halve the global incidence of civil war." Three key actions by the international community could reduce the risks of civil war: (1) substantial change in aid policy; (2) reductions in military expenditure in conflict zones, and better sequencing of military interventions, aid, and reform "to avoid gap periods of exceptionally high risk"; and (3) greater international governance of natural resources so that natural resource endowments realize their potential for poverty reduction rather than being associated with conflict, poor governance, and economic decline.[51] The key arguments concerning natural resources hinge on who controls this wealth and how it is used; on the extent of transparency in the allocation of exploration and production concessions, and the related payments by natural resources companies to governments; and on how the economic impact of revenue, and its volatility, are managed.

The finding that primary commodity exports substantially increase conflict risk[52] has triggered work by many researchers to investigate the strength of this risk relationship whether it holds true for all primary commodities or only some, and what the underlying mechanisms are. Michael Ross, reviewing fourteen recent cross-national econometric studies and many qualitative studies, finds robust relationships between the incidence of conflict and the presence of oil or "lootable" commodities such as gemstones, drugs, and perhaps timber.[53] He finds no relationship, however, between conflict and the export of legal agricultural commodities. This and other studies by various researchers using different data sets (in terms of the numbers of casualties defining a conflict)[54] consistently conclude that the production of oil is associated with violent conflict and particularly with secessionist conflict.

In a further study, Ross tests seven hypotheses on the way in which resources influence the onset, duration, or intensity of civil war.[55] Conclusions of particular relevance from his work include the absence of any evidence that looting from resource firms, and grievances associated with their operations, have contributed to the onset of nonseparatist conflicts, although they may have contributed to the rise of separatist conflicts and low-level conflicts. Where resource wealth is located in a region with separatist aspirations, it may help precipitate or escalate separatist conflict. Oil, in particular, can act as a catalyst in relation to separatist conflict: by gaining statehood, an oil-rich region can enter into contracts with oil companies and receive a share of the oil revenue, thereby realizing all the resource wealth for the subnational region instead of sharing it with the country as a whole. Intensifying the temptation to seek secession are secrecy surrounding oil revenues, distrust of companies, and ignorance of the oil industry, which together can lead to unrealistic expectations of the wealth that could become available.[56] In terms of conflict intensity, Ross finds the evidence contradictory. Whereas many wars have been fought over resource wealth, in most of the cases he examines, temporary or permanent peace was also achieved because of cooperation over exploitation of the same resources. Ross also notes that conflict onset and intensity may become linked through a negative spiral in which preemptive repression by governments against separatist political movements in resource-rich areas—partly motivated by the governments' interests in protecting their access to resource wealth—causes popular support for independence to escalate.[57]

Oil Revenue and Conflict

"I call petroleum the devil's excrement," said Venezuelan oil minister and founder of OPEC Juan Pablo Pérez Alfonso in 1975. He continued, "It brings trouble, waste, corruption, consumption, our public services are falling apart. And debt."[58] This section considers the role that government revenue from oil (and, to a lesser extent, gas)[59] production play in causing the troubles referred to by Pérez Alfonso. A brief outline of the scale of this revenue and its key attributes is followed by a discussion of the ways in which those attributes, if not properly managed, can present conflict risks. In chapter 4 this discussion is expanded to consider the scope for, and barriers to, oil companies' influencing revenue management to limit these risks.

Worldwide, estimates show that governments generally receive at least 45 percent, and as much as 90 percent, of the net value (i.e., after deduction of costs) of crude oil over the lifetime of an oil field.[60] For most oil-producing states this is a major source of government revenue. In some countries, however, oil revenue can outstrip other sources of government income, such as income taxes, business taxes, customs dues, and international aid. For example, in Angola oil revenue accounts for some three-fourths of government revenue; in Sudan and Azerbaijan, for approximately half—a proportion that will increase sharply after 2007, when large new oil and gas fields in both these nations come into production.[61] A flow of oil revenue is predictable for up to forty years once a field has been developed; however, its magnitude is highly volatile and sensitive to changes in oil prices and in the volume of output, which makes economic management of oil revenue a challenge for all oil-producing states. For countries with fragile economies, weak institutions, or limited capacity for peaceful resolution of political conflict, this is a particularly acute challenge.

The damaging effects of natural resource revenue on economies and governments, in the absence of appropriate policies for economic management and good governance, are well documented in the economics and political science literature.[62] In this light, for example, it is widely agreed that Norway has been the only state to successfully use oil wealth as a basis for transforming its economy and society. The central economic argument here is that dependence on natural resource revenue makes government spending programs vulnerable to revenue volatility and, hence, inefficiency; that the revenue provides a temptation for spending on "white elephant" projects; and that the revenue can actively weaken the nonoil economy by raising the value of the domestic currency and reducing competitiveness. The principal argument regarding resource revenue's effects on the quality of governance is threefold and centers on the way in which revenue insulates governments from the need to act in ways acceptable to their citizens and to international organizations such as the World Bank, bilateral donors, and the International Monetary Fund. First, without transparent tendering and reporting of concession contracts between governments and companies, there will be major opportunities for corruption. Second, oil revenues reduce the incentives for governments to invest in human capital and legal and institutional reforms, because a reliable domestic tax base—or donated aid funds conditional on reform—is less important than it would be without guaranteed oil revenue. Third, oil revenue provides the means for state-sponsored violence and for social control via patronage and repression.

The specific risks of triggering or exacerbating violent conflict that result from government receipt of oil revenue are a subset of these broad economic and political factors. Oil revenue can provide an incentive for conflict over control of the state,[63] as has happened in São Tomé and Príncipe[64] and Equatorial Guinea[65]—both emerging West African oil producers that have experienced attempted coups since oil reserves were first identified. (See also the discussion about Angola in chapter 6.) Oil revenue (or borrowing against future oil revenue streams) may also provide a source of funds with which to finance war, as in Angola's thirty-year war, the war in Sudan since 1991, and, as is feared might become the case, in Azerbaijan, over Nagorno-Karabakh.

A more complex set of connections between oil revenue and conflict risks concerns secession and economic/political mismanagement. Disputes over the allocation of oil revenue between oil-producing areas and the rest of the country have fueled both violent local conflict, as in the Niger delta, and secessionist conflict, as in Indonesia's Aceh Province, Angola's Cabinda Province, Biafra (Nigeria), and Southern Sudan. (The potency of oil in fueling separatism even in stable democracies is illustrated by the case of Scotland, where an independence movement grew up along with the oil industry, eventually leading to radical constitutional reform, which reduced the powers of the UK government and set up a Scottish Parliament.)[66] Economic mismanagement and poor governance, to which resource-based economies are particularly prone, can also contribute to violent civil unrest, as the next section illustrates.

The Example of Oil Wealth and Conflict in Nigeria

Violent conflicts in the Niger delta illustrate how the generation of oil revenue for government can exacerbate political tensions and contribute to their escalation into violent conflict.

In analyzing conflict in Nigeria, Rotimi Suberu identifies disputes over revenue sharing as one of the four linked and contested issues that undermine the establishment of a successful federal political structure in Nigeria as well as contribute to ethnic conflict.[67] Nigeria has been unable to agree on principles for revenue sharing between the federal government and the states since before the country became independent in 1960, when disputes focused on sharing export tax earnings from agriculture. Tensions have grown since the 1960s as state earnings from oil and gas exports have increased. The core issues concern how much of the country's oil wealth "belongs" to the areas where the oil fields are found, and—to the extent that these areas receive a share of revenues—which, precisely, are the areas that should benefit. Since 1946 nine separate commissions on revenue sharing have led to "neither the development of an acceptable state revenue sharing framework nor the elaboration of an appropriate framework of values and rules within which a formula can be devised and incrementally adjusted to cope with changing circumstances."[68] And pressures to define ever more tightly the areas to benefit from revenue—under the "derivation principles" that have been applied in various forms to oil wealth—have contributed to the increase in the number of Nigeria's states from four to thirty-six between 1960 and 2004, with a concentration of small states in the oil-rich delta.

The country experienced a brutal civil war (1967–70), an underlying cause of which was interregional conflict over control of growing oil revenues.[69] (Renewed calls for independence have been made since the early 2000s by the Movement for the Actualization of the Sovereign State of Biafra, or MASSOB, advocating secession to create the Biafran state over which the civil war was fought, leading in late 2005 to the detention of MASSOB's leadership.[70] In early 2006 a second organization, Movement for the Emancipation of the Niger Delta (MEND), launched a violent campaign to take control of the region's oil reserves by force, taking oil workers hostage in pursuit of political demands.)[71] Since the 1980s Nigeria has experienced civil conflict in many parts of the country, particularly the Niger delta, where violent conflict between ethnic splinter groups, crime, and lawlessness are often associated with calls for local control over oil wealth and with threats to shut down oil production. The seriousness of conflict in the Niger delta was highlighted in President Obasanjo's 2004 independence anniversary broadcast in October 2004, wherein he acknowledged the threat these conflicts present and reported that talks were underway for a cessation of hostilities. The president reminded listeners that 13 percent of revenues from onshore and offshore oil fields are now allocated to the Niger delta states, but noted, "So far not much impact has been made on the lives and living standards of most ordinary people of the Niger delta."[72] The 2005 National Political Reform Conference became deadlocked over oil revenue sharing, described as "the most contentious issue," following a recommendation to increase the share of the producing states to 17 percent, in contrast with the producing states' initial demand for 100 percent of revenues and subsequent demand for 25 percent as an interim measure.[73]

Management of Oil Revenue

Oil revenue carries the risk of contributing indirectly to violent civil unrest where it has a negative impact on economic development, wealth generation, and governance. Although resource wealth should be a catalyst for economic development—and in some cases has been so with spectacular success[74]—this is often not the case. Studies of post–World War II economies globally show that natural resource–abundant countries have systematically failed to achieve strong economic growth or poverty reduction.[75] Among the African developing countries, Botswana stands out as the single example of natural resource–based development accompanied by economic growth, democracy, and poverty reduction.[76] A task force convened in 2004 on behalf of the U.S. Department of State to examine the impacts of oil wealth in Africa recognized these risks and concluded that "An Angola, Nigeria, Chad, or Equatorial Guinea in distress could well become a vector for violence, crime, terror, and wanton disregard for democratic norms, human rights, equity, and stewardship of the environment."[77]

Work on the political economy of resource-based states also links oil wealth with high levels of corruption[78] and with authoritarian governments that are relieved of the need to secure public approval and a domestic tax base because of the revenue stream they receive from oil or minerals. The availability of resource revenues insulates corrupt, authoritarian, or ineffective government from internal and external pressures for reform. In the 2004 and 2005 Corruption Perceptions Index (CPI) published by Transparency International (TI), oil-rich countries had particularly low scores. According to the chairman of TI, introducing the 2004 report, "Oil rich Angola, Azerbaijan, Chad, Ecuador, Indonesia, Iran, Iraq, Kazakhstan, Libya, Nigeria, Russia, Sudan, Venezuela and Yemen all have extremely low scores. In these countries, public contracting in the oil sector is plagued by revenues vanishing into the pockets of western oil executives, middlemen and local officials."[79]

Many academics, policymakers, NGOs, and oil industry analysts are studying revenue "resource curse." A consensus is emerging on the main issues and the key components of revenue management required to avoid the curse. The central issue is not resource development per se but how the wealth is used. The broad characteristics of a revenue management system that would most likely lead to economic development, poverty reduction, stability, and democracy are macroeconomic controls, transparency in matters of state earnings, and acceptable rules on revenue allocation, including how producing areas will benefit. The specific measures most suitable to the circumstances of any one country, and the strategies to ensure that these are actually put in place, are much more contentious.

Techniques for economic management of revenue include putting oil revenue in savings, or stabilization funds, so that government income can be stabilized and oil "windfalls" spread over a longer period. Norway, Alberta, Alaska, Venezuela, Oman, and Kazakhstan have established oil funds with varying degrees of success. Another approach is to establish legally binding constraints on how government can use its oil receipts. For example, Chad's Revenue Management Law specifies the proportion of revenue that must go to debt service, to a "Future Generations Fund," to the oil-producing regions, and to development projects, under the oversight of a multistakeholder committee.[80] Policies are also needed to prevent oil-induced inflation from undermining the rest of the economy and to create employment (because oil production is not labor-intensive). In terms of transparency, the emerging—and plausible—international consensus is to reduce opportunities for corruption by making public information about oil contracts, the revenues paid by oil companies, and the allocation of revenues.[81] This builds on the experience in nonoil countries where the public dissemination of information about government resources and their allocation has reduced corruption and improved policies.[82]

The politics and economics of regional revenue allocation are a particularly challenging problem and have not been examined by policymakers and scholars to the extent that the macroeconomic and transparency issues have. Laws governing the regional allocation of revenue to producing areas show a tendency, worldwide, to provide for defined—and increasing—shares to producing regions. In Nigeria, the delta states now receive 13 percent of government oil revenues under the 1999 constitution, while Indonesia's 2001 "Special Autonomy" laws for Papua and Aceh formally allocate 70 percent of oil, gas, and mining revenue to those provinces. The Sudan Wealth Sharing Agreement of December 2003 provides for almost half of revenue generated from southern oil fields to be allocated to a new government of Southern Sudan. The agreement also provides for at least 2 percent to be allocated to the producing regions/states.[83] Chad's Petroleum Revenue Management Law allocates 5 percent to producing areas. However, there is little evidence to suggest that measures to share revenue are sufficient to stem existing conflicts or prevent violence in secessionist areas. On the basis of one of the few empirical studies, Ahmad and Mottu argue that subnational revenue sharing is the least preferable solution: "Such measures have generally not assuaged the aspirations of the oil producing regions and have exposed them to volatility in their revenue flows that they are generally unable to cope with."[84] Both Nigeria and Indonesia show few signs that oil wealth, once transferred to the regions, is any more cleanly or effectively used than by the central government, or that wealth sharing is contributing to an end to conflict. Both countries have experienced a domestic backlash over unfairly preferential treatment of oil regions.

Direct Distribution of Revenue

In light of the political challenges of inducing governments to improve their management of oil wealth, there is emerging discussion of more radical approaches whereby revenue would be distributed directly to the population rather than being held by government. The model for this is in Alaska, where one-half of oil royalties[85] is channeled into the Alaska Permanent Fund, and one-half of the fund's investment earnings is distributed to the state's residents in the form of annual checks. The objective of the Alaska scheme is to give citizens a stake in the development of the industry while also saving a share of this nonrenewable wealth for future generations. The first dividends were paid in 1982; in 2004 each resident received $919.84.[86] In late 2005, Alberta Premier Ralph Klein announced that one-third of the Canadian province's unbudgeted surplus from high oil revenue would be distributed to Albertans, each of whom would receive a Can$400 check in 2006.[87]

Some analysts argue that in states where the government has a record of failing to manage oil wealth effectively, all revenue should be transferred directly to citizens. This goes beyond the Alaska model by cutting out the fund that earns income from oil revenue, on the grounds that in such states the institutional capacity to monitor and exercise accountability is weak. Instead, proponents suggest direct, annual revenue distribution. Thus, Xavier Sala-i-Marta and Arvind Subramanian argue in a 2003 IMF working paper that in order to address the natural resource curse in Nigeria,

> ...oil revenues be distributed equally to the people, with each Nigerian or adult Nigerian having a right to an equal share in the proceeds... [This] proposal...could also apply to other countries that are dependent on oil and minerals and have been affected by the consequential curse of weak institutional quality. In some ways, countries such as Venezuela and Iraq may be even better candidates...because the [administration] costs...may be lower than in Nigeria.[88]

Nobel laureate economist Vernon Smith takes the case further, arguing in the case of Iraq that state assets, including subsurface rights and revenue streams, should be transferred to a fund directly owned by all Iraqi citizens. This would require, among other things, that the government obtain its income from taxes "levied on the citizens who are willing to elect them and finance their spending programs."[89] Regarding the tiny phosphate-producing island state of Nauru, one leading analyst argues that direct distribution of the remaining revenue wealth is one key component of a strategy to try to redress a situation in which most of the country's wealth has been stolen or misused by predatory institutions while its 11,000 residents face economic, ecological, and social disaster as the mineral reserves tail off without any alternative economic base.[90] The drawback to these approaches, recognized by the authors promoting them, is that of persuading the elites who benefit from ill-managed wealth to cede control. Nevertheless, it is to be expected that as more information about oil revenues becomes available in producing countries, and in the absence of improved governance resulting in real benefits to the citizens of resource-rich countries, there could be popular pressure for "Alaska-type" or even more radical solutions.

Revenue Transparency

In the early 2000s, making accurate information publicly available about extractive industry revenue paid to governments began to be a focus of international policy toward developing and transitional countries with oil and gas wealth. Voluntary government–extractive industry collaboration, as framed in the Extractive Industries Transparency Initiative (EITI, discussed in chapter 4) is bolstered by technical support and international leverage.

In their mid-2004 summit, the G8 nations launched the first Transparency Compacts, voluntary partnerships in which a developing country government sets out a plan to bring greater transparency and accountability to the management of public resources, with the G8 governments providing technical assistance and political support.[91] The IMF's managing director, Rodrigo de Rato, has stressed the importance of fiscal transparency, and its role as a key element in the recommendations it makes to oil-exporting countries. Revenue transparency is a condition for IMF financial support in Angola, for example. In Azerbaijan, the IMF helped the government to set up the State Oil Fund[92] and, in mid-2004, was applying open pressure on the government to develop a long-term oil revenue management strategy.[93] In 2005 the IMF published guidelines on revenue transparency:

> A high immediate priority should be given to improving the quality and public disclosure of data on resource revenue transactions, using either templates recommended as part of the EITI or alternative formats that provide adequate assurance of data quality. Transparency of current revenue transactions is an area in which many low and middle income countries can make immediate visible progress, if necessary with technical support. An equally high priority should be given to establishing clear policies for the use of resource revenues.[94]

During 2002–04 the World Bank Group undertook a thorough review of its policies concerning the extractive industries, and it is increasingly promoting transparency, anticorruption measures, and policies to actively promote the nonoil sector in oil-rich countries, through the Country Assistance Strategies that frame its operations and by its involvement in developing and implementing national poverty reduction plans, or poverty reduction strategy papers (PRSPs). The

World Bank Group became directly involved in oil revenue management policy in Chad by making oil-sector development loans conditional on the creation of a revenue management law. The group also
helped draft this law, design and establish supporting institutions, and
set up revenue management monitoring systems.

The case of Chad illustrates the political challenge of changing how
oil revenues are managed. Only a few years after the government of
Chad started receiving oil revenues, it substantially amended the Petroleum Revenue Management Law, cutting back on savings for future
generations, increasing the share of the general budget not subject to
civil society scrutiny, and allowing for spending on administration and
security as well as on health, education, and other development priorities. In January 2006 these changes caused the World Bank to withhold
new loans and grants and suspend disbursements on existing loans.[95]

The Local Impact of Oil: Changes, Tensions, and Violent Conflict

The second set of links between oil and conflict relates to the local environmental, social, and economic impact of the industry. The development of petroleum resources always brings physical, social, economic,
and political change in areas where production fields and pipelines are
located. This section discusses these changes and how they can lead to
local tensions and wider violent conflict.

Local Impact: Changes and Tensions

In his seminal history of the oil industry, Daniel Yergin shows how,
from the first oil boom in nineteenth-century Pennsylvania to the rise
of the current industry in South America, the exploitation of oil
resources has brought waves of change. His description of the effects of
an oil find at Pithole Creek, Pennsylvania, serves as an ominous example of oil's transformative power:

> The first well was struck in the dense forest land there in January 1865; by
> June, there were four flowing wells, producing two thousand barrels per
> day—one third of the total output of the Oil Regions—and people fought
> their way in on the roads already clogged with the barrel-laden wagons.

"The whole place," said one visitor, "smells like a corps of soldiers when they have diarrhea." The land speculation seemed to know no bounds. One farm that was virtually worthless a few months earlier was sold for $1.3 million in July 1865, and then resold for two million dollars in September....And by that same September, what had once been an unidentifiable spot in the wilderness had become a town of fifteen thousand people. *The New York Herald* reported that the principal businesses of Pithole were "liquor and leases."[96]

Yergin then notes what happened when the wells ran dry:

Pithole returned to silence and to the wilderness. A parcel of land…that sold for $2 million in 1865 was auctioned for $4.37 in 1878. Even as Pithole died, the speculative boom was exploding elsewhere and engulfing neighboring areas.[97]

Most modern oil production is more controlled than was the case in the nineteenth century, but it is also conducted on a larger scale and over a longer period, creating the potential for major local impacts from production wells, pipelines, and processing plants, as well as new roads, housing, and various infrastructure. The scale of impact varies from country to country and from oil field to oil field, depending in particular on how densely populated and industrialized the production area is when oil reserves begin to be developed, and whether oil fields and the supporting facilities are onshore or offshore. For example, most of Angola's current production is from onshore or coastal oil fields, but most new fields being developed will have minimal onshore impact since they are located far offshore and will load oil directly onto tankers from the floating platforms. By contrast, in the case of Azerbaijan, although the production fields are offshore in the Caspian Sea, there are onshore terminals and thousand-mile-long pipelines crossing three countries to take the oil to market. In Sudan both oil fields and pipelines are onshore, located mainly in very undeveloped but sparsely populated rural areas without any previous industrial activity.

A common characteristic of modern oil and gas projects is that they are capital-intensive and create little permanent local employment. Typically, large projects employ thousands of people during a one- to three-year construction period, and only a few hundred people over the decades during which they are producing oil. Much of the equipment needed is high tech, brought in from global suppliers. Local employment and business opportunities are likely to be restricted to a few individuals with the specialized skills, powerful connections, or landholdings required by the industry. In these circumstances, oil developments can bring destructive cultural change, disappointment, and inequality, altering the relationship between work and wealth. Anthropologist Karin Barber writes of the dislocation that oil wealth caused in Nigeria in the early 1980s:

> Wealth…has always been an attainable and a supremely desirable goal for Yoruba people…. But…wealth was always seen to be created by work…. Oil wealth, however, is not seen to be produced by work…. All the government has really had to do is to open its hands and receive the money…. In other words, gigantic sums of cash seem to have appeared as if from nowhere, being appropriated by those who contributed virtually nothing to its production, and in the process personally enriching a few Nigerians on a colossal scale.[98]

The process of economic and social change brought about by large-scale energy development has often led to conflict, in some cases to violent conflict. For example, in Iran in the early twentieth century, violent conflict between local tribes and oil drillers, and between tribes, caused Britain to send a small military detachment. In Venezuela geologists and drillers had to contend with hostile Indian tribes: "As late as 1929, Shell protected the cabins of its tractors with several layers of a special cloth, dense enough to stop Indian arrows."[99] Writing of the period leading up to the overthrow of the shah of Iran, Yergin describes how, by the mid-1970s,

> It had become evident…that Iran simply could not absorb the vast increase in oil revenues that was flooding into the country. The petrodollars, megalomaniacally misspent on extravagant modernization programmes or lost to waste and corruption, were generating economic chaos and social and political tension throughout the nation. The rural population was pouring from the villages into already-overcrowded towns and cities; agricultural output was declining, while food imports were going up. Inflation had seized the country, breeding all the inevitable discontents….The social fabric was unraveling.[100]

In the early twenty-first century, people who experience problems because of petroleum-related change are often vocal, organized, and effective in making their voices heard. This was evidenced, for example, in the Extractive Industries Review (EIR) carried out from 2001 to 2003 for the World Bank in order to investigate the impact of the extractive industry on poverty reduction and sustainable development. The report presented to the bank stated, "The EIR received many grievances from indigenous peoples and affected communities alike who believe that the extractive industries sector have had negative impacts on them and on other communities."[101] Specific grievances cited in evidence to the Review include loss of land and of access to land, resulting in loss of livelihoods and cultural erosion; human rights abuses; degradation of the environment and natural resources; lack of consultation; lack of credible and easily accessible grievance mechanisms; accidents; armed conflict; lack of perceived benefits from projects, and socioeconomic problems; and the absence of rights on the part of communities to decide whether extractive industry projects should go ahead, and under what conditions.

Local Impact and Violent Conflict

Evidence that oil projects can generate grievances is widespread. And as will be discussed in chapter 4, businesses in the industry are increasingly using the tools of corporate social responsibility to anticipate and avoid creating negative impacts that generate grievances and problems for their operations. What are less clear are the links, if any, between local grievances over oil projects and larger-scale violent conflict that escalates beyond local tensions and crime. Far more areas produce oil than are locked in intractable conflict.

One persuasive argument holds that the interaction of secessionist or ethnic politics with oil and gas projects that have caused local damage or failed to meet local expectations of benefits, combined with the capture of oil revenues by distant elites and the violent repression of secessionist activity, leads to large-scale and long-lasting violent civil conflict or civil war.[102] Outside these circumstances there is little evidence that grievances related to extractive industries, although widespread and sometimes provoking violence, have contributed to the onset of civil war. In a recent analysis of civil wars ending between 1945 and 1996, however, Barbara Walter argues that renewed war has largely been a function of individual citizens' incentives to rejoin a rebel group, and that hardship or dissatisfaction, combined with the absence of any non-violent mechanisms for change, creates such incentives. Thus, she argues, actions to improve the quality of life and enable political participation are essential to reducing the likelihood of renewed war.[103]

Conclusions

In assessing the risk that oil development may become either a catalyst for, or an exacerbator of, conflict, companies must accept that many other factors are also involved and that it is impossible to predict accurately whether or when conflict might erupt. The circumstances that increase the risk that investments will contribute to violent conflict occur (1) where revenues from oil are a substantial part of total government income; (2) where petroleum reserves are located in parts of the country with a distinct identity that is not recognized politically; (3) where there are unresolved conflicts or there has been civil war during the previous decade; (4) where the economic conditions of most people are stagnant or deteriorating; and (5) where government and institutions lack the capacity for effective management of revenues and for nonviolent management of conflict.

Walter's findings suggest that oil companies can make a valid contribution to peacemaking by avoiding creating the conditions for grievances and unfulfilled expectations and by contributing to economic development and democracy building. As discussed in chapter 4, companies can do much to avoid provoking or exacerbating local grievances, especially regarding new projects, through applying impact assessment and mitigation techniques, consulting widely before starting work, operating in developing countries according to the high environmental standards required in the West, and investing in high-quality social programs. Because the evidence shows that local conflicts, once started, are persistent, it is important that these steps be taken to avoid creating the grievances that give rise to violence. However, there are no guarantees that this type of "conflict-sensitive approach" will be sufficient to prevent social change from mutating into tension and violence, or to prevent projects from serving as catalysts for secession conflicts if governments mismanage revenues, allow widespread corruption, and react aggressively to political opposition.

4

Corporate Social Responsibility

ORPORATE SOCIAL RESPONSIBILITY (CSR) concepts and tools have taken hold within many international businesses, particularly those based in Europe. This has led to thinking, though more by NGOs and academics than by business executives, about the roles that socially responsible business might play in peacebuilding. This chapter begins by providing a brief outline of the development of CSR in general, then focuses in some detail on CSR developments within the oil industry and outlines the principal arguments being advanced about a business role in peacebuilding. The discussion considers the different levels of uptake of CSR among oil companies, and the limited appeal that explicit engagement in peacebuilding holds for most in the industry. The next section suggests that a new model for oil and gas developments, with the potential to reduce the conflict risks attendant on the development of oil resources, was initiated by the Chad-Cameroon project. The project includes comprehensive actions on revenue and local impact management as part of the development of a new oil field and export pipeline and, in doing so, sets a benchmark for oil companies and their host government partners. Drawing on and extending much of the CSR thinking in the industry, the project came about as a result of hardheaded corporate analysis of business risks and risk management strategies. The final section considers the differential uptake of CSR within the international oil industry, showing the links with the variation in priorities for the different types of company described in chapter 2.

From Corporate Philanthropy toward Social Responsibility

Corporations have a long-standing tradition of philanthropy, particularly in the United States, where corporate charitable contributions are estimated at more than $12 billion a year[104] and where a whole range of community, arts, education, and health projects are funded in part by grants from businesses. During the 1990s, concepts of corporate social responsibility—going beyond this traditional philanthropy—began to emerge among businesses in the West, in response to two main sources of pressure. Companies were increasingly targeted by nongovernmental organizations on the grounds that they had a damaging impact on communities and the wider society. And with the end of the Cold War and with globalization lowering trade barriers worldwide, businesses started facing new challenges as they invested in locations where individuals, communities, and governments had expectations, cultures, and values unfamiliar to Western managers. These dual pressures on businesses were reflected in the stream of new assignments for consultants, who were increasingly asked to advise business directors on human rights, and operational managers on dialogue with communities and NGOs.[105] Interest shifted from the value of charitable donations to the wider implications of the ways in which businesses operate and the extent of their responsibilities both to the communities where they operate and to the wider public.

A series of seminal events put CSR on the business agenda. In the 1970s antiapartheid campaigns led to development of the Global Sullivan Principles—one of the first expressions of recent CSR principles—for American companies operating in South Africa.[106] In 1984 the Bhopal chemical plant explosion caused an estimated 4,000 deaths and 400,000 injuries, exposing the risks of locating large-scale, complex facilities in countries lacking the legal or institutional capacity to regulate and control them. In the 1990s the "sweatshop" and child-labor campaigns against companies such as Nike, condemning the conditions under which consumer goods sold in the United States and Europe are produced, led to the development of voluntary "codes of conduct." The Enron and other scandals of the early 2000s resulted in a new focus on corporate governance and corruption. By the mid-2000s a much broader debate has started to emerge about the extent to which corporations are either a contributor or a key part of the solution to global poverty.[107]

Since the 1980s business management systems developed within multinational corporations to address environmental issues were extended to address social, community, and human rights issues.[108] Corporations developed company-specific CSR strategies, exemplified in social responsibility policies and programs, and groups of companies joined together or started to collaborate with NGOs, governments, or multilateral organizations to develop collective strategies. For example, in 1995 the World Business Council for Sustainable Development (WBCSD) was established as a coalition of businesses with "a shared commitment to sustainable development via economic growth, ecological balance, and social progress." By 2005 it had some 175 members, including major U.S. corporations.[109] In 1999 UN Secretary-General Kofi Annan set up the Global Compact, bringing together companies, UN organizations, and NGOs to support a set of nine principles in the fields of human rights, labor, and the environment. By mid-2005, more than 2,000 companies had signed up, and the nine principles had been extended to cover corruption.[110] According to the United States Council for International Business, most of its large member-companies employ managers who oversee corporate responsibility issues.[111] Reflecting consumer interest in corporate social performance, many financial institutions now offer "socially responsible investment" products and encourage companies to adopt specific social policies, for example, on labor practices, environmental performance, and stakeholder engagement. Systems such as FTSE4Good[112] and the Dow Jones Sustainability Index[113] were established for the benefit of socially responsible investors, to rank corporations in terms of their social and environmental performance, with the criteria applied by these systems sending signals to businesses about their expected behaviors. Although a few of these steps toward CSR were in response to new government regulations (such as

Sarbanes-Oxley),[114] most reflected a business response to changes in the marketplace.

A new phase of CSR thinking started in the early 2000s, focusing on how companies could benefit themselves and the wider society by seeking out "corporate social opportunities" through such actions as providing goods and services geared toward poverty reduction and alleviation.

CSR in the Oil Industry

The oil industry, along with the apparel industry, is at the forefront of CSR, largely because of the criticism it has taken and because of its business operations in developing and transitional countries with weak or authoritarian governments and poor records of protecting human rights or the environment. The discussion below examines how CSR thinking in the oil industry has evolved, the key industry approaches to CSR, and the evolving pattern of corporate-government-NGO partnerships in the sector.

Evolution

The international oil industry, especially its large companies, has long been the subject of public suspicion and NGO criticism. The 1989 Exxon Valdez oil spill focused attention on environmental damage issues. Numerous campaigns and legal actions have arisen over the destructive effects on communities living close to oil industry operations, for example, in the Niger delta and Ecuador. Allegations of human rights abuses, such as the use of forced labor or abuses by security forces protecting oil facilities, have been leveled at the industry, as have allegations that companies prop up authoritarian and corrupt governments through oil concession and revenue payments. A number of key triggers led the major oil companies to start taking these concerns seriously. The "boycott Shell" campaigns, in response to the company's 1995 plans for disposing of decommissioned drilling rigs in the North Sea, and to the execution of Ken Sara Wiwa by the Nigerian military regime in November of that year, led Shell to revaluate its business conduct and communications with stakeholders. Another important trigger was the 1997 allegations that BP hired paramilitaries with a reputation for human rights abuse to protect its oil installations in Colombia. This prompted a major rethinking of the company's approach to security, one outcome of which has been the industry-wide Voluntary Principles on Security and Human Rights, discussed below. A suite of cases brought under the U.S. Alien Tort Claims Act (ATCA), alleging corporate complicity in human rights abuses in countries including Burma, Ecuador, Nigeria, and Sudan, has influenced other companies to consider the potential financial and reputation costs of ignoring the behavior of the governments with which they have concession contracts. The point was brought home even more clearly with Unocal's 2004 settlement of an ATCA case alleging that the company had commissioned Burmese soldiers to protect its Yadana gas pipeline, knowing that the soldiers had committed murder and rape, and had used forced labor.[115]

Continuing expressions of concern about the impact of the oil, gas, and mining industries in developing countries, encouraged or supported in many cases through financial and technical assistance by the World Bank Group (WBG), led the WBG to set up an independent investigation of the extractive industries' impact on sustainable development, and the future role that the WBG should take. This resulted in an assessment, published in 2003, that was highly critical of the industry's performance in terms of both local impacts and the impacts of resource revenues. The Extractive Industries Review recommended that the WBG exercise its influence to ensure that investments in the extractive industries contribute to poverty alleviation, and stated that achieving this requires pro-poor governance of concessions and revenues, high standards for environmental and social protection, and insistence that extractive industry operations protect human rights.[116]

The major oil companies and the WBG responded to these criticisms by challenging the facts of specific allegations and, in many cases where they had not already started doing so, by developing social responsibility programs to alter their ways of operating. Thus, a 2003 World Bank study found that "most" of the eighteen oil exploration, production, and servicing companies operating in Angola had policy statements on social responsibility,[117] and in 2005 the NGO Business & Human Rights reported that fifteen oil companies had policy statements referring to protection of human rights.[118] A large number of the oil companies publish annual social and environmental reports (sometimes referred to as sustainability reports) that set out their nonfinancial objectives and report on what they are doing to achieve these.[119] In some cases, these reports are externally audited, like financial accounts. Many have adopted, and publish, codes of conduct covering social, environmental, and ethical performance. Some have developed and published guidelines setting out specifically what these codes of conduct imply in terms of the way business is carried out.[120] Several oil majors now have sociologists, anthropologists, and former NGO employees on their staffs or among their advisors. CSR is becoming established in the language of financial analysts, too; a 2004 report published by Goldman Sachs concluded, "In order to succeed, companies must be managed for the new world, that means...in a socially responsible manner."[121]

Key Components

Social responsibility approaches found in the oil industry have three substantive components. The first is based on systems to avoid creating negative social impacts while contributing positively to the communities and societies where they operate. This involves doing impact assessments of new projects, consulting with neighboring communities and NGOs in order to understand what the unintended impacts of investment might be and how these can be avoided, and financing community projects chosen to reflect community needs and priorities.[122] These assessments can involve making sure that people from oil field areas benefit from employment and business opportunities, often through elaborate training, hiring, and business development programs, because a consistent finding from all community consultations is that people want jobs as compensation for the changes introduced by oil industry development. Since around 2003, social and environmental impact assessments have become standard practice for large-scale oil and gas projects that have been undertaken by the majors or that have obtained financial backing from the World Bank's private-sector arm, the International Finance Corporation (IFC), or from the commercial banks that have signed on to the Equator Principles, which commit them to apply the IFC standards to projects that the signatory banks finance. (Many large-scale investments, including the development of oil fields, pipelines, and oil terminals, are partly financed by banks. Under the Equator Principles, launched in 2003, commercial banks provide project financing to projects costing $50 million or more only if the projects comply with the IFC environmental and social criteria. As of December 31, 2005, thirty-eight major financial institutions worldwide had adopted the Equator Principles, estimated to control more than 80 percent of the project finance market.)[123]

The second key element of CSR approaches in the oil industry is involvement in "trisectoral" partnerships, made up of companies, governments, and NGOs, to develop and implement voluntary systems that address specific issues. The first such initiative in the oil industry was the December 2000 Voluntary Principles on Security and Human Rights, negotiated by the U.S. and UK governments, six major extractive industry corporations, and a set of international NGOs. This was followed in 2002 by the Extractive Industries Transparency Initiative (EITI), which focuses on revenue management. It is predominantly the majors that are involved in these initiatives. (See below for a more detailed discussion of these two initiatives.)

The final element of CSR in the oil industry is for companies to become explicitly involved, as a matter of enlightened self-interest in collaborating with governments, businesses, and NGOs in activities aimed at preventing the "curse of oil" and ensuring that oil booms result in economic and social development.[124] This approach, promoted by some NGOs,[125] is reflected in efforts to encourage revenue management programs, large-scale and development-oriented social investment programs (targeted at super majors), projects to provide access to energy for people in hydrocarbon-exporting countries,[126] and projects such as the International Business Leaders Forum action plan for businesses in support of the Millennium Development Goals,[127] which, for example, encourages business to get involved in promoting international trade reform.

World Bank Standards and Impact Assessments

The WBG's policies on environmental and social safeguards, originally developed to guide World Bank lending to governments, are increasingly used by companies as the standards to apply to private-sector projects, and as the basis for determining how oil fields will be developed in those cases where concession contracts refer to the application of "international standards."[128] They also form the core of the Equator Principles. In essence, these standards require thorough impact assessment before a project starts, as well as consultation with those affected, and an understanding of actions to avoid, minimize, or make compensation in the event of adverse impact. In their latest form, put forth by the IFC in mid-2005, the standards require projects to be designed to provide development benefits as well as safeguard communities or the environment from "collateral damage" caused by business investments. They include standards for impact assessment methods, disclosure of information to the public and consultation with affected communities, land acquisition and compensation, employment conditions and labor rights, and environmental protections.[129] Applying these standards requires companies to go through a systematic process to incorporate the requirements into the planning and execution of new exploration and production projects and to solicit and respond to external views on their activities. This process breaks the usual pattern in the oil industry, by which companies and governments agree, in the absence of public scrutiny, on projects that often have a major impact on local communities and the wider society. The standards establish some clear benchmarks, for example, that companies and their government partners select project designs that do not require people to leave their homes or lands in order to allow for oil exploration, or, if this is unavoidable, that ensure that people's livelihoods are at least restored and, if possible, improved.

Up to the late 1990s, although environmental impact assessments were standard practice in the oil industry—and required in some form by many governments as part of the process of agreeing to new oil and gas projects—little attention was paid to the impacts of oil and gas developments on people and communities. With oil companies and their employees under threat in the Niger delta and occasionally elsewhere, and with expansion of the industry into countries where companies had little experience or local knowledge, businesses began to recognize the need to be more careful in planning their projects. Environmental impact assessments began to be expanded to include an assessment of social impacts, with the objective of identifying potential negative impacts and then avoiding, limiting, or compensating for them. At their best, environmental and social impact assessments (ESIAs) include detailed research in an effort to understand the social and economic fabric of the neighborhoods where oil wells and pipelines are to be built, as well as extensive consultation with community members, so that people have advance knowledge of the developments, and the opportunity to express their concerns and interests. The assessments require public disclosure of findings. They result in concrete, published plans for avoiding or compensating for negative impacts and for providing local benefits, and they include mechanisms for resolving any disputes and for monitoring implementation. The underlying aim of an ESIA is to develop new oil and gas fields in a way that avoids causing social damage and disruption, provides tangible benefits to the local population, and reduces business risks from social and environmental factors. This brings to countries lacking the legal and institutional framework something of the public scrutiny of major projects that is standard in Europe and the United States.

Government-Business-NGO Partnerships

The crux of the conflict risks presented by oil projects in developing and transitional countries—revenue management and damaging local impacts—cannot be fully addressed by companies developing individual projects in a socially responsible way. The need for collective action in dealing with host governments on revenue transparency and oil field security was recognized early on as some of the major oil companies developed CSR approaches. This resulted in the Voluntary Principles for Security and Human Rights and the Extractive Industries Transparency Initiative.

The Voluntary Principles on Security and Human Rights were negotiated in 2000 by a group of oil, gas, and mining companies, the U.S. State Department, the UK Foreign and Commonwealth Office, and NGOs with an interest in human rights and corporate social responsibility. The Principles aim to "guide companies in maintaining the safety and security of their operations within an operating framework that ensures respect for human rights and fundamental freedoms."[130] The business logic behind the Principles is to provide some objective standards for "socially responsible" security that could protect companies from allegations of human rights abuses, to have a widely endorsed framework to assist with negotiating project security arrangements with host governments, to reduce the risks of excessive and abusive responses by security forces to local disturbances, which only raise tensions and exacerbate conflict, and to have a process for developing expertise on human rights–sensitive security. The Principles define processes for planning and managing security (whether provided by state or private security forces) that safeguard human rights through the observance of international law enforcement principles, excluding individuals credibly implicated in human rights abuses; rules of engagement that limit action to preventive and defensive services; and public consultation and transparency about security arrangements. By signing on to the Voluntary Principles, companies make a commitment to try to ensure that these objectives are met, although it is explicitly recognized that in many countries the host governments have the ultimate decision-making power. One of the country case studies reported in chapter 5, "Azerbaijan," demonstrates how the Voluntary Principles have been explicitly incorporated into the oil and gas projects. Published security protocols illustrate how this has been done. In another case, the Canadian company Talisman, though not a member, tried to negotiate agreement with the Government of Sudan on a security protocol consistent with the Voluntary Principles but was unsuccessful.

The Extractive Industries Transparency Initiative (EITI) is a voluntary, government-led, multistakeholder program aimed at increasing transparency over revenue and concession payments by companies to governments, as well as transparency over the use of revenues by host governments. The underlying assumption is that increasing transparency and knowledge of revenue use will empower citizens and institutions to hold governments to account, and that mismanagement or diversion of funds away from social and economic development spending will become more difficult. Participants in EITI agree to a set of principles and to work actively to support the objectives of the EITI, including developing and testing methods for payments and revenue disclosure, seeking country-level agreements on reporting and disclosure, incorporating EITI principles into organizational policies and guidelines, and encouraging others to join the initiative. Standardized templates for revenue reporting have been developed, and member countries are encouraged and assisted in developing country-level multistakeholder programs for implementing transparency. Azerbaijan, Ghana, the Kirghiz Republic, and Nigeria have chosen to be "pilot" countries for the initiative.[131] All five "super major" oil companies (ExxonMobil, BP, Shell, Total, and Chevron Corporation) have joined EITI, as have their home country governments: the United States, France, and UK. Other oil companies have joined, including the state oil companies of Azerbaijan and Angola. But the governments of many oil-producing states have not yet joined; of the three countries analyzed in this study, in mid-2005 only Azerbaijan was a participant. Among countries outside this study, Nigeria has launched one of the most sophisticated, comprehensive audits of all 2004 EITI participants.

CSR, Conflict Prevention, and Peacebuilding

An important element in the development of CSR is advocacy, particularly from some NGOs and academics,[132] calling for business to take an explicit role in peacebuilding. These advocates propose systematic actions for businesses—at the corporate, operational, and collective levels—designed to protect local people from conflict risks and to yield wider social benefits. Several broad assumptions are suggested here: that much of the business world has a direct interest in operating in a peaceful environment, that businesses contribute to conflict in ways that should be identified and stopped, and that businesses, individually or collectively, can contribute to conflict prevention and resolution— especially by collaborating with partners in government and civil society. Much attention within the discussion about business and conflict focuses on the oil and gas industry because of its pattern of investment in conflict-prone countries and because of the growing attention to links between oil and conflict.

Jane Nelson, in her seminal 2000 report "The Business of Peace," focuses on the potential for corporate actions. She argues that the potential and reality of conflict is becoming an unavoidable business issue, that most businesses have a vested interest in stability and peace, and that the private sector "has a vital role to play in creating wealth and promoting socioeconomic development but also has a role in contributing—both directly and indirectly—to the prevention and resolution of violent conflict."[133] She identifies the natural-resource industries as one of three sectors that have a particular responsibility to understand and address their direct role as potential agents of conflict, and demonstrates how tools for conflict analysis and peacebuilding could be adapted for use by business. She advocates five "Principles of Corporate Engagement in Conflict Prevention and Resolution"—strategic commitment, risk and impact analysis, dialogue and consultation, partnership and collective action, and evaluation and accountability—to guide companies in creating social value and enhancing shareholder value in ways that contribute to conflict prevention and resolution.

Two years later, Andreas Wenger and Daniel Möckli, in "Conflict Prevention: The Untapped Potential of the Business Sector," made many of the same arguments about the overall business case for engagement in conflict prevention. They encourage individual companies to engage in conflict prevention by pursuing their business activities with a specific conflict prevention perspective and contributing to "economic peacebuilding," for example, by transferring know-how on private-sector development. However, they also propose a collective conflict-prevention initiative by the private sector "that orchestrates the activities of the business community in conflict prevention and serves as a contact point for other actors involved in international prevention activities." Doing so would provide a valuable business perspective to the planning and implementation of conflict-prevention operations, convince activists and consumers of the willingness of corporations to take on their share of global governance, and assist companies operating in conflict areas.[134]

In 2005 the London-based NGO International Alert, drawing on the results of research and consultation with NGOs, companies, and other sources, presented detailed guidance for companies in the extractive sector on minimizing the risks of conflict during operations and actively engaging in peacebuilding. They make the business case that applying conflict management strategies can help avoid costs incurred as a result of conflict—for example, higher security, capital, and insurance costs and disruption to operations. The guidance pack presents tools for identifying conflict risks, for undertaking "Conflict Risk and Impact Assessments," and for addressing nine specific "flashpoint" issues that commonly arise at the company-conflict interface. The guidance pack goes on to describe likely impacts and propose good practice in each area, for example, resettlement, protection of indigenous rights, and issues of corruption and transparency.[135] Wenger and Möckli encourage businesses to stimulate economic activity that creates employment and contributes to the development of government and civil-society capacity building.

There is little evidence that companies in the oil sector (or other industrial sectors) are persuaded by the argument that their social responsibilities extend to establishing policies and programs for conflict prevention and peacebuilding. Few corporate or industry policies make any reference to conflict prevention or peacebuilding, and it is not a topic to which industry CSR organizations are devoting visible attention. Discussions with company CSR managers reveal skepticism that explicit corporate commitments to peacebuilding would be viewed as legitimate or realistic, that their colleagues and shareholders could be persuaded that this is a valid activity to undertake, or that they have the skills needed to intervene successfully. Businesses are also wary of accepting concepts that might lead to a loss of control over decisions about where to invest, thereby creating "no-go" areas and leaving investment opportunities open to competitors less committed to social responsibility. The business case for corporate engagement in peacebuilding, moreover, is probably weaker than it appears, because of the perception of many in the industry—especially the globe-trotting engineers who typically lead new projects—that it is often possible to continue operating in conditions of conflict. There are cases where conflict has shut down operations temporarily, but these are few. In this view, then, while peace might provide a better environment, it is not considered essential; security arrangements can be called upon, if necessary, to insulate operations from the surrounding society. Indeed, one econometric study found that the share value of companies in Angola's diamond industry based in rebel-held territory fell in 2002 when Jonas Savimbi, the rebel leader, was killed and the war came to an end.[136]

Within the oil industry, however, there is greater interest in conflict prevention and peacebuilding in a restricted and operationally relevant way. Many of the specific ideas about how oil companies could operate to help prevent conflict and build peace are increasingly reflected in CSR systems, including, for example, the Voluntary Principles on Security and Human Rights discussed above. Without making any broad statements or developing ambitious policies and programs, some corporate social responsibility managers are starting to explore how their actions might contribute to conflict, and how to limit this; to consider the links between revenue management and conflict, and how companies might, without jeopardizing their relationship with host governments, facilitate effective revenue management, implement social investment projects with peacebuilding objectives, and provide financial support to postconflict reconstruction. For example, since 1999, the Norwegian part-private, part-state oil company, Statoil, has been supporting Amnesty International, the UN Development Program (UNDP), and Escuela Judicial, the latter in providing human rights training for judges in Venezuela.[137] In Colombia, where BP operates in an area where "outlawed military groups are permanently based in the province's foothills and grassy plains and guerilla groups have historically targeted foreign oil companies," the company supports the House for Peace and Justice, which trains judicial and social service officials in conflict resolution and provides conciliation services.[138] Many more projects attempt to counteract the underlying economic causes of conflict by seeking to stimulate employment and economic development. Such projects include multimillion-dollar partnerships between aid donors and corporations, such as that in Angola involving Chevron Corporation, the U. S. Agency for International Development (USAID), and the UNDP.[139]

The Chad-Cameroon Project[140]

The Chad-Cameroon Project set new standards for the development of oil resources in conflict-prone countries through collaboration between ExxonMobil and the World Bank. Its efforts resulted in comprehensive measures being applied to manage local impacts and government revenues. Chad's Doba oil fields are located in an undeveloped country with fragile institutions, communities, and ecology, unresolved civil conflicts, and few opportunities, other than developing its oil resources, for emerging out of poverty. Amid much controversy, after ten years of planning and negotiation involving oil companies, the governments of Chad and Cameroon, the World Bank, communities in the oil field areas, and national and international NGOs on mechanisms to develop the oil resources in a way that would be commercially and socially successful, the production fields and pipeline started operations in 2003. Innovative regulations and new institutions were established to manage the Chad government's oil revenues, including an Oil Revenue Law mandating transparency about payments; the allocation of revenues to development purposes, and a share to the producing areas; and an independent oversight committee to supervise revenue payments and use. There was in-depth consultation with communities, over a seven-year period, to explain the plans in the villages around the project area and to understand and address community concerns and expectations. Very thorough impact assessment was undertaken leading to detailed plans for land acquisition, impact management and community benefits, and a multilayered monitoring system set up to control the local impacts of oil production. A World Bank capacity-building and development program for government and civil society was also established.

The genesis of the Chad-Cameroon approach was the oil company's assessment that although there were commercially viable oil reserves in the Doba field, the political and security risks of the $4 billion project to develop the field and the export pipeline to take the oil to market were too high for the company to take on alone and needed to be shared with governments and multilateral institutions, through cofinancing and export credit guarantees. The core risks were conflict—the exploration phase had been interrupted several times by civil conflict in Chad—and the absence of a record of accomplishment, in either country, of large-scale, long-term investments. ExxonMobil, the operator of the concession, secured international (World Bank Group and French and U.S. governments) involvement in two ways: by seeking financial backing for the project from the IFC and the French and U.S. export credit

guarantee organizations, and by encouraging the government of Chad
to seek financing from the World Bank for its share of the project (rather
than lending this money directly to the government, as is often the
practice in oil projects). Because, unusually, no other companies at that
time were interested in undertaking exploration and production in
Chad (oil prices were low, and the country is landlocked), the operator
company and the World Bank were in a position to impose conditions
on the government of Chad. One consequence of the involvement of
the World Bank Group was the need to meet the conditions it imposed
that revenue management and environmental and social safeguards be
in place before work started on developing the fields.[141]

The relative effectiveness of the Chad-Cameroon model in overcom-
ing the "curse of oil" will not be evident for many years. However, three
lessons have emerged from the initial years of the program. One is that,
counter to much experience worldwide, it is possible to construct large-
scale oil and gas projects in a way that measurably improves the standard of living of the nearby population, even when that population is
mostly uneducated rural people with no history of industry or market
economies. Second, implementation of comprehensive programs for
revenue management and local impact management is more difficult
and resource-intensive than anticipated. And third, continued encouragement, support, and supervision and a strong civil society are needed
to ensure that the potential of the revenue management system is not
eroded as the government accrues wealth and, hence, independence
from conditions imposed by donors such as the World Bank. An early
indication of the difficulty of securing adherence to the revenue management regime was the 2000 use of part of an oil concession signature
bonus for arms purchases—clearly against the spirit, though not the
word, of the agreements with the World Bank. The 2005 decision by
President Deby to hold a referendum on extending the number of terms
a president can stay in power is interpreted by many as a signal that the
limited movements toward constitutionality in Chad may be under
threat. The huge difficulty of imposing systems of good governance of
oil revenues was made unequivocally clear in late 2005, when the government of Chad revised the Petroleum Revenue Management Law to
dilute its provisions and provide the government with a greater share for

the unsupervised general budget. This breach of contract led to the suspension of World Bank disbursements to the government and froze the movement of some of Chad's oil revenues. As of April 2006, the government of Chad and the World Bank were in the closing stage of negotiations to seek a resolution to the dispute.[142]

Differential Uptake of CSR

The adoption of social responsibility approaches is not uniform across the industry, with marked differences between types of company (major, state-owned, and independent) and according to country of origin. Within the very large companies there is also often a marked difference between head office–based corporate staff and in-country managers of exploration and production operations, with the former focused on protecting corporate reputation over the long term, and the latter on maintaining schedules and working to budget. The oil majors, with greater or lesser degrees of enthusiasm and expertise, are involved in social responsibility initiatives and are beginning to transform the ways in which they operate. A few are at the forefront of developing the new models for oil industry activity, comparable to those of the Chad-Cameroon project. For the oil majors, social responsibility is seen as a way of accomplishing several things: protecting or even enhancing reputation with governments, shareholders, employees, and customers; reducing vulnerability, for example, to community hostility that could undermine the returns from multimillion-dollar investments, or to possible future lawsuits; and securing what is described in the industry as "the social license to operate." Guidelines published by the American Petroleum Institute in 2005 on social and environmental reporting and on partnerships with community groups indicate the mainstreaming of these ideas.[143] The drawing up of collective agreements through which member companies negotiate a set of common standards with NGOs and governments is a powerful innovation to provide a quasi-regulatory framework for transnational activities, and a means of pressing operational managers and partners to higher standards. For industry participants, it is important that these be standards that businesses choose to adopt on a voluntary basis; there

remains an unresolved difference of opinion with the NGO participants who would prefer to see binding, universal, and enforceable
requirements applied.[144]

However, despite the changes taking place among the majors, most
of the hundreds of independents and state oil companies show little
interest in corporate social responsibility. They typically do not have
CSR policies, belong to CSR organizations, publish environmental and
social reports, or undertake impact assessments or community projects
(other than when required to by host governments), and stay out of
debates and initiatives on global issues, although they may make charitable donations. The exceptions[145] are largely found among the few
independents and state oil companies that have been targeted by NGOs,
for example, those companies investing in Sudan, those based in countries where corporate social responsibility is widely valued, such as Scan-
dinavia and Canada, and those that have long-term operations in developing countries and have aspirations to become major global companies.
In the case of the independents, the lack of interest in CSR reflects the
short-term focus of businesses under pressure to deliver financial returns
quickly; the low likelihood of being involved in an oil field throughout
the twenty-five years or so of its operation and, thus, limited interest in
the impacts of operations; and, as businesses without gasoline stations
and largely ignored by shareholder activists or campaigning NGOs, little exposure to reputation risk. Similarly, most of the state oil companies are protected from the risk of consumer boycotts or shareholder
pressure.

Corporate social responsibility approaches, if implemented fully
and expertly to the management of oil projects, have the potential to
significantly reduce the risks of local dissatisfaction exacerbating or triggering local conflicts. The private sector's application of the policies
developed by the World Bank Group is helping to systematize these
approaches. Similarly, as the role played by companies in establishing
the EITI and the Voluntary Principles on Security and Human Rights
illustrates, companies can play a part alongside governments and NGOs
in developing broader policies to address the wider issues posed by oil
and gas developments. However, under conditions of competition
between oil companies for concessions, and in the face of the resistance

by many governments of oil-producing countries to what is perceived as interference in their sovereign rights, the role of CSR is likely to remain limited, in many cases, to spending money on charitable projects and not addressing the more complex issues. Continued pressure from NGOs—particularly extending to the state-owned and independent oil companies—will be important in extending the CSR practices of the best companies to the rest of the industry.

5

Azerbaijan: Oil, Conflict, and the Business Role in Peacebuilding

THIS FIRST OF THREE CASE STUDIES turns to a specific country in conflict and a specific set of oil and gas investments, assessing whether there is or has been a relationship between oil and gas production in Azerbaijan and the "frozen" Nagorno-Karabakh conflict that dominates the country's political landscape. It reviews how the structure of the oil and gas projects, and the ways in which they are being implemented, affect this conflict, and considers the role that companies investing in Azerbaijan have played, and could play in the future, in contributing to its resolution.

The analysis draws principally on information published by BP, its financial backers, and the project-monitoring groups for information about the oil industry in Azerbaijan, and on discussions with individuals, including Azerbaijan government representatives and regional specialists, about links between oil and conflict. The discussion starts with brief descriptions of the background and status of the Nagorno-Karabakh conflict and of the oil and gas developments in Azerbaijan. It then considers the links between revenues and conflict and between the local impacts of the projects and conflict over Nagorno-Karabakh. Finally, it considers whether there are contributions, other than those relating to revenue management and the management of their operations, which the companies investing in Azerbaijan could make toward resolution of the Nagorno-Karabakh dispute.

Figure 5-1 Map of Azerbaijan[146]

The Nagorno-Karabakh War

Nagorno-Karabakh is a largely, but not historically exclusively, Armenian ethnic area. It came under Russian control in 1813, when Karabakh was formally incorporated into the Russian Empire. In 1921 Nagorno-Karabakh was allocated by the Soviet Union to Azerbaijan, and in 1923 the Nagorno-Karabakh Autonomous Region was created under the Soviet "minorities" system. From 1945 there were intermittent requests to Moscow from Armenian leaders seeking the reallocation of Nagorno-Karabakh to Armenia. From the 1960s, with the nationalist consciousness rising throughout the Soviet Union, Armenian and Azerbaijani tensions grew over Nagorno-Karabakh—"the only instance in the Soviet federal system wherein members of an ethnic group, which had its own Union Republic, were in charge of an autonomous region inside another Union Republic."[147] In 1988, as the Soviet Union was disintegrating, Nagorno-Karabakh used its hitherto dominant powers as an Autonomous Region to vote within the Regional Soviet for secession from Armenia. An increasingly strident political dispute followed regarding the status of Nagorno-Karabakh—whether it should form part of Azerbaijan or Armenia, or become a separate entity—a dispute that the decaying Soviet Union was unable to resolve and that eventually deteriorated into violent conflict.

The war that erupted between Azerbaijan and Armenia in 1991 led to more than seventeen thousand deaths and the displacement of over a million people out of a total population of eight million in Azerbaijan and almost four million in Armenia. It resulted in the loss to Azerbaijan of Nagorno-Karabakh and all or part of seven adjoining districts, amounting to almost 14 percent of the country's territory.[148] The war spanned the period of the collapse of the Soviet Union; thus, the countries were at war when they became independent in 1991.

The Nagorno-Karabakh conflict has been "frozen," in terms of formal resolution, since 1994, when fighting ended and a cease-fire agreement was signed. Since 1994, the Organization for Security and Cooperation in Europe (OSCE) has held a peacekeeping mandate for Nagorno-Karabakh that involves observation of the cease-fire but no deployment of forces. OSCE has also been involved in promoting a solution to the conflict, through a subset of members known as the Minsk Group. Nagorno-Karabakh is now a quasi-independent but not internationally recognized enclave republic with close political, economic, and military ties to Armenia.[149]

Despite several bursts of active peace negotiations—notably in 1997, 1998, 2001, 2005, and early 2006,[150] including the outlining of a peace deal and process—no substantive progress has been made. The border between Azerbaijan and Armenia is still closed, hundreds of thousands of displaced people remain in refugee camps, and the Azerbaijan enclave of Nakhichevan is cut off from the rest of the country. Failure to make peace is damaging the economic development of both Azerbaijan and Armenia—a study by the World Bank in 2000 concluded that lifting trade barriers would increase the two countries' gross domestic product by some 5 percent and 30 percent respectively.[151]

Although resolving Nagorno-Karabakh remains the highest-profile public issue for both countries, there are few signs of political will or popular support for compromise in either country. A NATO exercise in Azerbaijan, planned for September 2004, was canceled when Armenian military officers were denied entry visas; and public opinion polls in Armenia in mid-2004 found that almost half the "experts" polled considered the "liberation" of Nagorno-Karabakh to be the key accomplishment of Armenia since independence (although only 29 percent of the general public shared this view).[152] The line of conflict remains mined, and there are sporadic outbreaks of violence—hostilities escalated during 2004–5, with six servicemen reported dead in the first three months of 2005.[153]

Many analysts argue that Russia holds the key to securing a peace settlement in Nagorno-Karabakh; others feel that the role of regional and geopolitical factors is overstated[154] and that change on the part of the leaders and people of the region is key. Under the Soviet Union, the transport, telecommunications, and energy infrastructure of Armenia, Azerbaijan, and Georgia were integrated, and the countries shared Russian as a common language. Although these systems have broken down and communications are hindered by the use of national languages in the media and schools, local and international efforts are being made to encourage individual, organizational, and economic contacts throughout the three countries and to build constituencies for peace. For example, interparliamentary meetings have been held, such as that between the chairmen of the Azerbaijan, Georgian, and Armenian parliaments, hosted by the French government in November 2004. However, observers note that while there is often a good relationship between individuals meeting outside Azerbaijan or Armenia, public attitudes remain entrenched and antagonistic. In the words of Thomas de Waal, a veteran analyst of the Nagorno-Karabakh conflict,

> For Armenians, Karabakh is the last outpost of their Christian civilization and a historic haven of Armenian princes and bishops before the Eastern Turkic world begins. Azerbaijanis talk of it as a cradle, nursery, or conservatoire, the birthplace of their musicians and poets. Historically Armenia is displaced without this enclave and its monasteries and its mountain lands; geographically and economically, Azerbaijan is not fully viable without Nagorno-Karabakh.[155]

The Oil Industry in Azerbaijan

Azerbaijan is one of the world's longest-established oil producers. Reports by early Arab travelers note that by the ninth century political and economic life on the Absheron Peninsula (where Baku, the capital, is located) "had long been connected with oil" and that people used soil soaked in oil as a fuel. Industrial-scale oil production has a continuous history since the mid-nineteenth century, when Azerbaijan was one of the first places in the world where oil fields were developed. The first well was drilled in 1846, and the "oil boom" of 1885–1920 saw the construction of oil barons' mansions that still dominate the center of Baku. From 1920 to the 1950s, the Soviet Socialist Republic of Azerbaijan was responsible for the bulk of Soviet Union oil production. In 1941 output from Baku reached 23.5 million metric tons (compared to 19.9 million in 2004).[156] Both sides in the Second World War paid attention to securing the Baku oil fields and denying enemy access to the oil.

Since the dissolution of the Soviet Union in 1991, the government of Azerbaijan has pursued an economic and political development strategy based on use of the country's oil and gas resources. Since 1994 over twenty production-sharing contracts have been signed for exploration in the Caspian Sea and onshore. The first was the production-sharing agreement (PSA) for the Azeri-Chirag-Guneshli (ACG) block, widely referred to as the "Contract of the Century" because of the prospects it offered Azerbaijan as, for the first time, international companies secured access rights to develop the nation's oil potential, and the country looked set to become a major supplier to world markets.

The results of exploration in Azerbaijan have been mixed: two large fields have been identified—the ACG oil field and the Shah Deniz gas field—and some smaller new resources identified onshore, but other exploration has been unsuccessful. Disputed control of the Caspian Sea among the five littoral states also prevents exploration in some blocks.[157] The principal exploration activity concentrates on probing for additional resources in the fields already identified, rather than looking for new fields. Current estimates are that as of the end of 2005, Azerbaijan had proven resources accounting for only 0.6 percent and 0.8 percent of global resources of oil and gas respectively.[158] However, current investment in exploring there will lead to a quadrupling of Azerbaijan's output for about twenty years starting in 2007.[159]

Until the new fields are in full production, most of the oil produced in Azerbaijan is from fields operated by SOCAR, the State Oil Company of the Republic of Azerbaijan. SOCAR operates a large offshore field in the Caspian Sea, which came online in 1981, and forty older fields. However, production from these fields is stagnant or declining, and the expansion of Azerbaijan's output is being driven by the ACG and Shah Deniz fields, developed by consortia of international oil companies partnered with SOCAR, and led by BP as the operator.[160] This new output is destined mainly for export. Two largely parallel export pipelines have been built from Azerbaijan through Georgia, to Turkey, to export the oil and gas produced from ACG and Shah Deniz (and potentially other oil and gas produced in the region). The Baku-Tbilisi-Ceyhan (BTC) oil pipeline alone is a $4 billion investment.

As the operator of the ACG, Shah Deniz, and BTC projects, BP has a particularly high profile in Azerbaijan. It is responsible for the planning and execution of the projects—within the boundaries set by legal agreements, including the intergovernmental agreements on the pipelines, the annual work programs adopted under the terms of the PSAs with the government and the other consortia members, and the terms set by the international lenders financing the projects.

Revenue Management and Conflict Risk in Azerbaijan

The argument set forth in chapter 3 states that when oil taxes and royalties make up a major proportion of government revenues in countries without stable democracies, conflict risks are heightened. These risks are manifest directly, through disputed control of the state and its revenues, by financing violent conflict or by providing an incentive for secessionist rebellion; and indirectly, through increased poverty and inequality from failure to conquer the macroeconomic challenges of oil dependency, and because revenues facilitate authoritarian and repressive government.

To what extent are these risks evident in Azerbaijan? The picture is mixed. Oil wealth was not a factor causing or contributing to the Nagorno-Karabakh war. The first PSA yielding revenues to the government was signed in 1994, after the Nagorno-Karabakh cease-fire was negotiated. Unlike in many other oil-rich countries, there are no indications that anticipated oil wealth was a factor encouraging or facilitating this conflict. Nor are the oil fields located in or near Nagorno-Karabakh. In contrast, since 1994 the prospect of securing further oil wealth because of foreign investment has been a stabilizing factor contributing to the "freezing" of the conflict. Anticipated investment under the "Contract of the Century" provided an impetus for the cease-fire, and the existence of contracts with international oil companies has subsequently been an incentive for maintaining stability in order that companies will go ahead with promised investments, which are expected to continue, in a phased development of the fields, until 2010. Indeed, when Azerbaijan first opened up to international investment in the early 1990s, there was discussion in the international community and the oil industry of trying to use the development of the country's oil as an active agent for peace. The idea of building a pipeline through Armenia to take Azeri oil to market was tentatively explored in the mid-1990s. However, in the absence of commitments by either country to permanent peace, the "peace pipeline" was deemed unacceptable by the government of Azerbaijan, because it would have given Armenia leverage over Azerbaijan's earnings, and was seen by investors as too risky.

Looking to the future, there is a risk that this effect will reverse. As new wealth materializes, it will become destabilizing and could play a critical role in enabling renewed active conflict if no resolution has been reached in the meantime. The main flow of Azerbaijan's oil revenues will occur between 2007 and 2024, with anticipated annual receipts of some $2 billion a year, compared to 2002's GDP of just over $6 billion.[161] Unless there are large new finds—thought unlikely—then Azerbaijan's oil boom will be short.

The revenues might contribute to a resumption of armed conflict in two ways. First, increased revenues will allow for a buildup of the Azerbaijan army and consequently enable serious consideration to redressing Azerbaijan's military weaknesses and losses in the war with Armenia. According to de Waal, writing in 2003, "A wealthier and more confident Azerbaijan will inevitably begin to consider the option of going to war again to capture its lost lands."[162] While such a military buildup might be intended simply as posturing (and some argue that this might be necessary to put pressure on Armenia to negotiate), in a volatile environment it could lead to unplanned escalation of tensions, and preemptive action by one side or the other, resulting in resumed conflict. In mid-2004, analysts from the Washington-based Central Asia Caucasus Institute urged NATO to take more seriously the risk of resumed conflict in Nagorno-Karabakh (and elsewhere in the South Caucasus):

> If the present deadlock continues, as seems likely, the public and elite mood in Azerbaijan will continue to tilt gradually towards war. Meanwhile, Azerbaijan is recovering economically, and is beginning to receive substantial oil revenues. It is also building its armed forces with Turkish assistance—and Armenia's population is shrinking. Azerbaijan may hence feel the odds are in its favor.[163]

In 2005 one-quarter of Azerbaijan's budget was allocated to military spending, doubling the previous year's sum.[164]

Public statements by Azerbaijani leaders that reiterate the importance of resolving the conflict and, while emphasizing commitment to a peaceful resolution, implicitly or explicitly keep open the military option, underpin concerns about oil revenues and popular frustration fueling support for a military solution to Nagorno-Karabakh. In his New Year message for 2003, former President Heydar Aliev noted, "Sometimes there are ideas in our society that this problem [Nagorno-Karabakh] should be resolved in a military way. This method has never been ruled out."[165] Fifteen months later, his son and successor, Ilham Aliev, stated in an interview, "Our position is that we intend to resolve the conflict by peaceful means. However there should be a set date, i.e., we do not want the process to be eternal, there are limits for talks and we believe that fresh proposals will be drawn up and we shall be able to resolve the conflict on a just basis and in line with the norms of international law."[166] Then, in March 2005, he was quoted as stating, "Our army should be strong to solve the Armenia-Azerbaijan conflict over Nagorno-Karabakh."[167] An NGO project carried out in 2003, investigating the conflict implications of the BTC pipeline, reportedly found that "BTC is having a huge impact on the region—people expect it to allow them to get Nagorno-Karabakh back."[168] With the Azerbaijan State Oil fund holding approximately $994 million in early 2005,[169]—that is, before the major revenues start to flow—these concerns about the scope for military spending are justified.

The second risk of Azerbaijan's oil boom leading to renewed conflict is linked to the government's ability to manage oil revenues and deal with corruption and governance issues in the country. If revenues are mismanaged and there is no perceptible improvement to the population's standard of living, domestic political instability may ensue, creating incentives for the government to recommence diversionary military aggression in Nagorno-Karabakh.

In terms of economic management and transparency, the record to date in Azerbaijan has been better than in many other emerging oil-producing countries. Over the long period between the signing of the "Contract of the Century" and the start of principal revenue streams to government, the government put in place several of the policies put forward by the International Monetary Fund (IMF) and others, including the World Bank, to avoid the "curse of oil." There has been real GDP growth, a steady exchange rate, and low inflation following hyperinflation and economic collapse in the mid-1990s[170] (although in 2005 inflation started to accelerate once more). A key step was the establishment in December 2000 of the State Oil Fund of Azerbaijan, to take in most of the oil revenues in order to manage their use and their macroeconomic impacts. Oil fund receipts and spending are disclosed publicly,[171] and the government is participating as one of three pilot countries in the Extractive Industries Transparency Initiative (EITI). A national committee on the Extractive Industry Transparency Initiative was set up by a cabinet decree in November 2003, and an initial framework for reporting and auditing revenues has been agreed on between oil companies, the government, and NGOs. Among developing-nation oil producers, Azerbaijan is unusual in permitting its contractor companies to publish in full the PSAs for the ACG and Shah Deniz fields, and the intergovernmental agreements and host-government agreements (HGAs) for the export pipelines.[172] In late 2004 the government defined a strategy for macroeconomic management, particularly to address the risks of oil price vulnerability, and a long-term strategy for the use of oil revenues consistent with Azerbaijan's State Program on Poverty Reduction and Economic Development (SPPRD). In so doing, it resolved a dispute with the IMF, which had publicly reported concerns about delays in developing this strategy.[173]

On the other hand, there remain important weaknesses in terms of governance within the revenue-management system for Azerbaijan. The state oil fund was set up under presidential decree, and the presidential administration controls its expenditures. According to the Open Society Institute, which sees the establishment of oil funds in both Azerbaijan and Kazakhstan as "important steps," "for these oil funds to endure they must be embedded in a democratic system that gives the various branches of government oversight of another, a system that is transparent in its handling of public monies, and that allows the public to hold civil servants accountable."[174]

In terms of addressing the governance risks associated with oil revenues, little progress is evident except on revenue transparency. Corruption remains a major problem—in 2004 Azerbaijan ranked 140 out of 145 countries in the Transparency International Corruption Perceptions Index[175] (with 145 the worst), although the local chapter of Transparency International reports a sharp fall (from 60 percent to 28 percent) in surveys on how often individuals have to pay bribes.[176] The country also continues to score poorly on measures of political freedom and civil liberties.[177]

The intent of Azerbaijan's ruling elites to maintain their hold on power was illustrated in the November 2005 parliamentary elections—widely criticized for interference with opposition campaigns before voting day, and widespread rigged vote counting.[178] This failure to prevent corruption has ripple effects on the economy, preventing the growth of small businesses that create employment. In turn, oil revenues may have to be diverted away from progressive social and infrastructure spending in order to meet short-term welfare needs created by high unemployment because of systemic corruption.

Oil Companies and Revenue Management

Unusually for an oil project, the companies developing the ACG, Shah Deniz, and BTC projects have published their views on the potential links between the projects and conflict, and the concomitant responsibilities they have as investors. They acknowledge, "Some research suggests that governments have in the past used energy revenues to purchase military goods, which in turn triggered new conflict or has underwritten new conflict." However, they maintain, "The disposition of state revenues is a government prerogative, not one to be decided by investors."[179] In terms of their own responsibilities to contribute to conflict prevention, the companies identify their commitment to work with other stakeholders to raise public awareness about the revenues earned by the projects and to ensure new opportunities for local economic development.

More public information is available on oil revenues in Azerbaijan than in the other cases considered in this study, and, as discussed above, more elaborate systems are in place to manage revenue use. The driving force behind the revenue-management system in Azerbaijan has been the national government, working with the IMF and the World Bank. The companies involved in the ACG, Shah Deniz, and BTC projects have, however, taken some significant actions to support effective revenue management. In particular, the project consortia have explicitly and publicly set themselves the objective of "creating a model for investments in extractive industries that will leave a lasting, positive legacy on the host countries."[180] Since revenue management is a key influence on the legacy of the projects, the companies have been active in discussing revenue management issues with government and civil society, collaborating with the EITI, and disseminating more information than is usual in the sector. For example, all the legal contracts, including the PSAs, have been published, along with a "Citizen's Guide to the BTC Project Agreements,"[181] as have reports that include revenue projections. An influencing factor behind BP's negotiations with the government to publish the PSAs is that Azerbaijan's parliament approved the contracts, so they have the status of law. It should be noted that securing parliamentary approval for the PSAs and thereby providing, many years later, the legal basis allowing their publication had little to do with issues of transparency. Rather, both parties agreed to publication in order to provide themselves with an additional layer of legal protection in the uncertain post-Soviet environment.

Local Impact and Conflict Risk in Azerbaijan

Chapter 3 showed that oil and gas projects risk being a catalyst for tension and violent conflict in the area where they operate if they negatively affect livelihoods (for example, through land appropriation or environmental damage), provoke increased military activity, stimulate social change that the community is unprepared for or unwilling to accept, or generate unrealistically high expectations of benefits. These risks are heightened if the area is already experiencing ethnic or secessionist unrest, and reduced or eliminated where oil and gas reserves are offshore. To what extent are these risk factors present in Azerbaijan, and how are companies dealing with them?

The ACG, Shah Deniz, and BTC projects all involve local environmental and social impact. Although production is from subsurface wells in the Caspian Sea, the development requires onshore terminals and the construction of two thousand-kilometer pipelines, buried about a meter belowground, running westward across Azerbaijan, Georgia, and Turkey, with aboveground pumping, metering, and monitoring stations at various points along the route. According to the impact assessments carried out during project planning, the 443-kilometer BTC pipeline that crosses Azerbaijan affects some 2,500 hectares (approximately 6,200 acres) of land, owned and used by 4,082 households in 131 villages. Access to land was curtailed while the pipelines and facilities were being built, but even after they became operational, land use within a fifty-eight-meter-wide tract—the "protection zone"—remains restricted along the length of the pipeline. Within this zone, constructing buildings, planting trees, or engaging in activities that carry fire risks, such as fertilizer storage, are all prohibited.

While under construction, the pipeline was highly visible and disrupted farming activity, although now that it is in operation, buried and invisible, it has minimal impact on people's lives. But like all other oil and gas facilities, the terminals, pump stations, and pipelines require security, including an emergency response system to protect against accidents, vandalism, sabotage, theft, or terrorism. The potential for negative local impact, in addition to the need to provide pipeline security in a region driven by conflicts, has led to much international attention and controversy. International NGOs and, notably, some in-country NGOs have voiced concern that the projects will not, in practice, bring positive economic and social development benefits to the people of the region. The possibility of oil spills causing environmental damage and the fear that providing security would exacerbate tensions and "militarize" affected areas were also topics of discussion.

Oil Companies and Local Impact

The PSAs and host government agreements for the ACG, Shah Deniz, and BTC projects are unusual in that they include clauses requiring environmental protection and impact assessment. These stipulations provide an opportunity for including social and environmental safeguards, and for recovering the costs of their implementation, in the development of the oil fields. They bind both government and company to apply "international standards" and to conduct impact assessments before construction starts.

The projects are being carried out simultaneously and are being undertaken by similar (though not identical) consortia of companies, with BP the operator company in each case. The projects have financing from a Project Lenders' Group that includes the World Bank's International Finance Corporation (IFC), the European Bank for Reconstruction and Development (EBRD), the Export-Import Bank of the United States, and the (U.S.) Overseas Private Investment Corporation, as well as other export credit guarantee organizations and commercial banks. The sponsor companies and many of the financing organizations have policies and commitments requiring efforts to identify and then avoid, minimize, or compensate for any damage caused by the projects, and also to make positive contributions to the communities affected by projects.

Each of the funding institutions has slightly different specifications, but the broad requirement is to apply World Bank/IFC policies and standards for impact assessment, public consultation and disclosure, and deal with involuntary resettlement of people or disruption of their livelihoods, forced labor, and harmful child labor. As a result, and in a manner broadly similar to that of the Chad-Cameroon project (discussed in chapter 3), the projects have realized numerous accomplishments. These include carrying out extensive environmental and social impact assessments, including consultation with all affected communities; developing environmental and social management plans to avoid, limit, or compensate for damage; undertaking land use surveys, including identification of, and compensation for, every case in which land use has been affected temporarily or permanently by oil and gas projects; requiring contractors hired to build pipelines and facilities to implement the same environmental and social standards; setting up systems to ensure that the majority of unskilled work goes to people from the communities close to operations; establishing programs to resolve complaints and grievances; and supporting community social and environmental projects. In the area of human rights, the projects have established independent human rights monitoring groups focusing on labor, communities, and security, and negotiated and published security protocols consistent with the Voluntary Principles on Security and Human Rights (see chapter 4).

An important area identified by BP as part of a conflict prevention strategy is support for local economic development. Large-scale oil and gas projects acquire the bulk of their equipment and supplies from nonhost-country companies specializing in the oil industry. In Azerbaijan efforts are being made to provide more opportunities to local businesses to sell goods and services to the major projects than might otherwise be the case. These efforts include setting up the Baku Enterprise Center, to help Azerbaijan-owned and -based companies develop businesses to supply the international oil industry; collaborating with other companies and NGOs in a business development alliance; targeting specific opportunities for local businesses to supply goods and services to the projects; and developing a community investment program that provides grants to NGOs and civil society organizations for employment creation projects. BP has also announced that it will provide up to $25 million for a new regional development initiative to be funded jointly by the EBRD and other companies in order to support employment- and business development–related projects, such as microfinance, training, and infrastructure development. These projects are in the early stages. No information is available yet on how the initiatives are working in practice, and it will be several years before their long-term impact can be evaluated.

Three separate monitoring systems have been set up, designed to produce public reports to evaluate the effectiveness of these approaches (to the extent possible, given that the projects are still at an early stage). One monitoring system, carried out on behalf of the Project Lenders' Group, monitors the implementation of the detailed Environmental and Social Action Plans (ESAPs) resulting from the environmental and social impact assessments (ESIAs). A second is the Caspian Development Advisory Panel (CDAP), commissioned by BP's chief executive to advise more broadly on the economic, social, and environmental impact of the company's South Caucasus projects. Local NGOs run the third monitoring system, co-coordinated by the Open Society Institute and reporting to BP and the public, under an arrangement put in place in 2004.[182]

In terms of the conflict risks associated with local impact, the monitoring reports published through mid-2004 suggest that while impact and response strategies have been correctly identified and are being implemented in practice, the potential remains for local grievances to surface because of poor implementation or supervision, and unmet expectations. In particular, CDAP recommended that a large-scale regional development program be established to ensure local benefits, that human rights monitoring be carried out, and that tighter controls be exerted over contractors. The ESAP monitors also recommended that some additional specific training and procedures be put in place. Initial NGO monitoring raised concerns about the amount of compensation paid to some individuals, the fairness of hiring systems, and the selection of community investment projects.

Together, these steps reflect serious efforts to avoid the negative impact (including becoming a catalyst for tension and violent conflict) that the sponsor companies and financiers, their advisors, and the NGO critics of the oil industry have seen in other oil and gas projects. Meanwhile, continuing scrutiny from NGOs will continue to be influential in ensuring that the companies pay close attention to social and environmental issues.

A Business Role in Conflict Resolution?

Beyond seeking to exercise positive influences on revenue management and economic development, and avoiding negative local impact that creates grievances and tensions, do the large international companies investing in Azerbaijan have a role to play in the resolution of the Nagorno-Karabakh conflict? Could they help to "unfreeze" this conflict or prevent Azerbaijan's oil wealth from enabling its resolution by military means, and if so, would any such actions be in the interests of the companies?

The major investors in Azerbaijan's oil and gas industry are the twelve international oil companies and the multinational financing organizations, including export credit guarantee organizations and commercial banks. The business case for engagement in active peacebuilding for Nagorno-Karabakh is that renewed conflict could directly affect the projects if their infrastructure should become the target of attack. Unlike many other types of investment, oil and gas facilities, particularly buried pipelines, cannot be removed if conflict erupts. On the other hand, the legal status of the investors, as contractors to the Azerbaijan government, acts as a disincentive to undertake any actions in pursuit of peace that could jeopardize contracts and working relationships with the government—for example, engaging with Armenian groups.

In terms of conflict prevention, many regional specialists have been concerned about rising tensions and the low level of international attention paid to the region, although events in Georgia, Ukraine, Kyrgyzstan, and Uzbekistan during 2004–05, and growing awareness of the emerging security issues, have brought some international attention back to the region. Individually or as a group, Azerbaijan's investors could help maintain attention on the region, and its conflict risks, with their home governments and communicate any rising tensions observed in the areas where the companies have a presence. The companies building and operating pipelines cutting across Azerbaijan have local knowledge likely to exceed that of embassies based in capital cities. Companies could also contribute to conflict prevention without jeopardizing their relationships with government or taking on an overtly political role, by stating publicly the importance to current and prospective investors—particularly those outside the oil industry who have a wider choice of investment locations—of a peaceful resolution to the Nagorno-Karabakh conflict.[183] They could also play a role in stimulating the development of a positive vision for Azerbaijan's future as a peaceful and democratic country—for example, by promoting awareness of how transformation has been achieved in successful oil states such as Norway. This is advocated to all concerned with peace in Nagorno-Karabakh by Thomas de Waal: "…be storytellers, contradicting the bellicose and rejectionist language that issues from the two ex-combatants, holed up in their prison fortresses, with a patiently told tale of how things could be different."[184]

Conclusions

The large-scale oil and gas projects in Azerbaijan provide one of the strongest examples of corporate social responsibility in reducing conflict risks presented by oil revenues and the local impact of the oil industry. The application of a strong CSR approach has been helped by several factors that could potentially be replicated in other countries. For one, a pattern of constructive engagement between the government, the oil companies, multilateral organizations, and NGOs has been deliberately established in the effort to overcome the "curse of oil." Second, the concession contracts and legal agreements include requirements for environmental and social safeguards and allow for transparency in contract terms and revenue reporting. Third, having the World Bank Group, with its rigorous safeguard policies and influence on revenue management, involved through IFC financing, coupled with the long time taken in exploration and in field and pipeline development, has allowed revenue management systems to be put in place. Fourth, one company with strongly developed CSR policies and long experience engaging in such issues is the operator for each of the principal projects in the country.

How effective these CSR approaches are in reducing conflict risks will become clear only in the years following 2007, when Azerbaijan oil production will reach full capacity. What is clear is the risk that unless Azerbaijan's public and political mindset changes in support of a negotiated peace in Nagorno-Karabakh, the country's oil wealth could be wasted on renewed conflict. The oil companies can help create a climate for peace and press the international community to encourage peaceful resolution. They can also encourage revenue transparency and prevent local impact from catalyzing conflict.

But if conflict arises because of the mismanagement of oil revenues, there is little that companies can do to prevent this other than by taking on the high-risk strategy of halting production. There is little business case for doing this unilaterally, since the structure of the industry (as outlined in chapter 2) means that once oil infrastructure is in place, the companies to operate it are substitutable. But given the increasing risk of attempts to resolve the conflict by force, the oil companies could make known to the government that an escalation in violent conflict over Nagorno-Karabakh would lead to immediate shutdown of operations. This could probably be done by triggering the force majeure conditions in the oil field and pipeline contracts, but would need to be carefully coordinated with the governments of the United States and UK (as the "home" countries of the main companies involved) to reduce the risk of the government inviting other oil companies to take over operation of the assets.

6

Angola: Oil, Conflict, and Postconflict Reconstruction

ANGOLA IS THE KEY CASE around which much of the analysis of oil production and producer-country conflict has developed, because, while undergoing almost thirty years of war starting in the 1970s, the country also became a leading exporter of oil. This chapter outlines the history of conflict and peacebuilding in Angola since the mid-1970s, the development of the oil industry over this period, and the links between oil and conflict, focusing on the civil war. We then review the development of revenue management issues, and the role that investor companies have played in them. We look briefly at local impact management—less of an issue in Angola than in either Azerbaijan or Sudan because most of Angola's industry is offshore—and at the secession conflict in Cabinda. Finally, this chapter proposes a role for oil businesses in Angola's postwar reconstruction.

Angola's Civil War

The conflict in Angola, an independence struggle that turned into a Cold War–influenced civil war, lasted through much of the period from 1975 to 2002. It originated in the early 1960s, as separate liberation movements sought independence from Portuguese colonial rule.[186] The armed struggle by the People's Movement for the Liberation of Angola

Figure 6-1 Map of Angola[185]

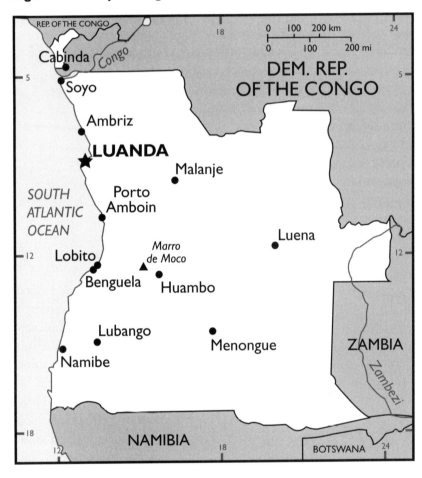

(MPLA) started with an attack on a prison in Luanda in 1961. In the same year there was rebellion in the northwest of the country, organized by the National Liberation Front of Angola (FLNA); and in 1965 the National Union for the Total Independence of Angola (UNITA) was formed.

When the Portuguese revolution in 1974 led to the sudden decision to grant independence to Angola, the three key nationalist movements— MPLA, FLNA, and UNITA—opposed one another as well as Portuguese rule. They each had distinct ideologies and regional bases of support, as well as different external backers.[187] In January 1975 the three groups signed on to the Alvor Accords, designed to put in place a power-sharing regime until elections could be held later that year. However, this was never implemented, and fighting between the groups resulted in the MPLA gaining control of Luanda, while the FLNA largely went into exile and UNITA regrouped in southern Angola. (The Cabinda-based liberation movements were not parties to the Alvor Accords, and Cabinda separatists still contest the inclusion of Cabinda within Angola.)

The Portuguese departure on November 10, 1975, was followed the next day by a declaration of the independence of the People's Republic of Angola, under an MPLA government. From then until the late 1980s Angola suffered continuing civil war between the MPLA and UNITA, contesting control of the country. War waxed and waned in intensity and was exacerbated by the active support both sides secured from the Cold War powers and their proxies. Paul Hare (the U.S. special representative for the UN-sponsored Angolan peace process during 1993–94, which resulted in the 1994 Lusaka peace agreement) explains:

> Following its independence and throughout the 1980s, Angola became a pawn in the Cold War. The Soviet Union provided loans, military advisors and weapons to support the MPLA government in Luanda. The Cubans sent troops numbering, at their height, fifty thousand. Although the Clark Amendment in 1976 prevented continued American military support to any Angolan group, including UNITA, South African forces crossed Angola's borders periodically to attack SWAPO [South-West Africa People's Organization] bases in Angola.… The South Africans also attacked Angolan targets in order to curb Soviet and Cuban interference in the region. If South

Africa had not supported UNITA during this period, its chances for survival would have been slim.[188]

After repeal of the Clark Amendment in 1985, Hare notes, "the [U.S.] administration also resumed assistance to UNITA."[189]

Toward the end of the 1980s, after a series of particularly fierce encounters leading to thousands of casualties and extensive loss of equipment, and with the waning of the Cold War, the Soviet Union, the United States, and South Africa sought to extract themselves from the war in Angola. Under the New York Accords of December 1988, South African and Cuban forces withdrew from the country. But there was no reconciliation between the MPLA and UNITA, both of which continued to receive military support from the superpowers, while also being encouraged by them to negotiate a settlement. Donald Rothchild writes,

> Both the Soviets and the United States continued to back their local allies with military assistance while supporting Portuguese mediatory initiatives..... In 1990, for example, Soviet military aid amounted to an estimated $800 million. Meanwhile the United States insisted upon continuing support for UNITA.[190]

From 1988 until 2002 intense war was interspersed and overlapped by peace initiatives, negotiations, and periods of peace such as that triggered by the Lusaka peace agreement. By this time the ideological differences between the two sides had largely disappeared, and although each side was concentrated in different parts of the country, the MPLA-UNITA conflict was not fundamentally based on regional or ethnic issues. It was a "struggle for power and domination."[191] Civilians were drawn by dint of circumstance into a conflict based on rivalry between competing elites. Anthropologist Inge Brinkman discussed this issue in her fieldwork:

> Most civilians only expressed casual loyalty for the party to which they belonged. They had had no choice: residence determined which party one belonged to: "We were in MPLA, because we were in town." If the rival party took over the area, the civilians' membership automatically shifted. Ideological differences, ethnic loyalties, and regional rivalries hardly inspired civilians' accounts of the war.[192]

In 1991, the Bicesse Accords led to a cease-fire, followed by the September 1992 presidential and national assembly elections, contested by both the MPLA and UNITA. These first-ever elections in Angola had a 90 percent turnout, and the United Nations certified, "With all deficiencies taken into account…the elections could be considered free and fair."[193] The elections confirmed the divide in the country between the MPLA and UNITA supporters but gave the MPLA a clear overall victory. (The MPLA's José Eduardo dos Santos received 49.5 percent of the vote compared to UNITA's Jonas Savimbi, with 40.1 percent; in voting for the national assembly, the MPLA received 54 percent of votes, and UNITA 34 percent.)[194] Before the second-round presidential election could be held, Savimbi withdrew the UNITA troops from the combined army and resumed fighting.

Bitter fighting during the years 1992–94 ended with the successful negotiation of the Lusaka Protocol. This agreement built on the Bicesse Accords, addressing some of their weaknesses. It included, among other changes, provisions for postwar power sharing, through formation of a government of national unity, and a distribution of provincial administrative posts. The 1994 peace was followed by four years of "quasi peace,"[195] during which there was sporadic fighting, partial quartering of troops, and de facto division of the country into areas controlled by the government or held by UNITA. Failing to meet its commitments under the peace agreement, UNITA became the target of UN sanctions starting in 1997, including a prohibition of sales of diamonds from the areas it controlled. In late 1998 open war broke out again, and Angola remained in conflict until the April 2002 cease-fire, which followed six weeks after the death in battle of UNITA's leader, Jonas Savimbi. The Luena Memorandum of Understanding, signed on April 4, restored the Lusaka peace process, and the peace between the MPLA and UNITA has held since then. Unusually for post–World War II civil wars, the end of Angola's civil war was not brokered by the international community, nor did it involve any significant restructuring of the power holders at the national level.

The anticolonial war, surrogate Cold War, and civil war led to an estimated 750,000 deaths from conflict-related causes, including famine and disease; 440,000 refugees; and the displacement of over four million people from their homes.[196] The country has lost thirty years of potential development. Much of the infrastructure existing in 1975 was destroyed, including railways and many roads, and the population of Luanda and other cities and towns increased far beyond their capacity as waves of people fled the war in the countryside. Reintegrating people forced to move by conflict and rehabilitating the country's infrastructure are key priorities of Angola's Strategy to Combat Poverty, released in February 2004.[197]

Secession Conflict in Cabinda

The 2,800-square-mile oil-rich enclave of Cabinda, with a population variously estimated at 100,000–300,000,[198] lies north of the Congo River, separated from mainland Angola also by a twenty-five-mile-wide strip of land belonging to the Democratic Republic of Congo. The location of much fighting during the independence struggle, Cabinda remains the scene of intermittent low-level violent conflict, and no substantive peace process has been under way despite intermittent flurries of activity and discussion of potential autonomy.[199] Whereas the civil war was about control of the entire country, conflict in Cabinda involves groups fighting for independence for the enclave—initially against Portugal, and since 1975 against Angola. During 2002–03, following the end of the war between the government and UNITA, the Angolan army launched a counterinsurgency campaign in Cabinda,[200] and persistent reports emerge of human rights abuses against the civilian population,[201] as well as of civil society pressures for peace. Jean-Michel Mabeko-Tali, a historian of the MPLA, has labeled meetings between the government and independence groups over 1986 and 1989 "a dialogue of the deaf,"[202] and argued in 2004 that a compromise solution based on far-reaching autonomy had become less likely as the government had failed to engage in serious dialogue and civil society leaders in Cabinda had become more radical.[203] In early 2006 the Government of Angola reportedly sent a document to the Cabinda Forum for Dialogue, outlining principles for a solution including a cease-fire and the principle of special status for Cabinda. As of April 2006, negotiations had not started.[204]

The Oil Industry in Angola

Angola's oil industry started in the 1950s and has been expanding ever since. In the 1950s and '60s onshore and shallow offshore fields in Cabinda and northern Angola were developed, followed by expansion into additional offshore fields starting in the 1980s. In the 2000s attention is focused on the deep (water depths of over 500 feet) and ultradeep (over 1,500 feet) offshore fields in Angola's Exclusive Economic Zone (EEZ) along the Atlantic coast. Exploration has been successful in several but not all of these offshore blocks, and ongoing exploration is expected to yield further finds.[205] With peace, the government is also opening up onshore blocks for exploration, including in Cabinda.[206]

Sonangol, the state oil company, is in charge of leasing oil concessions and also operates, or is a shareholder in, many of the production blocks. As of November 2005, thirty-four blocks had been delineated, eighteen were in the production phase, and five had been abandoned because no oil was found.[207] With so many concessions let, many international oil companies are involved in Angola including four of the five super majors, several of the majors, an increasing number of independents, and several government-owned companies, including those from Brazil, China, Malaysia, Norway, and Portugal.

Angola accounted for approximately 5 percent of U.S. crude oil imports in 2005.[208] It is by far the largest-scale producer of the three countries profiled in this study. Production rose from less than one million metric tons in 1965 to 61 million metric tons in 2005[209] and is predicted to grow a further 60 percent by 2008.[210]

Exploration and production in the deep and ultradeep blocks is a high-technology, capital-intensive activity led by the super major oil companies. Oil is transferred directly from offshore production platforms onto tankers. Four of the five largest companies are operators in Angola, with Chevron Texaco responsible for the largest share of production, followed by ExxonMobil. Many other companies—majors, independents, and state oil companies—have shares in Angolan concessions.

War and the massive increase in oil production radically changed the country's economic profile after independence. Although once a major producer of coffee and other commodities, the Angolan economy is now highly dependent on oil, which accounts for nearly half the country's GDP and about 90 percent of government revenues and export earnings. Agriculture and other nonoil economic activities have contracted drastically. Diamond mining has continued, on both an artisanal and a capital-intensive basis, with earnings reported at some 10 percent of those from oil in 2003.[211]

The expanding oil sector is largely disconnected from the rest of the economy and society (except via the impact of oil revenues, as discussed below). Physically, the main new oil developments are far offshore, not visible from the coast. Economically, as is the case with the industry worldwide, the industry is capital-intensive and creates few employment opportunities for citizens. Most of the equipment is imported from the handful of specialist international companies that service the global oil industry, and where local businesses do supply goods and services to the oil industry, they are largely subsidiaries of the state oil company or otherwise associated with the elite. The four "oil bases," in Lobito, Luanda, Soyo, and Cabinda, that service Angola's offshore industry were built during the war as self-contained, self-sufficient complexes, largely isolated from the nearby towns. One well-informed person, who wished not to be identified, describes the situation:

> Under the PSAs, all expenditures have to be approved by the government. Many times companies have to hire specific companies because these are linked to particular businesses. The risk for the (oil) companies is being perceived (by civil society) as part of the elite—making money and preventing others from having opportunities. For example, the houses that companies rent belong to people in high places, the security companies are owned by generals, and goods and services are purchased from elite-owned companies.[212]

Oil and Conflict in Angola

The interaction between oil industry operations and Angola's conflict has been limited—most of the operations are offshore, and none of the warring parties wanted to risk destroying the country's wealth basis.[213] Investment and production continued through the war, except for a six-month period when production from Cabinda was suspended (September 1975 to March 1976). According to Piero Gleijeses, "at the request of the Ford administration, Gulf suspended operations in Cabinda and put the $125 million in taxes and royalties it owed the State of Angola in escrow, to be paid when Angola had a government 'generally recognized by the world community.'"[214] Exploration activity on some onshore blocks was also curtailed beginning in the mid-1970s because of the security risks presented by conflict, and in 1992 the northern oil-producing area around Soyo was captured first by UNITA, then retaken by the MPLA in fighting that damaged oil industry buildings and equipment. The fighting resulted in the capture of two oil industry employees and caused short-term shutdowns in production. The MPLA recapture of Soyo was assisted by the involvement of a private company, Executive Outcomes (EO), which provided private military forces. Accounts differ on whether EO was originally brought into Soyo by international oil companies before being contracted by the government.[215] Additional reports of links between the oil business and conflict include unverified claims that UNITA secured some of its financing by promises of oil field concessions[216] and that shares in some oil field concessions were let in return for arms supplied to the MPLA.[217]

Of greater significance is Angola's oil wealth, which has had a major effect on the country's conflicts in two main ways. First, the MPLA's control of Cabinda and its oil revenues, and thus the revenues from the expanding oil industry, gave the party the competitive advantage that enabled it first to win control of the government, from a position of relative weakness, during the independence struggle and eventually to win the war. When the Cold War powers stopped supplying Angola's armies, oil revenues (signature payments on new PSAs, the state's share of production, and loans taken out against future revenues) took over the financing role. Thus, the estimated $800 million of Soviet military aid to the MPLA in 1990[218] compares with the $900 million paid in signature bonuses for blocks 31–33 in 1999—money that "helped finance the government's military operations."[219] In the late 1990s observers predicted that the steady increase in oil production would allow the government to get the upper hand and eventually to win, as indeed happened.[220]

Second, the Cabinda conflict itself is directly related to its oil wealth. It fuels demands for independence while making Cabinda essential to Angola as a major source of government income. Cabinda's oil has also provoked external interference. In the 1970s both Congo and Zaire supported Cabindan separatist movements. A National Security Council report cited by Piero Gleijeses notes that "both…looked covetously at Cabinda's oil";[221] and one of the leaders of FLEC (the Front for the Liberation of Cabinda, the Cabindan secession movement) was the deputy director general of the Elf oil company subsidiary in Brazzaville.[222] Further, political interference by oil companies in the 1970s may have played a part in making the status of Cabinda more difficult to resolve. According to Jean-Michel Mabeko-Tali, the belief that oil companies in Cabinda were colluding with separatists and foreign powers to control Cabinda's oil wealth was a factor in the MPLA's change of policy away from support for a decentralized state and toward the creation of a highly centralized state, in which there was no place for Cabindan autonomy.[223]

Revenue Management in Angola

The questions of how oil revenues were secured and used up to the end of the war and how future revenues will be used are politically charged issues, both within Angola and in Angola's relations with the international community. As of early 2005 there is little public disclosure of government oil revenues or of the terms of concession agreements, nor is there any structured arrangement for protecting the country from the economic risks associated with oil dependency. Since about 2000 a consensus has been building among multilateral organizations and Western bilateral donors about the importance of effective oil revenue management to economic development and stability in Angola. This has been accompanied by recognition of the need for concerted external pressure on, and encouragement of, the government to put appropriate policies in place.

The government of Angola argues that in the past, "political and military conflicts in the region, resulting from the Cold War, made it impossible for its sources of energy to be used for causes such as poverty alleviation and the eradication of imbalances."[224] Others claim that massive corruption also lies behind "missing" oil revenues. In October 2002 an internal IMF report is said to have "found that nearly $1bn disappeared from Angola Government finances last year."[225] And in January 2004, Human Rights Watch claimed that "more than $4 billion in oil revenues disappeared from the Angola State coffers between 1997 and 2002, an amount equal to that spent by the government on all social problems in the same period."[226] The government strongly rebuts these claims, arguing that there are discrepancies totaling much less than one billion dollars (US$673.5 million) during 1997–2002 and that these derive from recognized inadequacies in budget and financial-sector management systems and statistics.[227]

Looking forward, the Washington-based consultancy PFC Energy estimated in December 2003, "The country will receive a total mean expected value of $94 billion in the 2002 to 2019 period for offshore production alone," equivalent to some $480 per capita annually over this eighteen-year period. These numbers could be larger if further oil finds are made as a result of ongoing exploration, or oil prices are higher than estimated.[228] These earnings are equivalent to a more than 50 percent increase in wealth—gross national income per capita in 2003 was estimated by the World Bank at $740.[229]

The international community is trying to use its leverage during the postwar period to put a revenue management system in place for two reasons: Angola's financial needs are high because of reconstruction costs and debt servicing, and the large new oil projects are not yet releasing their full revenue flow to the government, because companies are recovering development costs. Still, in the words of one interviewee (who does not wish to be identified), "Now with peace, the biggest challenge is wealth distribution. Those in power are using their position to get rich and select the beneficiaries—this could send us into new conflict."[230]

Because the IMF is insisting on revenue transparency as a condition for assistance, other donors are largely holding back from major aid or debt relief programs in Angola until agreement with the IMF is reached. For example, the World Bank's Transitional Support Strategy (TSS), launched in March 2003, was a relatively small program totaling

$125 million over twelve months, a principal component of which was technical assistance in establishing a more transparent and efficient public finance framework. Conditions for further lending beyond the TSS included progress on revenue management, no reemergence of conflict, and no deterioration in governance.[231] Unusually, no postconflict donor conference has been held for Angola, despite widespread recognition of the large scale of the country's humanitarian, reconstruction, and development needs. Donors are calling on the government to stamp out financial mismanagement, arguing that Angola's own finances are not being put to the best use.[232]

Some steps have been taken toward financial reform and transparency. In particular, the Ministry of Finance, in 2004, published a long-awaited report by accountants on the petroleum sector, analyzing and disclosing information on reserves, production, revenues, and their distribution, and projecting future data and making recommendations on revenue monitoring and management.[233] By late 2004 there was international recognition that some progress had been made. A World Bank spokesman announced that a further, expanded support program was in negotiation and that a donor conference would be held in 2005— conditional on finalization of the poverty reduction strategy and agreement with the IMF.[234] Similar statements were made on behalf of the UN Development Programme (UNDP).[235] In July 2005 the IMF reported, "important improvements have been made in the last two years in the fiscal accounts and the transparency of oil transactions."[236] In late 2005 Sonangol for the first time released to the public information on new concessions to be let, the list of companies qualified to bid, and the generic terms of the production-sharing contracts (without financial information included).[237] In April 2006 the government-controlled *Jornal de Angola* published for the first time the value and origin of the winning bid for a new oil concession.[238]

The government is also being encouraged to sign on to the Extractive Industries Transparency Initiative (EITI) as an indication of commitment to transparent and development-oriented use of its oil revenues. Representatives from the government and the state oil company attended the EITI launch conference and confirmed that they were observing the process. In November 2004 the deputy prime minister, Dr. Aguinaldo

Jaime, told a London conference that the government would join, saying, "The priority is finishing an arrangement with the IMF, which would include measures on governance and transparency.... Having said that, when the time comes—and I think it will come very soon— we will consider EITI."[239]

But by early 2006 the pace of change seemed to have slowed down. The government of Angola announced that it was no longer interested in borrowing from the IMF, since the country could now obtain huge loans from foreign governments. (In March 2004, for example, Angola signed a $2 billion credit line with Exxonbank of China.)[240]

The allocation of oil revenues to producing areas—particularly Cabinda, but also the provinces close to other new offshore fields—is not at the forefront of the revenue management debate. But it is likely to become increasingly important in the context of the Cabindan conflict, new onshore developments, and expanding output, especially if slow progress continues on delivery of the peace dividend in mainland Angola. In March 2005 one Angolan interviewee suggested that the peace process in Sudan, with half of revenues allocated to southern Sudan, and commitment to a referendum on independence (see chapter 7), will influence the Cabinda conflict, strengthening demands for independence. A series of decrees and resolutions passed since 1992 allocate 10 percent of oil revenues originating there to each of the two provinces—Cabinda and Zaire—where there is currently production. But little is known about how these transfers are used or what transfers will be made, and to which provinces, in relation to newly developed offshore fields.[241] A plan announced by the government in June 2004 to spend some $370 million by 2010 on economic and social development projects in Cabinda received a skeptical response from civil-society organizations for not being developed in consultation with the population and for not addressing "the fundamental frustration of the province."[242] There is also a risk that local tensions might develop in neighboring Zaire Province, if revenues from oil produced offshore of that province do not translate into positive change and the promised national and local elections do not take place. (Although there is no secessionist movement in Zaire, there is a history of Kongo nationalism and hostility toward Luanda, sharpened by the Bloody Friday massacres in Luanda in 1993, when northerners were attacked and "churches, schools and houses were destroyed, women were raped, numerous people were wounded and killed.")[243]

The political climate in Angola reflects the centralized, authoritarian system typical of oil-rich developing countries and states at war. In the four years since the end of the war, few steps have been taken toward building the foundations of a democratic postwar state. Efforts to rewrite the constitution, started immediately after the war, have stalled. Presidential and parliamentary elections, though promised, have not been scheduled, nor has critical preparatory work, such as drawing up voter lists, begun. The postwar agreement included amnesty provisions for all involved, so there has been no process to address war-related crimes or grievances.[244] While some independent newspapers and radio stations have started up in the capital, this opening up of the media has not extended to the rest of the country. And Angola remains one of the world's most corrupt countries, ranking below both Azerbaijan and Sudan in Transparency International's 2005 Corruption Perceptions Index.[245]

Oil Companies and Revenue Management

When the civil war resumed in the late 1990s, much international attention was focused on restricting the sale of diamonds from UNITA-controlled areas. At the same time, the oil companies operating in Angola started to come under pressure from NGOs about the way in which oil revenues provided the government with financing that enabled it to wage war. The key arguments made were (1) that secrecy surrounding the financial aspects of oil deals was enabling the huge revenues to be used to fund the conflict and line the pockets of the elite; and (2) that international companies should implement ethical policies and disclose the payments made for oil concessions, thereby acting as a lever to stop the war and the pilfering.[246] Pressure was heightened by a series of scandals about oil-backed loans and bribes to secure oil concessions.[247]

Under the terms of Angolan PSAs, companies are required to maintain confidentiality about their terms. The state can terminate contracts if information is disclosed without prior agreement "if disclosure causes prejudice to Sonangol (Angola's state oil company) or the state."[248] Disclosure is, however, permitted where this is required "by an applicable law, decree or regulation including, without limit, any requirement or rule of any regulatory agency, securities commission or securities exchange" on which the companies are listed.[249]

In 2001 BP, one of the companies operating in Angola, stated that it would make available information on production from the blocks in which it had a share, and that information on signature bonus payments it had made was available in its routine filing to the UK companies regulator (Companies House). This led to a strong response from Sonangol, which made clear in writing that this was unacceptable and could be construed as grounds for terminating the company's PSAs. The letter was copied to the other oil companies operating in Angola.[250] The incident was a catalyst for the development of the EITI, and the launch of the Publish What You Pay campaign, which lobbies for changes to stock-exchange and company-regulation systems such that disclosure of payments to individual governments becomes a legal requirement placed on companies, and one that cannot be constrained by PSAs. The letter also helped to raise the profile of revenue-management issues among the international institutions and to create the current situation whereby, in the words of one commentator, "in the end this is all causing so many problems for the government that it just has to be dealt with."[251]

In 2004 there were indications of a shift in attitude on the part of government and companies. Two companies succeeded in coming to agreement with the government to release information about the bonuses paid on signature of PSAs that were revised that year,[252] and interviews with oil executives suggest that several companies are discreetly seeking opportunities for constructive engagement with officials regarding revenue transparency and management, and encouraging Angolan membership in EITI.

The Local Impact of the Oil Industry, and Impact Management

Because it is largely an offshore industry, the local "footprint" of the oil industry is smaller in Angola than in the other countries covered in this study. Issues of land acquisition and resettlement, environmental

impact, and major social change in oil field areas, which have contributed to social tension and conflict elsewhere in Africa, have not been
present to any significant degree except in Cabinda.[253] In the future this
could change substantially if plans to develop new onshore blocks are
implemented and if the proposed onshore Liquefied Natural Gas Plant
in Soyo and the new refinery in Lobito go forward. These developments
will greatly increase the onshore impact of the industry.

One area where the offshore industry does have some limited local
impact is in the hiring of local people and the procurement of goods and
services from local sources. Where there is local conflict, this can make a
contribution to peace. According to one Angolan interviewee with a good
knowledge of the oil industry, "Chevron helped the seccessionist movement (in Cabinda) by not doing this…but in the last few years they have
been helping companies to set up, empowering local companies, things
are starting to change and there are now plenty of opportunities."[254]

Long-standing Angolan legislation requires oil companies to meet
targets for employment of Angolan nationals, and more-recent legislation requires that the oil industry buy certain goods and services only
from Angolan firms.[255] Several of the companies operating in Angola
identify efforts to increase "local content" as an important demonstration of corporate social responsibility. A World Bank study on corporate social responsibility in the Angolan oil sector concluded that a
range of initiatives related to employment, training, business development, and capacity building could benefit communities, businesses,
and postconflict transformation. Studies by companies have reached
similar conclusions.[256] Some companies report limited success in
expanding the numbers of local vendors, implementing a transparent
local content strategy, and recruiting employees from around the country rather than from Luanda or Cabinda. But in the current context in
Angola, these steps are not easy—some report, for example, that it is
difficult for new firms to set up and operate independently in a state
described as a "kleptocracy."[257]

The oil industry's other major local impact in Angola is through
social investment. The pattern since the late 1990s is for companies to
spend some money on community projects in and around areas where
they have onshore bases and to provide some funds to NGO-run proj-

ects, such as for mine clearance. There is no overall data on the sums spent, and the levels of spending are believed to vary widely between companies. In late 2003 Chevron Texaco, the largest operator in Angola, launched by far the largest corporate social project in Angola, in the form of cofunded parallel partnerships with USAID (United States Agency for International Development) and UNDP, to support economic diversification through education, training, and projects to encourage small-scale business development.

Starting with blocks 5 and 6, companies have also been obliged to contribute to "social funds" in bids to secure exploration concessions. Since 1997 it is estimated that Sonangol has received at least $165 million from oil companies for social projects; however, these funds are controversial. There are disputes between companies and Sonangol about control of the funds and about what projects will be supported, and wider concerns about how the funds are spent and who is really paying, given that these social contributions are a "cost-recoverable" element within the PSAs.[258]

Postwar Reconstruction and the Role of the Oil Industry

Determining the role that business can play in postwar reconstruction is complicated in Angola because of the stalled status of the postwar transition. Having won the war, the same party that has governed since 1975, the MPLA, remains in power. No firm dates for presidential and parliamentary elections have been announced, and the constitutional reform that has been underway since 1997 remains incomplete and contentious.[259] Despite some steps toward transparency, and the development of policies to reduce the extensive and deep poverty in the country, there is little evidence that the ruling elite is prepared to share wealth or power. Humanitarian and development needs are high. Angola's poverty reduction strategy spells out the huge needs for social and physical infrastructure in order to make any significant progress toward meeting the internationally agreed "millennium development goals," which include halving the number of people living in acute poverty (people living on less than one dollar per day) by 2015. A set of projects costing some $3 billion is identified for 2003–05 alone.[260]

The case of Angola illustrates the limited incentives for, and possibilities of, oil-sector investors taking an active role in peacebuilding in circumstances where their involvement is neither essential to successful business nor welcomed by the government. Incentives to contribute to peace were limited because offshore operations were unlikely to be directly affected by the conflict. This remains largely true with the Cabinda conflict. Further, the limited onshore presence of oil companies translates to limited demand for involvement in local development activities. In this context, companies, individually or as a group, can contribute to the consolidation of peace in four main areas:

(1) The use of Angola's oil revenues is key to the country's future. A priority for companies is therefore to support and promote revenue transparency and to find opportunities to encourage and contribute to public debate about how these revenues are spent. For example, the strategy of participatory poverty reduction presents opportunities for company involvement in Angola's development at the national level. Also, impact assessments carried out for individual oil projects provide scope for openly discussing revenues and their uses. Companies that are not yet participants in the Extractive Industries Transparency Initiative should join, and provisions for publication of PSAs and revenues should be included in negotiations for new or revised concession agreements.

(2) The development of a strong civil society and political culture in a country that has been at war for most of the time since its independence is vital to sustained peace. Companies can contribute to the strengthening of civil society by involving a wide range of organizations in consultations about projects and in planning, delivering, and monitoring social investments. They can also partner with a range of nongovernmental organizations on social projects, and they can support progressive policies and debate, for example, by supporting research and discussion forums. When elections are held, companies should encourage employees to participate, and enable them to volunteer as participants in the process, for example, as election monitors.

(3) Maintaining peace also depends fundamentally on the Angolan people's access to employment and on opportunities to make a living through business, commerce, and farming. Companies can contribute primarily through maximizing national content and employment in oil projects, but also by contributing to the policy debate on, for example, land reform and business regulation—both issues in which business has an interest and to which business can contribute experience. Social investment projects, such as microcredit programs, can also help support livelihoods.

(4) The oil industry in Angola is beginning to have a larger onshore footprint. Oil companies and their backers involved in onshore activities should ensure that high standards of consultation, impact assessment, and management are applied (comparable to those applied in Azerbaijan or on the Chad-Cameroon projects), including standards for project security that protects human rights. Most of the super major companies, each with extensive experience in environmental and social impact management, are present in Angola, alongside smaller-scale operators with less experience and fewer resources, holding onshore concessions. There is a strong case for the major companies to work together to encourage high standards across the industry—for example, by developing a voluntary environmental and social code of conduct that embodies the standards defined by the International Finance Corporation, which would complement the national legislation that is currently being revised. As explained by one Angolan source,

> In the past, most people thought that oil was just a strategic thing for the government—now they see it impacts their lives.… This has a profound impact,…and people living in poor social conditions look at the companies making huge profits…they [the oil companies] need to rethink and restart the model of their operations in Angola.[261]

While moving from peace to development is the challenge for mainland Angola, the conflict in Cabinda has still to be resolved. Detailed information is scarce, but there appear to be typical "oil and secession" characteristics in Cabinda, whereby the separate identity of Cabindans has been reinforced over the years by the oil wealth of the enclave, dissatisfaction with the oil industry, and reaction to violent efforts to suppress the independence movements. Ethnic links between the Bakongo population of Cabinda, provinces in northern Angola, and neighboring areas of Congo (Brazzaville) and the Democratic Republic of Congo, together with extensive movements of people, trading links across the area, and a history of regional political intrigue, combine to make Cabinda a flashpoint.[262] Failure to establish peace in Cabinda risks spilling over into neighboring Zaire Province as the oil industry grows there, too. Although the intermittent conflict in Cabinda impinges little on the day-to-day operations of the oil industry, it does expose the companies operating there to criticism from the media and NGOs, and hostility from some of the independence groups. According to one such group's Web site, in material published there until July 2005, "Chevron Texaco continues doing good business in Cabinda, by collaborating with the Angolan invaders, stealing the oil of Cabinda, and destroying the future of the next Cabinda generations."[263] A security assessment in 2004 determined that "FLEC is far too weak to effect secession but does seem to have considerable support among the impoverished local population and may still be able to disrupt onshore elements of the enclave's critical oil infrastructure."[264] Local tensions associated with oil operations are likely to intensify as new onshore operations get under way.

The history of external interference in Angolan conflicts suggests that direct pressure from oil companies concerning Cabinda would be neither welcome nor effective. Specific contributions that oil companies in Angola could realistically make to limit the risks of escalation and encourage peaceful resolution include, at the operational level, applying the highest standards of corporate social responsibility—focusing particularly on environmental protection and security and human rights systems, which are an ongoing source of grievance. On a larger scale, the industry could seek opportunities to collaborate with the provincial government and local civil society to debate and develop strategies for ensuring that the province's growing oil sector benefit the community, in a similar way to that being done in São Tomé and Príncipe, another small area rich in oil (see chapter 8).

Conclusions

The historic link between oil and conflict in Angola is patently clear, with oil revenues financing the continuation of the civil war after its sponsorship by the Cold War powers came to an end. It is also clear that oil revenues could potentially finance a transformation of Angola from a country whose people are among Africa's poorest to a middle-income country with modern infrastructure, health, and education services. But the politically dominant elite that has remained in power since independence in 1975 shows no sign of putting in place the policies to enable such a transformation to happen.

To date, the international community has had very little success in pressing for change in Angola despite significant efforts to do so through withholding financial aid. Rising oil revenues and the ability to take out bilateral and commercial loans backed by future oil revenues have enabled the government to withstand this pressure.

The oil industry has had little direct involvement in the negotiations between the Government of Angola and the international community. To a limited extent, some companies have tried to change revenue transparency, and in recent years this has had some positive effect. But in a climate where the government has made clear that political as well as commercial factors determine the allocation of concessions, where there is a political culture of resistance to externally imposed views, and where companies are in competition and have offshore operations, which are insulated from social and economic conditions in the country, most have not engaged with Angola's postconflict development at all.

For the next decade, unless the industry as a whole takes a longer-term view, looks for ways of encouraging wider political debate and economic reform in Angola, and makes much greater efforts to spread the direct economic benefits of its investments in Angola through "local content" programs, both the oil companies and the citizens of Angola are likely to experience renewed instability.

7

Sudan: Oil Wealth, Civil War, and the Peace Agreement

S UDAN IS THE LARGEST COUNTRY IN AFRICA, with an area just over a quarter the size of the United States. It was established within its current borders in the early twentieth century, as a colony jointly administered by Great Britain and Egypt.[265] It became independent in 1956. The experience of Sudan since the 1980s illustrates powerfully the potential of oil to serve as a force exacerbating conflict; historically, it provides the first example of the explicit integration of oil revenue management into the terms of a civil war peace agreement. Because of the history of sanctions and effective pressure on companies to divest, Sudan's experience provides valuable insights into the implications of invest-or-divest decisions in today's global oil industry. Lessons can also be drawn concerning the effectiveness of corporate social responsibility approaches where companies either gain limited leverage over government or fail to recognize the need to exercise what influence they have at the critical stage before production facilities and export pipelines are up and running.

This chapter examines the links between oil, conflict, and business behavior, beginning with a short introduction to Sudan's civil wars and oil industry. The main focus then shifts to revenue management in relation to Sudan's conflicts, the 2004 wealth-sharing agreement,[266] and the role of investor companies concerning transparency, the local impact of

Figure 6-1 Map of Sudan[267]

the oil industry, and associated corporate social responsibility (CSR) initiatives. The conclusion discusses the key oil-related priorities and opportunities following the December 2004 peace agreement, and the lessons learned from Sudan about sanctions and divestment.

Sudan's Civil Wars

When Sudan formally became a state, it had deep religious and ethnic fissures. The population consists of over fifty ethnic groups, of which some 60 percent are African and 40 percent Arab, and of which about 70 percent are Muslim and the remainder Christian or adherents of traditional religions. The north is predominantly but not exclusively Arab and Muslim, and the south is predominantly but not exclusively African and non-Muslim. The two regions also have different geographical characteristics: the south is more fertile, containing most of the known natural resources; the north is largely dry savannah and desert with fewer natural resources.[268]

Since at least the early nineteenth century Sudan's northern-based groups have sought to govern, tax, and convert the peoples of the south, and have engaged in slave raiding and slave owning—the latter in part as a response to northern impoverishment due to higher taxation and changed forms of land ownership.[269] During the late 1890s, when the Anglo-Egyptian condominium[270] was establishing control over Sudan, north and south were already divided by religion, ethnicity, culture, and history. Divisions were reinforced and institutionalized by the 1922 Closed Districts Order and other measures (the "southern policy") that restricted and controlled northern traders and Muslim proselytizers from going to the south, and by policies that concentrated education, infrastructure, and economic development in the north.

Until the late 1940s the British administration was ambivalent on whether southern Sudan should form part of a future independent Sudan. The southern policy was reversed in 1946, "but not before creating and fortifying psychological and emotional boundaries between southerners and northerners that would live on after independence."[271] Moreover, the unequal distribution of educational and other opportunities that were available in the south contributed to disunity, tensions, and (later) conflict between the diverse ethnic groups in the south, providing justification for divide-and-rule policies by the northern-dominated government.[272]

As Sudan moved toward independence, the issue of the south's status was raised, with southern politicians articulating demands for the south to become an autonomous state within a federal Sudan or, failing that, to have the right of self-determination, including the option of complete independence from the north. This was not resolved, however, and the immediate preindependence period saw an increase in "Sudanization," manifest in an influx of people from the north and in efforts to impose a "northern" perspective on the entire country. This was marked by a "rapid increase of Northerners in the South as administrators, senior officers in the army and police, teachers in government schools and as merchants."[273] Anne Mosely Lesch, writing on the sharp distinction in the views of the northern and southern elites, notes that, "The Muslim Arab politicians in the North, who lead the drive for independence, conceived of the Sudan in their own image and hoped to transform the South into that image; in contrast, southern leaders sought to preserve their autonomy and cultural identity."[274]

The First Civil War

At independence in 1956, two key issues, which have been the central focuses for civil war during most of the time since then, remained unresolved: the status of Islam in Sudan as a whole, and the extent of northern political control over the south.[275] Since the birth of independent Sudan there has been resistance and civil conflict in the south, and the basis for what Francis Deng describes as "an internecine war of visions."[276] There were profound economic inequalities, with GDP per capita in the south approximately two-thirds the average for the rest of the country.[277] Moreover, neither north nor south was a homogenous region; divisions of particular importance during the first civil war period included deep differences in terms of political ideology and Islamic religious affiliation among the northern elites.[278]

From the preindependence era until 1972, including two periods under parliamentary democracy (1956–58 and 1965–69) and a period of military dictatorship (1958–64), civil war raged in the south as guerrilla armies fought against northern domination. This period was also marked by fragile government control over the mountain areas in the economically underdeveloped west, the devastating impact of the Sahel drought, and the involvement of Sudanese forces in rebel movements in Chad, and vice versa.[279]

Peace: 1973–83

Faced with the recognition that "renewed attempts of the government to reach a military solution were failing…(and) a recognition that Khartoum had finally come to terms with the fact that Sudan's future depended on a peaceful process of nation building,"[280] President Ja'far Nimeiri and the southern leaders negotiated the 1972 Addis Ababa Agreement on the Problem of South Sudan, which ended the north-south civil war. It addressed the long-standing issues of regional autonomy, religion, and equality by providing for a single, elected regional government in the south, with revenue from local taxes and fees and transfers from the north to help narrow the economic gap.[281] The 1973 constitution described Sudan as a country with dual Arab and African identity, with respect for Islam, Christianity, and "noble spiritual beliefs," and provided for equal legal rights for all.[282]

The Addis Ababa peace deal lasted, under increasing pressure, until 1983. After a series of about-faces on provisions within the agreement, and residual guerrilla warfare, the northern government unilaterally abrogated the agreement, redivided the south into three subregions, and imposed Islamic law. "Step by step, then, Nimeiry subverted the very agreement he had helped to create,"[283] and what is known as Sudan's "second civil wars" began.

The Second Civil War(s)[284]

The second phase of civil wars started in an overall context of economic collapse and institutional breakdown. It involved both north-south conflict and conflict between southern groups and is therefore often referred to as a set of civil wars. Renewed war was the outcome of political pressure within the north to respond to the demands made by Islamic fundamentalist elements and those factions that had opposed southern autonomy all along,[285] the strengthening of the Sudan army as a result of U.S. (and Chinese) support designed to oppose Soviet-aligned Libya and Ethiopia,[286] and the discovery of oil in southern Sudan after the peace agreement.[287]

Oil finds in southern Sudan stoked the tension in many ways. First, political conflict developed over north-south boundaries, with unsuccessful efforts to redraw them to include the oil fields in the territory belonging to the north.[288] Second, disputes arose over control of oil revenue. Oil wealth was not anticipated when the Addis Ababa Agreement was negotiated, and no rules for its allocation between north and south were explicitly spelled out in its terms. A third issue concerned the location of the refinery to process oil for domestic use: should it be built near the oil fields in the south or the main markets in the north?[289] Meanwhile, the forcible expulsion of people from parts of the oil field area created anger and distrust.[290] Moreover, the knowledge of oil wealth gave added impetus to the struggle for autonomy from the north. Anthropologist Sharon Hutchinson cites the explanation of one "determined Nuer fighter," who compares the first and second phases of civil war thus: "We fought for seventeen years without even knowing the wealth of our lands. Now we know the oil is there, we will fight much longer if necessary!"[291] At an early stage in the renewed war there were attacks on the oil fields, and both companies operating in Sudan ceased operations.

Sudan's "second civil wars" were increasingly brutal and increasingly complex. Douglas Johnson wrote in 2003,

> The current civil war has intensified in complexity the longer it has been fought. Multiple local grievances have created numerous motives for armed confrontation, and shifting alliances within the wider conflict have produced a pattern of interlocking civil wars, now being fought on different levels…it has not been confined to the South: fighting has taken place in… parts of the "Muslim" North…. Since 1991 the number of internal civil wars has multiplied, paralleled by a deepening involvement of the Sudan government in the internal politics of neighboring countries…. These multiple civil wars have each fed into and intensified the fighting in the overall "North-South" war.[292]

Since 1983 there have been at least five efforts to make peace. Moreover, in 1996 and 1997 the government signed "political charters" with southern officers who had defected from the main southern army, and in 1997–98 the government agreed to the concept of an internationally supervised vote in the south, following a peace agreement.[293] As discussed in the following section on the oil industry, some investors misread these and other political moves as meaning that peace was likely.

Renewed oil investment in the 1990s, particularly in the construction of an export pipeline, enabled the government to double its military expenditures since 1999 and to pull out of the economic crisis of the mid-1990s.[294] Since the mid-1990s Sudan has been subject to UN sanctions (in force from 1996 to 2001 but scarcely implemented) and a range of U.S. sanctions. The 2002 U.S.-Sudan Peace Act threatened additional sanctions and restrictions unless the government of Sudan and the Sudan People's Liberation Movement (SPLM) engaged in good-faith negotiations to achieve a permanent, just, and equitable peace agreement.[295] Since 1983 the war has caused an estimated two million deaths and led to about four million internally displaced persons.[296]

The Machakos Peace Process and 2005 Peace Agreement

The signing of the Machakos Protocol in July 2002 led to a cease-fire in the north-south civil war, coming into force in October 2002.[297] The Protocol addressed the historical issues of the south's status and Islam through agreement that at the end of a six-year "interim period," which would follow the signing of a "comprehensive peace agreement" (CPA), there would be an internationally monitored referendum allowing the southern Sudanese to confirm Sudan's unity or vote for secession. The Protocol also agreed that a southern regional government would be set up and that southern states would base their law on "popular consensus and local custom" rather than Islamic law. The Protocol was supplemented by a series of more-detailed agreements on specific issues.[298] These included an agreement on wealth sharing, dealing mainly with the issue of oil revenue sharing (discussed in detail in the section below on revenue management). An intense negotiation period in 2003–04 led to the signing of the CPA on January 9, 2005, and the implementation of the Machakos Protocol agreements.

During 2003 civil war also flared in Darfur, in western Sudan. By September 2004 this conflict was estimated to have killed some seventy thousand people and caused the displacement of two million more. In 2004 U.S. Secretary of State Colin Powell described it as genocide.[299] African Union forces in Darfur since June 2004 have been unable to meet their mandate of protecting citizens, with violence and displacements continuing into 2006. During 2005 low-intensity conflict also developed in east Sudan. The January 2005 peace agreement does not address these conflicts, although its underpinning concept—the decentralization of political and economic power—potentially offers the route to their resolution.

As of early 2006, the north-south peace has held and withstood the challenge presented by the death, in a helicopter accident, of the south's leader, John Garang, in August 2005. The CPA is being slowly implemented, although, as discussed below in relation to implementation of the wealth-sharing provisions, there is little evidence of emerging trust between north and south, lessening confidence in the long-term durability of peace. In a public meeting in Washington, D.C., in November 2005, Salva Kiir Mayardit, the new president of Southern Sudan, reported that the wealth-sharing agreement remained contentious, as did the related issue of the demarcation of boundaries between regions.[300]

The Oil Industry in Sudan

Sudan is a relatively small-scale producer of oil, accounting for 0.4 percent of global production in 2004.[301] But production is rising, and because of the war many areas have not yet been developed or explored, so the future contribution of Sudan to world oil supplies could be on a greater scale.[302] All current production is from onshore fields in central and southern Sudan, with a pipeline running northeast to refineries and an export terminal at Port Sudan on the Red Sea. Some seventeen concession blocks[303] had been delineated by 2001, of which several had been subdivided; many of the large areas remained unlet.

Sudan's oil resources were developed in two distinct stages. The first began in the 1950s, when intermittent exploration resulted in few noteworthy finds. Work to bring the first fields into production started in the late 1970s, after Chevron made several substantial finds near the towns of Bentiu (Unity State), Malakal (Upper Nile) and Muglad (southern Kordofan), under a concession granted in 1974. This phase of the industry was short-lived, however. In 1984 a southern rebel force attacked a Chevron facility, killing four workers. Chevron halted its operations, followed soon afterward by Total, which was exploring in a neighboring block. Chevron's production ceased permanently when it became clear that oil facilities (and other components of the economic infrastructure) would continue to be targets of violence.[304] The oil industry started again in earnest in the 1990s, when the government subdivided the former Chevron concession and let new production-sharing contracts to independent companies. Production restarted on a small scale in 1996, and additional investors with greater resources were subsequently brought into the concessions. In 1998 work started on the rapid construction of an export pipeline linking the oil fields to a Red Sea export terminal. This pipeline has been operating since mid-1999. It enabled Sudan to become an oil exporter and provided a basis for the subsequent expansion of export production.

With the signing of the peace agreement between the government of Sudan and the SPLM/A[305] on December 31, 2004, a third phase of oil development began. New concessions were granted to state oil companies and several small-scale independents, exploration work started in other areas—including, reportedly, in Darfur—and new oil fields came onstream. In August 2005 Sudan's first offshore concession was let for exploration off the Red Sea coast.[306] Tensions flared over the right to establish new concessions, when political leaders from southern Sudan claimed the right to override the concession previously negotiated between Total and the government of Sudan, in favor of deals with other companies, which reportedly provided a faster flow of revenues into southern Sudan.[307] Industry newsletters report that further exploration activity is expected if peace takes hold. [308] The pace of exploration and form of investments will depend first on how secure the country appears to investors as the 2011 referendum on the status of the south looms on the horizon, and second on whether the post-CPA governments in the north and south are successful in bolstering the country's battered reputation, so that Sudan can be seen as a place where companies concerned about their own image should invest.

A range of oil companies have been involved in the stop-go development of Sudan's oil industry. In the initial phase of active development
in the 1970s and '80s, the key companies involved were U.S.- and
European-based majors.[309] Canadian and European independents and
small European state oil companies started the second phase of development, in the 1990s. But NGO and shareholder pressures for divestment
on human rights grounds led to the withdrawal of all Western oil companies from active operations in Sudan in the early 2000s. Their interests were taken up by state oil companies from China, Malaysia, and
India, as well as by some small independents and Sudanese firms. The
Asia-based state oil companies are taking the lead in the successful
expansion of Sudan's output.

From the very beginnings of the oil industry in Sudan there has been
tension over how the industry should be developed—between companies
and government, and between northern and southern interests. In the
1980s, for example, a dispute occurred between Chevron and the government over how quickly the fields would be developed (Chevron wanting
to move slowly because of low oil prices, and the government seeking
rapid development to meet domestic fuel needs and cut the import bill).
In the same decade, the central and the southern regional governments
argued about whether a refinery would be built close to the oil fields in
southern Sudan or in the north. The central government's coincidental
decisions to build a refinery at Kosti, in northern Sudan, and to construct
the Jonglei Canal to take water from southern Sudan to the north, were
widely seen in the south as the theft of southern resources for the benefit
of the north, as were attempts to redraw the north-south boundary.[310]
Then, in the 1990s, the decision to build the export pipeline through
northern Sudan to the Red Sea, rather than through Kenya to the port of
Mombasa, reinforced this view. These tensions have continued since the
peace agreement, as deals made by the SPLM in 2005 appear to violate
the CPA provision that existing concessions would be honored.

Revenue, Conflict, and Peace

The sections that follow show how oil has played an increasingly important role in Sudan's economy since 2000, examine how the economic

and political challenges of revenue management have been addressed in the years up to the CPA and how the provisions of the wealth-sharing agreement (WSA) have changed the allocation of revenues, and explore how companies operating in Sudan have approached the issues of revenue management.

The Role of Oil in the Economy

Since 2000 oil has been a major force in Sudan's economy, accounting for 80 percent of exports, the bulk of foreign investment, and some 40 percent of government revenues. In 2000 Sudan experienced its first trade surplus after more than twenty years of consecutive deficits.[311] The development of the oil sector played a significant part in the early 1990s, when Sudan emerged from an ongoing economic crisis characterized by loan defaults, hyperinflation, and a shortage of hard currency. By the end of the decade macroeconomic stability had been achieved, albeit accompanied by highly skewed wealth distribution and high poverty rates. In 2002 crude oil revenues accounted for 39 percent of central government revenues; by 2004 it had risen to 52 percent (5.55 trillion dinars out of total government revenues of 1.072 trillion dinars).[312]

Oil revenues have been important in financing conflict. In the 2003 Country Economic Memorandum, designed to provide the data and analysis needed to plan for a postwar Sudan, the World Bank, confirming the view of many commentators, stated that oil had "emerged as one of the major factors that keeps the war going." Spending on defense and security in 2002 was estimated at approximately $1 million per day,[313] government oil revenues at around $1 billion per year.[314] The U.S.-Sudan Peace Act of 2002 includes a commitment on the part of the U.S. government to "take all necessary and appropriate steps to deny Sudan government access to oil revenues in order to ensure that the funds are not used for military purposes," should the United States find that the government of Sudan has not engaged in good-faith negotiations or has unreasonably interfered with humanitarian efforts.[315]

Steps have been taken to address the macroeconomic risks presented by oil dependency. In mid-2002 the government set up an oil savings account (OSA) to save revenues above a defined threshold in order to provide protection from revenue volatility. According to the International Monetary Fund, Sudan's assets had reached 85 billion dinars by December 2004.[316] Under the CPA, this system will be maintained through the Oil Stabilization Account and a Future Generations Fund (to be set up when oil production exceeds a set threshold). In terms of revenue transparency, data is published on both aggregate revenues and revenues paid by (some) individual companies, and forecasts are produced and disseminated as part of the peace negotiation process. The specific terms of the Sudan production-sharing agreements, however, are not publicly disclosed documents.

Revenue Management before 2005

Revenue management has been contentious in Sudan since the early days of the oil industry. Key issues concern the regional allocation of revenues—particularly the share accruing to the south—and who holds the power to establish exploration and concession contracts with oil companies.

The arrangements for control of the industry and the allocation of revenues have been contested since oil was first discovered in the south. Since the mid-1950s the central government has issued all oil contracts. Fifteen percent of oil revenues were transferred to state authorities in those areas controlled by the central government, including oil-producing and other regions. The large areas of southern Sudan controlled by the SPLM were excluded and did not receive transfers from the federal budget.[317]

The 1972 Addis Ababa Agreement, signed before oil was found, did not specify how any oil resources or revenues should be controlled. Its wording allowed for differing interpretations. For example, Article 11 referred to the responsibilities of the Southern Regional People's Assembly as including "mining and quarrying without prejudice to the rights of the Central Government in the event of the discovery of natural gas and minerals"—it did not define the "rights of central government" or whether oil was included. Similarly, Article 25 included as a source of income for the southern region "revenues from commercial, industrial and agricultural projects in the Region," and "profits accruing to the Central Government as a result of exporting products of the Southern Region."[318]

In the various attempts to craft peace agreements since then, "natural resources" have been featured as a negotiating item. For example, the unsuccessful Abuja Conferences in 1992–93 drew on the experience of revenue allocation in Nigeria to develop alternative models for revenue sharing and enunciating the principle of "equitable sharing of national wealth." And the agreement signed between the Sudan government and some of the southern rebel groups in 1997 (sometimes referred to as the Khartoum Peace Agreement) included tables showing how wealth, including oil revenues, would be shared among local, regional, and central governments.[319] This became important because at least one of the companies investing in Sudan's oil industry in the late 1990s took it as evidence that revenue-sharing issues had been resolved, although this proved not to be the case.[320]

Revenue Management under the 2005 Peace Agreement

The wealth-sharing agreement (WSA) was signed by the government of the Republic of Sudan and the SPLM/A on January 7, 2004, as part of the Intergovernmental Authority on Development's (IGAD's) Peace Initiative on Sudan. The terms of the WSA will apply during the interim period between signing of the CPA and the referendum in the south six years later. The WSA deals with land, oil, and taxes. The issues of revenue sharing, transparency, and a "power sharing" approach to issuing and managing concessions are addressed, to varying degrees, in its provisions.

In allocating revenues from the oil resources of southern Sudan, the agreement states that government revenues should be distributed as follows: first, any revenues above an agreed benchmark price will be placed in an Oil Revenue Stabilization Account; at least 2 percent of revenues will be allocated to producing states/regions, and the balance of revenues will be divided equally between the planned new government of southern Sudan (GOSS) and the national government and states in northern Sudan. Further, once oil production reaches two million barrels per day, a Future Generations Fund will be established.[321] (GOSS will also have regional tax-raising powers and receive half the national nonoil revenue raised in southern Sudan.)

Under the separate protocol on the resolution of the conflict in Abeyei (which straddles north and south Sudan), net oil revenues from that area will be split between the national government (50 percent), GOSS (42 percent), the Bahr el-Ghazal region (2 percent), western Kordofan (2 percent), and locally with the Ngok Dinka and Misseriya people (2 percent each).[322] The Protocol on Southern Kardofan/Nuba Mountains and Blue Nile States provides for a small share of revenues to be allocated locally: "[The] oil producing state is entitled to two percent of the oil produced in that state, as specified in the Wealth Sharing Agreement."[323] The agreements do not mention oil wealth deriving from the north.

The wealth-sharing provisions are controversial in both north and south. As soon as the agreement was published, articles emerged in the northern press criticizing the decision to "give away" wealth; opinion polls in southern Sudan found wealth sharing to be one of four major areas of concern about the peace accords. Some challenge the overall north-south division; others argue that the bulk of revenues should go to the people who live in the localities where oil is produced. According to a report on focus-group opinions in October 2004,

> Sharing oil wealth is not fair. Many people believe that the allocation of the revenues they have heard about is not fair, especially in Abeyei and other oil producing areas. Indeed the severe development needs in the South persuade many that the bulk of revenues should be used closer to home, rather than shared with Khartoum.[324]

The agreement makes limited provisions for revenue transparency, which focus on the transparency of transactions between the governments of north and south but exclude wider dissemination of information. It specifies that all funds and special accounts referred to in the agreement (and future accounts) shall be "on budget" operations, thus open to tracking. Furthermore, the SPLM/A "shall appoint a limited number of representatives to have access to all existing oil contracts" and the right to engage technical experts, but those who have access to the contracts must sign confidentiality agreements. The agreement also provides for the establishment of a National Petroleum Commission (NPC) to negotiate all future oil contracts (see below). In a document signed in Naivasha on December 31, 2004, the government and SPLM/A set out in greater detail the conditions for implementing the agreement. Both parties agreed that a high degree of confidentiality will be maintained in regard to the terms of concession contracts and the formula for revenue sharing between companies and government, and that the SPLM/A technical team will have access to this information for only thirty to sixty days after signing of the CPA—and only after signing confidentiality agreements.[325]

Given the history of distrust over control of oil resources in Sudan, and the link between oil and conflict, it is arguable that stronger transparency provisions will be needed in order to build confidence in civil society as a whole that all revenues due the government are being paid and are then properly allocated. Moreover, in a context where both the government in the north and the SPLM have "a history of manipulation and nontransparent use of resources,"[326] systems are needed to ensure that the oil revenues will provide the peace dividend for reconstruction and development purposes. Stronger transparency measures may include building on the experience of Azerbaijan, that is, by publishing all production-sharing agreements (PSAs) in full, requiring oil companies to disclose all payments made, participating in the Extractive Industry Transparency Initiative (EITI), setting up a revenue-management oversight committee with civil society membership and external technical support (such as that established in Chad), and making transparent tendering for new concessions mandatory. GOSS will in turn require economic stability, transparency, and local revenue-allocation rules to ensure that its oil income does not destabilize.

Besides setting out how revenues will be shared, the wealth-sharing agreement introduces shared north-south responsibilities for deciding on the future development of the oil industry and developing "guiding principles for the management and development of the petroleum sector." The guiding principles specify that there should be "sustainable utilization of oil consistent with the national interest and the public good, the interests of affected areas and the interests of the local population in affected areas." The principles address the national environment and cultural heritage, encourage foreign direct investment, promote macroeconomic stability, and provide for consultation with land users.

Also stipulated is an independent National Petroleum Commission (NPC), which will formulate policies and guidelines for the development and management of the petroleum sector, negotiate and approve (before signature by the minister of petroleum) all exploration and production contracts, and ensure that contracts provide benefits to local communities affected by the development.

The NPC was established in October 2005 with ten permanent members drawn equally from the national government and GOSS, and up to three representatives from oil-producing areas.[327] But five months later it still had not started on its work, including developing technical specifications for how revenues will be allocated. According to the United Nations mission in Sudan (UNMIS), "Despite various statements by politicians and other high-ranking officials, little progress was made with regard to providing clarity on the oil discussions…there were no agreements on the rules of procedure for the commission or the mandate and composition of the secretariat."[328]

Oil Companies and Revenue Management

Two of the oil companies operating in Sudan in the early 2000s— Lundin Petroleum and Talisman Energy—made efforts to influence the way in which the government managed revenues, although in the absence of adequate leverage (at the time the issue surfaced, the production fields and export pipeline were already in operation), these efforts had little impact.

Lundin Petroleum, a Swedish independent that obtained exploration and production rights to Block 5A in 1997,[329] recognized the importance of revenue sharing to the north-south peace. According to one of its managers, the company explicitly voiced support for the revenue-sharing arrangement in place under the Khartoum Peace Agreement and argued in discussions with the government that even though revenue management was a government, rather than a company, responsibility, there would be adverse consequences for the company if the revenue-sharing arrangements were not honored. (Company managers were also concerned that there were unrealistic expectations in the south about how soon the revenue flows would start—there was little recognition that the project was still in the exploration phase and that it would be several years before production started, and longer still until costs were recovered and the bulk of government revenues came through.) Lundin also discussed revenue sharing with external stakeholders.[330]

Talisman Energy, a Canadian independent, bought into the Greater Nile Petroleum Operating Company (GNPOC; operator of blocks 1, 2, and 4 and of the export pipeline) as a nonoperating shareholder in 1998 and sold its holding in 2002. Talisman also understood at the time of its investment that the Khartoum Peace Agreement was a substantial step in the peace process and that through it the south stood to gain from its oil wealth.[331] As NGO and shareholder pressure on the company built up after oil shipments through the pipeline began in 1999, the company developed a set of "high-level principles" and a code of ethics. The principles included advocating wealth sharing and required company managers "to support peace processes and ensure that revenues were not being used for war." This led managers to raise the subject of revenue management in meetings with Sudan's president and minister of energy. In 2001 the company secured agreement from the government of Sudan to publish audited data on production volumes and revenues as a step toward transparency. Talisman also sought to engage in peace processes by offering "constructive input to whoever wanted it." This included verifying data on oil production and revenues, collaborating with U.S.-based organizations working to brief the incoming Bush administration on Sudan, and providing oil-sector data and analyses for the preparatory work of the Machakos peace process.[332]

Although no clear policy has been articulated on this, the leadership of South Sudan is seeking alternative models for securing oil revenues to the royalty or production-sharing agreements typical in the industry. The 2005 agreement with the White Nile Company gives a large equity share in White Nile to the Nile Petroleum Company, which is intended to become the government oil company of south Sudan. Thus, to the extent that the share value rises, so Nile Petroleum will profit.[333]

The Local Footprint of Oil Operations and Conflict in South Sudan

Oil operations in Sudan, like oil revenues, have become enmeshed with conflict almost from their start. Most of the potential problems associated with oil production in ethnically divided areas with unresolved conflicts have come to pass in an extreme form in Sudan, leading to the absence of any of the leading oil majors, and extensive turnover in the companies operating there. The legacy of this situation includes problems of compensation for past environmental damage, and the need to raise the industry's social and environmental management standards in a postwar setting. Key issues have been attacks on oil facilities and the forced relocation of people to accommodate oil facilities and security zones.

Oil Facilities as Targets

Oil facilities have been a repeated focus of attack. The first of these came in 1984, when the civil war had restarted following rising tensions over the oil fields and between rebel groups. Chevron was operating the only active oil fields in the country at the time. While the company was constructing a runway at Bentiu—a sensitive project because of its dual use for military purposes—rebels attacked a work crew, killing four Chevron employees. After several stops, suspensions, and restarts, the company determined that it would not be possible to ensure the future safety of its employees and that there was no way of controlling the risk. Then, in the words of a Chevron advisor at the time, "They walked away from a two-billion-dollar investment in what we thought would be a nice oil field."[334]

Since oil operations restarted in the 1990s there have been several periods of fighting centered on oil facilities, including the pipeline.[335] Oil facilities were designated a legitimate target by the SPLM/A up to the 2002 cease-fire, and according to human rights organizations, the development of new oil fields brought conflict into areas that had until then had little value to the government and where SPLM/A control was not previously contested by government forces. In a detailed account linking oil developments and human rights abuses, Human Rights Watch argues,

Without the pipeline, the oilfields in Block 5A would have remained as Chevron had left them, undeveloped, attracting little government attention. This was an area the government had long ago conceded to the rebels as of no strategic interest and having a particularly difficult, swampy environment; but with the GNPOC pipeline only a short distance away, it became economically feasible to develop the oil there. Block 5A shot up in strategic importance and became a military priority for the government.[336]

Making Areas Secure for Oil Development

Sudan has a history of forced displacement of people for economic projects, abrogation of customary rights to land use, and conflict over access to scarce resources between different groups of pastoralists and between pastoralists and the settled population. Several examples illustrate these problems: the resettlement of the people of Wadi Halfa was carried out in 1960 because of construction of the Aswan High Dam, "despite their near unanimous opposition";[337] many confrontations over tenure between agrarian producers and the state took place, especially from the 1970s, when the government's economic policy focused on large-scale, capital-intensive farming; customary land rights were abolished by law in 1970; and the recognition of customary land rights by the courts was prohibited in 1990.[338] According to Douglas Johnson, "the wholesale appropriation of land has been one of the government's underlying economic objectives in the [north-south] war."[339] This provides the context in which, even without the added factor of ongoing civil war, forcible displacement was a predictable risk of oil development.

Since oil development began in Sudan, and particularly since the construction of the pipeline in the late 1990s, there have been persistent reports of government forces or militias clearing civilian populations from oil field areas—destroying homes, crops, and livestock; causing death and injury; and leaving thousands of people exposed to famine in order to create an area free of rebels and rebel supporters. Since 1999 a succession of reports on these human rights violations in the oil fields has come from the United Nations and the Canadian government,[340] as well as from human rights NGOs, particularly Human Rights Watch.[341] While there are disputes about specifics—and those companies that have responded publicly to criticism have contested that displacements have occurred in the areas they operated in[342]—it is widely accepted that overall, oil development has caused large-scale and brutal population displacement. In 1999 the Canadian mission found,

> It is difficult to avoid…[the] conclusion that a "swath of scorched earth/ cleared territory" is being created around the oilfields. Over the years, the series of attacks and displacements are leading to a gradual depopulation, as only a percentage of people who flee return after each displacement.[343]

In 2003 the U.S. State Department's country report on human rights practices noted,

> Government forces pursued a scorched earth policy aimed at removing populations from around the oil pipeline and other oil production facilities, which resulted in deaths and serious injuries…. Scorched earth tactics by the Government and government-supported forces along parts of the oil pipeline and some key oil facilities decreased significantly after the signing of the Addendum to the Memorandum of Understanding (cease-fire) in February. These forces seriously injured persons, destroyed villages, and drove out inhabitants to create an uninhabited security zone. There was a significant decrease in indiscriminate government bombings of civilian locations in the south throughout the year. Such bombings often were associated with military actions by both sides or continuing government efforts to clear the population from near the oil producing areas in Western upper Nile and adjacent areas.[344]

Managing Local Impact

During the first phase of oil field development in Sudan, in the 1970s and 1980s, systematic social-impact assessment and management techniques had yet to be developed; wherever companies operated, they typically focused on drilling and field development while relying on government to provide land and a safe operating environment for those groups affected by operations. Occasional and unsystematic "goodwill" projects were carried out to build relationships with local communities, but impact assessments were undertaken only when specifically required by host-country legislation. While additional documentation is needed, existing accounts from people involved in Sudan in the 1970s suggest that this approach of minimal social concern was the norm, with some acceleration in local involvement and philanthropy over time (for example, Chevron's building of a hospital in Bentiu), but with little overall understanding of the social context and potential impact of the companies' operations.[345]

By the 1990s, when the second phase of oil development in Sudan started, the international oil industry was becoming aware of the risks—to operations and reputations—of developing projects that didn't attempt to protect the environment and minimize the negative impact on neighboring communities. The majors, such as ExxonMobil, BP, and Shell, were beginning to set their own standards for environmental and social impact assessment for projects in countries where there were no effective environmental impact assessment regulations. For example, ExxonMobil started its seven-year preconstruction local consultation on the Chad-Cameroon pipeline in 1993. But the Sudan oil developments were carried out by companies that had not adopted these new systems, and without the detailed level of impact assessment and public consultation that has since become the standard in the industry for major onshore projects. Sudanese law required no prior assessment, and the 1990 model production-sharing agreement does not specify any impact assessment or environmental or social standards, which are implicitly discouraged by stringent restrictions on costs treated as "recoverable" under the PSA.[346] Moreover, because no multilateral agencies, such as the World Bank, were involved in the projects, there was no requirement on either the government or the companies to adopt those agencies' stringent standards for impact assessment, consultation, and resettlement.

The independents and state-owned companies involved in Sudan in the 1990s did not have CSR policies or standards in place when they entered into consortia, although in some cases these were subsequently developed. This lack of experience and commitment on the part of the investor companies meant that a vital opportunity was missed for negotiating high environmental and social standards at the initial investment stage, when the companies may have had some leverage because of the government's desire to secure new oil-sector investors.

Although at least two companies (Lundin Petroleum and Talisman Energy) undertook some analysis of social and political conditions, this later proved inadequate in terms of understanding the complexities of the sociopolitical environment. Their analyses were based on a poor understanding, particularly of land-use patterns, and did not result in binding and monitored commitments for impact management by either the companies or the government.[347] For example, the Harker Report concluded in 2000 that Talisman appeared to have relied on northern Sudanese security officials for local information, had failed to understand the long-standing pattern of population displacement related to oil, incorrectly saw local conflict simply as "traditional interplay between armed cattle herders," and failed to prevent the government of Sudan from using the oil field landing strip for military operations.[348]

Oil Company Responses to Local Impact Issues

Since 1996 eight international companies have been involved in Sudan as members of consortia holding concessions for blocks 1, 2, 3, 4, 5A, 5B, 6, and 7. Of these, Talisman Energy and Lundin Petroleum have made efforts to apply CSR approaches to their operations, although Talisman has sold its interests in Sudan, and Lundin holds an interest only in Block 5B, where operations have been suspended.

Talisman became the focus of hostile campaigning by human rights groups, particularly over forcible removal of people from land around oil facilities. During the latter stage of its involvement, and stimulated in particular by the findings of the Harker Report, Talisman developed a comprehensive CSR strategy for Sudan. The key issues of revenue use, uncompensated and forcible population removal, security and human rights, military use of industry infrastructure, and the need for social and economic benefits for local populations were all explicitly recognized by the company. Its strategy included the development of Sudan Operating Principles, based on the International Code of Ethics for Canadian Business,[349] the setting of specific objectives for implementation of the Principles, extensive stakeholder consultation, and independently verified and publicly disclosed performance reporting.

Talisman's objectives included working within the Greater Nile Oil Production Consortium (GNOPC) to achieve higher environmental and social standards, for example, on compensation for land acquisition, giving preference to local suppliers in tenders, and formalizing a security agreement based on human rights principles. The company also put in place substantial community development programs. The policies, objectives, and results of all these activities and programs are reported extensively in Talisman Energy Corporate Social Responsibility Reports.[350]

Company reports show that while this program achieved some successes—for example, in providing human rights training to employees and setting up community development projects—little progress was made on key issues requiring collaboration from the government or GNOPC partners. In particular, the company was unable to secure agreement from the government for external, independent human rights monitors to identify, review, and verify the human rights situation in and around the concession area. Talisman's published CSR report for 2001 states, "Concerns regarding the perceived infringement of national sovereignty expressed by the Government of Sudan continues to hamper our efforts in this respect."[351] Talisman also reported failure to negotiate agreement on a security agreement based on human rights principles:

> The Government of Sudan ultimately rejected the draft security agreement on the basis that the provision of security is the prime responsibility and prerogative of governments and that these issues were not appropriate to be addressed by a company residing in and operating under the laws of Sudan.[352]

Moreover, Talisman failed to prevent use of the airstrip by the military for nondefensive purposes.[353]

In 2001 the Presbyterian Church of Sudan and a group of villagers filed a claim under the U.S. Alien Tort Claims Act, citing the Sudanese government's ethnic cleansing of Christian and other non-Muslim minorities in southern Sudan. The suit alleges that Talisman aided and abetted the government's military assaults on minority villages in order to help the government clear the way for Talisman's oil exploration.[354] Talisman regards the allegations as entirely without merit and is vigorously defending the case,[355] but as of early 2006 it had failed in attempts to have the case dismissed.[356]

In 2002 Talisman Energy sold its shares in Sudan. On leaving, the company set up an office in Sudan to maintain its community projects until the end of 2005. Discussing this history in 2004, a company representative took the view that Talisman's efforts were hindered by the company's role as a nonoperator member of the consortia it was involved in and by its failure to anticipate the issues and negotiate the required standards as a condition of investment, which was the point of maximum leverage.[357]

In the case of Swedish-based Lundin Petroleum, which has held shares in blocks 5A and 5B, staff met with key representatives of the local community on its first visit to the concession area, and understood from this encounter that oil activities were welcomed "as the only way to promote long-term economic development." In 1999, in the light of security concerns and criticisms directed at oil investors in Sudan, the company commissioned a sociopolitical assessment. The main recommendations of this study were that the company should continue monitoring sociopolitical developments and reinforce the ongoing approach to building relationships with the local community through meetings, local hiring, improving the infrastructure in the area, and a community-development/humanitarian-assistance program. Community projects carried out by Lundin included drilling water wells, building and supplying schools, providing medical and veterinary assistance and training programs, and assisting in humanitarian relief.[358]

In 2001 Lundin developed a code of conduct that set out its vision and values, responsibilities and principles, and attitudes toward employees, host countries, and local communities.[359] The company also started consulting with a wider set of stakeholders. It recognized, however, that the intensification of conflict at that time was making operations increasingly difficult to conduct safely. In 2003 Lundin sold its interests in block 5A at a profit. Activity in block 5B remained suspended, although, following signature of the peace agreement in January 2005, the company expressed the hope that this would pave the way for new oil industry activity, including in block 5B.[360]

Both Talisman and Lundin sought explicitly to promote peace in Sudan—in different ways and with little evidence of success. The veteran Swedish diplomat Carl Bildt, a member of Lundin Petroleum's Board of Directors, met with peace negotiators. One company employee described the meeting in a paper about Lundin's experience in Sudan:

> The situation encountered in Sudan…was exceptional, and the company needed to make clear to the protagonists in the conflict that it saw peace as the best way to ensure sustainable oil operations.… In a series of trips to Brussels, Cairo, Khartoum, Nairobi and Washington, Bildt met with high-level representatives of the Sudanese government, including the President… and the main representatives of the Nuer community,…as well as with representatives of the key nations acting as peace negotiators. Bildt delivered the same message to all: oil represented an incentive for peace as far as oil activities provided the material basis for a sustainable peace. The company's repeated suspensions of activities were a proof that oil activities could not flourish in a conflict situation.[361]

Talisman's efforts were lower-profile but included supporting peace initiatives in ongoing dialogue with the Sudanese government and foreign diplomats involved in the peace process, as encouraged by the Canadian government–sponsored Harker inquiry.

Postwar Risks and Opportunities

Sudan's history of intermingled oil operations, conflict, and human rights abuses leaves a complex legacy for the postwar period, a period in which further expansion of the industry is expected. The two major priorities will be to address the problems of the past—redressing or compensating for the displacement that has occurred—and to develop standards for environmental and social management of oil projects that incorporate effective protection of human rights, the environment, and the interests of the local population in production areas. The wealth-sharing agreement alludes to both priorities, though without any detail on how they will be achieved. Human Rights Watch, with a long-standing focus on displacement issues, has articulated the most detailed recommendations regarding the issue of redress for the past, stating that an independent enquiry should be set up to compile an authoritative and credible survey of civilians forcibly displaced from the oil concessions, and that return and/or compensation should be paid according to UN standards.[362]

In setting future standards for the oil industry, the most needed steps are to include in all PSAs requirements for environmental and social impact assessment, public consultation and disclosure, management of involuntary resettlement, provision of facility security, and protection of indigenous peoples in accordance with international standards, and to introduce legislation setting industry-wide environmental and social standards. In late 2004 Total announced that it had taken steps in this direction, renegotiating the block 5 PSA in anticipation of a peace deal, "to take account of new international industry standards, particularly in relation to corporate social responsibility."[363] None of the other concession holders has made any comparable statements, and in 2005 the Total concession was under challenge from southern Sudan politicians, who started negotiations with speculative oil independents to develop part of the concession under different (unreported) terms.

Invest or Divest: The Impact of Conflict on Oil Company Decisions

Sudan is an unusual case in which the direct effects of conflict on oil operations, alongside U.S. sanctions and intense civil society campaigning, have caused Western companies either to withdraw from the country or to suspend their operations. The only companies actively involved in exploration and production at the time the 2005 peace agreement was signed were the international branches of state oil companies from Malaysia (Petronas), India (ONGC Videsh), and China (CNPC), although one super major—Total—and Lundin held shares in blocks where activity was suspended.

In assessing the consequences of this divestiture on Sudan's north-south conflict and on peace negotiations, the picture is mixed.

Oil production has continued to increase, thus increasing government revenues, and new areas have come under exploration and development despite the withdrawal of Western companies. This illustrates how difficult it is to choke off oil revenues through international pressure and sanctions when many companies are both able and willing to continue oil exploration and production. This situation is likely to continue, and to grow, as the technical and financial capacity of independent and state oil companies grows, as illustrated by expanding investment by Petronas, CNPC, and ONGC Videsh in other parts of Africa, too. Most observers agree, however, that the Sudan government is keen for Western companies to invest, especially the super majors. One observer believed that this motivation "played a tremendous role in the [north-south] negotiations.... The way in which the companies divested, especially Chevron, to be replaced by more marginal companies was one of the incentives on the government to negotiate—they want the bigger companies in."[364] New investment (or a removal of Total's twenty-year suspension of activity in block 5) would be seen as providing an international seal of approval on the peace agreement and would likely lead to other majors expressing interest, as well as to wider market access for Sudan's oil. The attractions of Western investment are countered, though, by the absence of unwanted political "strings" with state oil company investment. As described by one Sudanese official, "Chinese companies are liked because they never interfere in politics."[365]

More difficult to assess is whether the presence of oil has changed the logic of the war—for example, by providing something to negotiate over as a means of financing peace, or through encouraging engagement by the United States. Indirectly, the presence of Western companies was of some importance in raising media and public interest in Sudan's wars, particularly with audiences in Europe and Canada.

Conclusions

Sudan has suffered increasingly complex civil wars that started before the country's independence in 1956 and continued until 2005. There was an eleven-year peace between 1972 and 1983, during which time significant oil reserves were first found and developed. In the 1990s and again since 2001 there were internally and externally brokered efforts to negotiate peace, during which time Sudan's oil resources were further developed. While oil was not the root cause of these conflicts, oil revenues financed their intensification, the existence of oil resources raised the stakes over control of oil-bearing territory, and the process of opening up and securing areas for oil development in the midst of civil war led to large-scale, brutal population displacement.

Looking forward, Sudan's oil resources could contribute to a sustainable peace if all parties make a profound effort. The international community and oil company investors have a role to play in seeking to beat the "resource curse" that has so damaged the country, by encouraging and supporting the development of a clear vision for, and commitment to, effective and transparent revenue management and the highest standards of environmental and social impact management in the industry, building on the lessons from countries such as Azerbaijan and Chad. But whether or not the peace process results in the emergence of two oil states rather than one, without effective and transparent systems of revenue management, and requirements for investor companies to act in a responsible way, there remains potential for future conflict between—and within—north and south Sudan.

8

Conclusions

I N THE EARLY TWENTY-FIRST CENTURY, petroleum is as central to economies across the world as it was for most of the previous century: world oil and natural gas production is rising; countries with no history of oil production, such as Nepal and Sierra Leone, are offering up exploration concessions in the hope that new technology will lead to oil discoveries; new producer countries, such as Equatorial Guinea, are becoming significant suppliers to world markets; and volatile oil prices have considerable economic and political consequences for producing and importing countries. This book has examined the implications of oil export for producing countries, focusing on links with conflict and peace, and the capacity of oil companies to affect the risks of conflict and the prospects for peace through the way they conduct business.

There are two principle links between oil and conflict in producing areas. The first and most important derives from competition for, and misuse of, the income that oil production generates for the governments of oil-rich states. Consider how competition between elites for control of this wealth was a key factor in the continuation of Angola's civil war long after the independence struggle and Cold War proxy conflicts were over. Also, oil wealth can mightily exacerbate secession tensions between oil-rich areas and the rest of the country. This was an important factor in Sudan's civil war, so much so that to make the 2005 north-south peace agreement it was necessary to split oil revenues between the two sides. Oil wealth can also be an enabler of violent conflict. The scale and duration of the civil wars in Angola and Sudan were extended because of the weapons and armies that oil revenues financed; in Azerbaijan, recent oil income is allowing the government to accelerate military spending and take an increasingly belligerent stance on Nagorno-Karabakh's status as an integral part of Azerbaijan. The second linkage between oil and conflict lies in the local tensions caused by the presence of the oil and gas industry in places where most people are poor, without the institutions and rights to protect themselves from pollution and land seizure, and unable to benefit from the industry's presence, because they lack education, skills and capital. Further, the places where both the historic and the prospective links between oil and conflict are greatest are where oil and gas industries are located in minority areas, even where the distinct religious or ethnic identity of the minority is not politically expressed at the time that oil production starts.

Drawing on these conclusions, this chapter addresses three questions: What are the trends of oil investment in countries in conflict or at risk of conflict? What might be done to mitigate the risks? And, what particular contributions can oil companies make?

Oil Industry Investment Trends

The international oil industry comprises several hundred companies that contract with governments to explore for and produce oil and gas from subsurface reservoirs, both onshore and offshore. These firms include the five U.S.- and Europe-based super-major corporations (ExxonMobil, BP, Total, Shell, and Chevron), which are among the world's largest businesses; a group of twenty or so very large companies, known as the majors; and a more numerous group of smaller independents that includes internationally active, state-owned companies, such as China National Offshore Oil Company, Petronas (Malaysia), and India National Overseas Group.

Investment by all types of international oil companies is taking place in an expanding number of countries, particularly in the developing world and the former Soviet Union, and including areas that have recently experienced conflict or are on conflict "watch lists."[366] Oil companies are being invited to bid for concessions to explore for oil and gas—both onshore and offshore—within the two-hundred-mile Exclusive Economic Zones (EEZs). For example, by mid-2004, half the sub-Saharan African nations, including countries with ongoing or recent conflicts, such as Angola, the Democratic Republic of Congo, Côte d'Ivoire, Eritrea, Liberia, Sierra Leone, and Sudan, had announced tenders.[367] The government incentive for offering these concessions is the potential revenue receipts if oil is found. The motivating force for the oil industry is competition: the only route to business success is to be better than competitors at finding new resources; producer companies have little control over the sale price of their product.

This trend of investment in an increasing number of developing countries is likely to continue, for four main reasons. First, demand for oil is growing. In Europe and the United States, oil consumption has increased by 20 percent since 1970, as increased energy efficiencies have been offset by economic growth.[368] In Asia, led by China and India, oil and gas consumption have been greater than in Europe since 1999. In the decade before 2004, China's oil consumption more than doubled, while India's rose by almost 80 percent. In 2002 China became the world's second-largest consumer of oil, after the United States.[369] The U.S. Energy Information Administration predicts that global demand for oil will continue to increase, from 78 million barrels per day in 2001 to an estimated 119 million barrels per day in 2025.[370]

Second, the international oil industry is largely excluded from exploration and production in the Middle East, which holds almost two-thirds of the world's proven oil reserves, and where government-owned companies (state oil companies) have managed most production since the mid-twentieth century nationalizations of international companies from the 1950s through the 1970s. While tentative steps are being made to allow foreign oil companies to compete—notably in Iran, for gas rather than more politically sensitive oil projects—this is very controversial in the region and, even before the Iraq war, was marked by stop-and-go negotiations.[371]

Third, resources are being depleted, and hence business opportunities are declining in North America and Western Europe. Though the

United States is the world's third-largest oil producer, its output is declining annually, and the North Sea oil fields shared by the United Kingdom and Norway are producing less.

Fourth, oil companies, unlike many other types of investors, are often insulated from the business risks that others face whether because of the location of their investments (particularly offshore) or the shared interest with host governments (and even warring parties) in preserving revenue-generating assets. Thus, investment and production increased in Angola and Sudan even as these countries endured civil wars; and in Azerbaijan, despite the unresolved conflict over Nagorno-Karabakh, billions of dollars in production facilities and pipelines have been invested. Unless demand for oil drops, there will be a growing presence of oil companies of all types exploring for and producing oil and gas from growing numbers of conflict-vulnerable countries.

Oil-Related Conflict Risks and Their Mitigation

However risky a prospect it appears—even if the United States or other countries place sanctions on investment, or individual companies (including banks whose financing underpins many oil and gas investments) choose to avoid conflict zones—many companies are likely to continue to do business in conflict-prone areas because they deem the commercial terms worthwhile. The concern, as shown in chapter 3, is that the development of oil resources in these areas can fuel or exacerbate conflict because of poor management of oil revenue, competition for that revenue, or ineffective control of the negative impact of production on local environmental and social conditions. The conflict risks are at their greatest when oil resources are located in areas with a distinct ethnic or religious identity or a history of political marginalization. The discussion below outlines the options for addressing the challenges of revenue management and harmful local impacts.

Revenue Management: Avoiding the "Curse of Oil"

Since questions of the "resource curse" became part of the policy agenda at the turn of the twenty-first century, much attention has been directed at finding ways of mitigating the risks. At the broadest level, the solutions lie in establishing "democratic, consensual and transparent processes…to ensure that the fruits of a country's wealth are equitably and well spent."[372] The emerging mainstream consensus is that the solutions require two conditions: (1) transparency in all aspects of dealing with revenue; and (2) economic measures to control the use of revenue and insulate the nonoil economy from "Dutch disease" (whereby currency appreciation resulting from an influx of oil revenues makes the nonoil economy less competitive, leading to a decline in output and employment).[373] There is also a need for mutually agreed-upon rules of revenue allocation, especially for oil-producing areas—an issue that is so politically charged that it has been neglected by policymakers and scholars.

Revenue transparency is a critical first step. It has been shown that providing public information about government income and its allocation to ministries and subnational entities can directly combat corruption and increase real spending on poverty-reducing activities such as health and education services—which themselves help to reduce conflict risks. Transparency can also reduce the ability of rebel groups or rebel leaders to mislead supporters about the wealth that might be realized after secession. And it enables policymakers to develop realistic programs. The International Monetary Fund (IMF) and World Bank are actively encouraging governments to allow more transparency in regard to revenue and to put in place the necessary macroeconomic measures.

A few countries are experimenting with new approaches to revenue management. In Chad, where oil production started in 2003, the 1998 Revenue Management Law provides for transparency and specifies that 10 percent of revenues be held in trust for future generations; 80 percent be spent for development purposes such as health, education, and infrastructure; and 5 percent be earmarked for regional development in the producing area. But as discussed in chapter 3, since the revenues have started flowing this approach has come under threat from the government, which has taken steps to loosen these restrictions on spending. São Tomé and Príncipe, which received its first oil revenues from signature bonuses in 2005, passed an Oil Revenue Management Law in 2004, which sets rules for spending and saving revenues, takes account of international expert advice, and establishes a nationwide consultative process. In the words of the republic's president, Fradique de Menezes,

> We want to ensure that oil is a blessing in São Tomé and not the proverbial curse that it has been to virtually every country that has oil today.... But the prospect of oil has shaken our society to the core.... We hope our law will serve as a model of how to guarantee the best possible use of our oil income, while ensuring prosperity for future generations of São Toméans.[374]

Other countries have adopted aspects of these approaches with varying degrees of success. Several have oil funds to manage economic risks; a few, notably Nigeria and Indonesia, have laws that allocate a proportion of revenue to producing areas.

The examples of Azerbaijan, Angola, and Sudan illustrate the varying but limited extent of effective revenue management systems in countries at risk of conflict exacerbated by oil. Building on advice from the IMF and other international organizations, the government of Azerbaijan has established the State Oil Fund of Azerbaijan to hold and invest oil and gas revenue and make information on revenue and its use publicly available. With this and other measures, Azerbaijan has so far been successful in managing macroeconomic issues associated with oil. But there remain few institutional or political constraints on how the president uses the rapidly accumulating wealth. Evidence suggests that using oil wealth to prosecute war would be politically popular. Thus, one of the critical conflict risks associated with oil and gas revenues remains, especially given the lack of progress in resolving the Nagorno-Karabakh conflict, which dominates the political and security landscape.

In contrast to Azerbaijan, as of mid-2005 neither Angola nor Sudan had in place the components of a revenue management system likely to contribute to peacebuilding. There is little revenue transparency and no rules on the use of revenue for development purposes, although some steps are being taken to direct it into savings for future generations. In both countries, oil revenue has been used to finance conflict; in Sudan, however, under the terms of the 2005 outline peace agreement, oil revenue from southern Sudan is to be shared equally. But in the absence of transparency and measures to manage the macroeconomic impacts, this division in practice creates two oil-dependent, at-risk states where before there was only one.

Beyond these approaches, a number of more radical and controversial strategies for oil revenue management have been tested or proposed. The most interesting is to remove the root cause of revenue risks by channeling revenue directly to citizens rather than to government, and requiring government to tax this income.[375] This approach posits that governments can never be trusted or effectively constrained to manage resource wealth and therefore must be bypassed. The underlying idea of direct distribution of revenue in developing countries is that it could function in a way similar to microcredit, empowering people to build livelihoods as entrepreneurs independently of government or donor programs; it could also, "at a stroke," curtail authoritarian or aggressive governments.

Direct distribution, however, faces formidable obstacles. The most important is the political problem of persuading elites to relinquish control of the revenue that provides them with power. A second problem is how to put in place the legal and commercial systems that would enable people to use the shares of revenue they receive as capital rather than as income, as illustrated by the case of Nauru's phosphate wealth, discussed in chapter 3. Also, there are formidable practical problems, including defining and identifying eligibility and establishing tax systems that enable government eventually to receive a share of revenue and to deliver on its obligations. In a postconflict environment, the practical problems are particularly acute.

A second approach to preventing oil revenues from fueling conflict is for the international community to take control, as in the Iraq "Oil for Food" program. While this approach is unlikely to be repeated in the near future, both because of the need to secure UN Security Council backing and because of the scandals associated with the program's implementation, it could become a possible tool for international action in circumstances where oil revenues are clearly seen to be financing violent conflict. Thus, joint control of Liberia's mining and timber revenues by the government and the international community is being exercised in postwar Liberia under the Governance and Economic Management Assistance Program (GEMAP). International supervisors have cosignatory powers with national counterparts in major ministries and sources of revenue, and monitor all earnings and expenditures;

adherence to the program is a condition of international aid and debt relief.[376]

The other tool potentially open to the international community is the imposition of sanctions on oil sales where such sales finance conflict. But the difficulties experienced in maintaining sanctions on Iraqi oil exports, and the failure (since 2004) to secure international agreement on sanctions on Sudan's oil in response to the Darfur conflict, suggest that sanctions can be effective only where there is nearly universal support internationally or where the sanctions are backed by a wide array of commercial and military mechanisms. These are always likely to be rare circumstances.

A significant gap in the work on revenue management concerns wealth sharing between producing and nonproducing areas. The key problem is how to agree on distributing shares of oil wealth between producing and nonproducing parts of a country, especially where there is an existing conflict. Although the trend is for governments to allocate a proportion of revenue to producing areas to prevent or resolve conflict, the evidence to date is that where oil wealth is already a factor in secession conflict, a share less than 100 percent carries little weight. Another area that has not been adequately addressed by policymakers or in the various revenue transparency initiatives is the need for effective revenue management systems (including transparency) at the subnational level.

Managing Revenue for Peace

Effective revenue management, including limits on the use of revenue by governments for aggressive military purposes, and control of the local impact of oil projects, is an important first step toward the limitation of conflict risks. In the long term, countries need to develop a national consensus on how to use resource wealth. Events in Bolivia in 2004—when opposition to plans to produce and export gas triggered a political crisis, violence, a change of government, and a referendum on gas policy—illustrate a dynamic that can be expected to occur in other countries. The effort in São Tomé to build such a consensus, through a "decentralized National Forum" involving fifty-six public meetings, disclosure of information on oil revenues, and a questionnaire on priorities for their use, is the first systematic attempt to achieve this.[377]

Despite growing clarity about what policies are needed to reduce oil-related conflict risks, creating the political climate for "making it happen" is a huge challenge. Oil revenue insulates governments from domestic political processes and from leverage by donor governments and multilateral institutions if votes can be "bought" and governments supported without donor aid. Nonetheless, a number of interlinked civil-society and international-community efforts are being made, using the tools of information, technical assistance, peer pressure, international standards, and conditionality.

The Open Society Institute's Revenue Watch program uses research, information dissemination, and advocacy to try to improve fiscal accountability. For example, the program trains journalists to investigate and report on revenue management in Azerbaijan.[378] The Extractive Industries Transparency Initiative (EITI) links volunteer governments, companies, and NGOs in developing country-specific revenue-transparency programs.[379] In 2004, new World Bank standards required the disclosure of revenue figures for major new extractive industry projects that it supports,[380] while the IMF made the disclosure of information on revenue a condition for financial assistance to Angola.[381] Two intergovernmental partnership programs launched in 2004—the G8 Transparency Compacts[382] and the U.S. Millennium Challenge Account[383]—link technical assistance and aid to progress in transparency and good governance.

These initiatives are important first steps in building a common definition of policy priorities and in creating stimuli and incentives to apply them. To a large extent, this progress has been made possible by a convergence of interests between the development, human rights, and security communities as the various threats presented by the "resource curse" are understood, and has been encouraged by continuing pressure from NGOs. But there remain inherent tensions between these interests, and built-in obstacles to maintaining the interest of governments and international organizations in preventive and long-term strategies, especially where outcomes are difficult to measure. It cannot be assumed that the progress made over the early years of the 2000s will necessarily be maintained, or that weaning governments from policies that make oil wealth a curse rather than a blessing will be easy to achieve.

Managing the Local Impact of Exploration and Production

The other main sources of conflict risk associated with oil projects are local grievances and the negative impact resulting from the ways in which oil concessions are granted and managed. The principal approaches being applied to reduce these problems are the use of social, environmental, and conflict impact-assessment techniques, and extensive public consultation, to "design out" risk factors, accompanied by community-development projects to ensure that local benefits result from the presence of oil and gas developments. The International Finance Corporation (IFC) branch of the World Bank has developed standards and guidelines that cover all aspects of this approach. Based on experience in backing projects in the extractive and other industries, and through consultation with NGOs, companies, and donor organizations, these guidelines have become the benchmark standards for the industry and are increasingly required by private-sector banks backing oil projects.

Evidence from case studies shows that oil companies are beginning to apply these approaches, but on a on a case-by-case basis. In Azerbaijan, IFC standards were applied to development of oil and gas fields in the Caspian and to the Baku-Tbilisi-Ceyhan (BTC) pipeline; in Sudan and Angola, by contrast, they have not been applied to any of the many projects that have been developed since the late 1990s. The difference reflects the involvement of the IFC in the Azerbaijan projects, the potential scale of onshore impact (which is less in Angola, where most oil and gas developments are offshore), the high level of NGO pressure applied to BTC, and the recognition by project teams in each country that applying higher standards than are normally adopted could help protect the investment and the reputations of the companies involved. Whereas oil companies have involved NGOs in monitoring projects and implementing community investment projects in Azerbaijan, these contributions to strengthening civil society have not yet been matched by similar initiatives in Angola or Sudan.

What Contribution Can Oil Companies Make?

Given the risks presented by oil revenues and the local impacts of the industry, and the emerging consensus about what is needed to reduce these risks, what role can individual companies be expected to play? This is, and will continue to be, a function of business logic—what the corporate rewards are likely to be—and of the tools available to companies through corporate social responsibility approaches. Each aspect is discussed in the sections that follow.

The Business Case and Its Limits

In order for businesses to play a role in conflict prevention and peacebuilding, two criteria must be met. First, a business logic designed for such efforts is needed. Second, actions and behaviors should be formulated such that, if undertaken, they can realistically be expected to make a positive contribution.

The business logic for oil company engagement in conflict prevention is twofold. Conflict in producing countries puts investments at risk, so it is worthwhile for businesses to undertake actions that mitigate this risk. Also, companies, especially the super majors and majors with global operations and consumer brands, are under pressure from NGOs, socially responsible investment houses, and sometimes from consumers, employees, and shareholders, to demonstrate their social responsibility. (This latter case is weaker for government-owned and hybrid companies that do not have to fear consumer boycotts or shareholder motions.)

Several important factors limit the extent to which individual oil companies apply this logic and implement actions to reduce conflict risks. First, businesses, and the managers leading operations in any given country, have very different levels of awareness of the risks that their operations might exacerbate conflict. A greater level of awareness exists in those companies that have been "hit," that is, where operations had to be stopped because employees or facilities could not be protected, as Chevron experienced in Sudan in the 1980s, or where campaigning by NGOs has affected share value, as occurred with Talisman following its investment in Sudan in the 1990s. Generally, however, a top-level commitment to conduct business differently will be required before company managers feel able to focus on conflict prevention and not just on providing additional security as a means of protecting business interests.

A second set of limiting factors surrounds the relationship between investor and host government. Whatever the top management commitment, companies are constrained by the dominating need to maintain good relationships with government and to work within the terms of the contracts with government. Thus, unless concession agreements permit disclosure of information about revenues, specify standards for environmental and social impact management, and incorporate human rights protections, companies risk losing concessions if they are perceived as hostile to government or as breaching contractual terms. In Angola, BP was threatened with loss of its concessions if it disclosed information in breach of contract terms; in Sudan, Talisman failed in attempts to negotiate security arrangements different from those embodied in its contracts. Companies are generally open to "constructive engagement" with governments, but not to confrontation; and most firms would rather not invest in countries where they see a high potential for conflict, for they are keenly aware of the risk that they could acquire a reputation for being hostile to host governments, meddling in politics, or infringing on sovereignty.

A further limiting factor on the business case for involvement in conflict prevention or resolution is the "insulation" effect. Case studies show that the industry is largely insulated from civil war, especially if operations are offshore, and that companies may not need to respond at all. Thus, Angola's government secured large-scale oil investment while civil war was raging over much of the country.

Finally, there is no convincing evidence that once oil production is under way, corporations have the leverage to promote peacemaking, through persuasion or divestment, to governments engaged in violent conflict. In Sudan, one company deployed (without success) a former international diplomat on its board in efforts to encourage peace negotiations. Nor did the withdrawal of other companies from that country make any tangible difference in either oil production or government attitudes toward peace. As an official from Azerbaijan explained, referring to the scope for investors to influence government policy on peace negotiations in the conflict with Armenia, "We know the companies have stakeholders. If they need to talk about peace, that's fine. But we will make peace only when the time is right for us."[384] One hardheaded evaluation made by a Sudanese diplomat serves as a warning: "We do want the American companies—but on the other hand, the Chinese don't try to interfere in politics."[385]

Generic Corporate Social Responsibility Tools

It is common practice for large businesses to have corporate social responsibility (CSR) programs, often characterized by spending on community projects; setting policies on diversity, community involvement, ethics, and human rights; and adopting voluntary standards that are more demanding than those set out in the legislation of the host country. The UN Global Compact, with a membership of over 1,500 companies committed to support a set of principles on environmental standards, human rights, labor conditions, and business ethics, exemplifies this trend.

Among the companies operating in the three countries profiled in this study, there are wide differences in the scope and sophistication of their CSR systems. Generally, the very large, shareholder-owned companies have the most advanced systems. The business logic for this, as expressed by one corporate executive, is that "CSR is not about being philanthropic, it is about protecting shareholder value."[386]

Within the CSR framework, ideas are being explored regarding the role that companies could, and should, play in conflict prevention and resolution. Some companies—including several super majors—have decided that social responsibility is essential to business success and they are beginning to consider how social responsibility approaches can mitigate the risks of operating in countries affected by conflict. These companies will benefit from the four principal elements of the emerging CSR strategies for conflict prevention and peacemaking: (1) company actions that avoid exacerbating conflict; (2) company involvement in policy processes that help create environments conducive to peace; (3) employment creation that reduces the attractiveness of insurgency; and (4) social projects that bolster the capacity of communities to resolve conflict.

Companies in the oil sector are also developing systems for self-regulation on environmental, social, and human rights issues, including setting company policies, commissioning impact assessments and social and environmental audits, and publishing reports on these issues for stakeholders. Some companies, working with other firms, governments, and NGOs, have also played a significant role in two innovative, standard-setting partnerships that address the specific issues of revenue transparency (the EITI) and the principles on managing the impact of facility security on human rights (the Voluntary Principles on Security and Human Rights). In their early stages, both initiatives appear to be yielding some positive results, such as the strong movement toward revenue transparency in Nigeria and the expanding use of the Voluntary Principles as a basis for negotiating inclusion of human rights safeguards in security arrangements. One publicly documented example of the application of these principles is in BP's Tangguh project in Indonesia's Papua province, where there is a low-level secession insurgency as well as a record of human rights abuses by the military, including in defense of mining companies.[387] Still, the scope for corporate influence must not be overestimated. When oil prices are high the influence of individual companies (and that of foreign governments) on the governments of oil-rich countries is low because these governments can pick and choose who is allowed to operate and can set the terms for their operations.[388]

These trisectoral voluntary agreements set a valuable precedent in approaching complex problems by facilitating constructive engagement of parties often in opposition to each other, and enabling leaders in business, NGOs, and government to develop and test approaches that can then be taken up by others. The long-term effectiveness of these initiatives will depend largely on the extent to which corporations and governments that have endorsed them maintain their momentum, and on whether the many businesses and governments that have not yet begun to apply these standards will do so. NGOs are promoting more regulatory approaches to supplement these voluntary approaches. Advocates of regulation, for example, would like to see a requirement that companies declare all payments to individual governments as a condition for stock-exchange listing worldwide (the Publish What You Pay program).

Priorities for Action by Oil Companies

The oil companies could contribute more to reducing conflict risks associated with their operations. This requires four principal steps. The most important, but also the most difficult, is to facilitate effective revenue management in the countries where they operate. The second step, more within the industry's control, is to apply high standards of environmental, social, and human rights management to its operations in order to avoid creating grievances. Third, companies could focus more of their social investment on employment creation to counteract grievances over the small number of jobs that oil exploration and production create. Fourth, and not yet tested anywhere, companies could ally with local governments and donor organizations to recast their investments as local economic development projects. This would mean aiming from the start to achieve the dual objectives of commercial success and being a catalyst for economic and social development, thus going beyond the "do no harm" philosophy to be a deliberate agent of transformative change.

Influencing Revenue Management

Timing and relationships are key to exerting influence. The greatest opportunities for companies to influence the way governments manage oil revenues occur in negotiations for concessions or before oil begins flowing on new developments, in relationships of mutual trust between company and government, and in cooperation with local and international initiatives such as the EITI. It is essential that concession contracts should allow for revenue transparency; ideally, the full terms should be a matter of public knowledge. The terms of oil concessions (licenses) and the revenues paid are in the public domain in oil-producing states in North America and Europe; companies should press for this practice in the other parts of the world where they operate.

Case studies show that individual companies can have an impact on revenue transparency. In Azerbaijan, production-sharing agreements have been disclosed in full, at the instigation of the industry. Companies and governments have also agreed to publish information on revenue payments and forecasts, providing a counterpart to the preexisting regular publication, by the State Oil Fund of Azerbaijan, of information on receipts, resources, and spending. BP, the largest operator there, has involved itself in the public policy debate on revenue management, by organizing seminars, sharing expert advice on revenue modeling, participating in consultations on the country's poverty reduction strategy, and being closely involved in the EITI.

In Sudan, some companies have contributed to helping southern politicians plan for management of oil wealth in a postconflict environment. Following the 2002 cease-fire, two companies with investments in Sudan—Talisman and Lundin—contributed to the discussion of revenue-sharing systems that took place during the preparations for peace negotiations; Talisman also initiated an agreement with the government in 2002 to publish information on revenue payments made.

In Angola, disclosure of signature bonus payments made by BP without the prior agreement of the Angolan government was treated as a serious breach of contract that could jeopardize the company's future operations, and other companies were warned not to follow suit. But four years later, after the civil war had ended, and following extensive international encouragement and pressure for revenue transparency (stimulated in part by this experience), the government of Angola and Chevron Texaco agreed to public disclosure of the $290 million in bonuses paid by the company on extension of the Block 0 concession.[389]

Influencing Impact Management

The second principal way in which oil companies can contribute to conflict prevention is by not creating grievances. A new model for oil projects that incorporates extensive actions to avoid negative impact, generate local benefits, and influence management of oil revenue is being developed by some of the largest companies in response to corporate assessment of the business risks associated with major capital investments in politically volatile regions. This new model incorporates CSR approaches in terms of impact management (as well as extensive disclosure of information and recognition of revenue management issues). It requires that before any construction work starts, an environmental and social impact assessment be carried out; communities, local government, civil society organizations, and local business be consulted; compensation be agreed upon with people who will lose access to land; community development projects be set up; security protocols consistent with human rights protections be agreed upon with government; and systems for dispute resolution and independent monitoring be established.

The principal examples of this new model are BP's Azerbaijan projects and the Chad-Cameroon oil field and pipeline project in Africa. Both represent a significant effort to extract petroleum resources in a way that not only is commercially successful but that also avoids local environmental damage and economic and political instability (as witnessed, for example, in Nigeria). In both cases, the World Bank Group is involved, with its private-sector lending branch, the IFC, bringing additional expertise and political leverage.

This new model for oil projects is difficult to put into practice. Implementing these standards demands new skills, resources, and partnerships, and it takes time. In Azerbaijan (as in Chad), the pace of implementing social-impact management was slower than that of construction of production facilities, because of shortages of resources and skills and because of the inherently slow speed of community consultation and consensus-based approaches. Companies that have been built on the skills of geologists, engineers, and accountants need now to extend their skills base to include historians, anthropologists, sociologists, and social development professionals, deploying tools and techniques such as participatory community consultation and partnership building. The shift requires cultural, organizational, and operational changes within companies, the scope of which is only beginning to be appreciated. It also requires that community organizations and NGOs adapt to collaborating with business.

This new model is controversial and will require many years to prove its effectiveness in reducing tension and conflict associated with oil projects, and to enable communities to benefit from those projects. Some observers, particularly environmental NGOs, express doubts that the model is robust enough or that companies are investing the adequate resources and efforts needed to implement it. But many people within companies, NGOs, and policy organizations are working to refine the approaches, for example, through the addition of human-rights impact assessments and greater community involvement. There can be no doubt, though, that these efforts are an improvement on practices still common in much of the industry, where companies consult only with governments, follow only local environmental laws, however inadequate, and rely on government to clear land and handle the environmental and social dislocations resulting from oil production.

Creating Employment

Businesses can also contribute to conflict prevention and peacebuilding by redesigning the way in which they operate and by reconfiguring their social projects to focus on creating employment. This is especially important in countries emerging from conflict, where a key to stability is finding livelihoods for former combatants and people displaced by war. When Angola's civil war ended in 2002, for example, there were some 113,000 soldiers to be demobilized, and four million displaced people and refugees to resettle.

Oil companies can encourage employment in three ways: by maximizing the use of local laborers and contractors (making such hiring a condition of construction contracts, for example); by maximizing the proportion of goods and services purchased locally, including helping local companies to develop needed technical and commercial skills; and by investing in social projects focusing on the nonoil economy, because this sector is always likely to be a greater source of employment. Some oil companies are beginning to put effort into host country employment creation. Examples are Chevron's economic diversification partnerships with UNDP and USAID; Angola's support of small business development, vocational training, and agricultural development; and the Enterprise Centre in Baku, set up by BP and its partners as a "one-stop shop" where Azerbaijan companies can learn about business opportunities, receive training, and hold meetings.

Business as Development: A Transformative Approach to Oil and Gas Development

In those countries where governments are aware of the risks of oil and gas development and are open to transparency, impact management, and the importance of local economic development, there is also the possibility of companies radically changing the ways in which they operate, by starting out with the vision of oil and gas development as a social development project. The reason for considering such an approach, which will probably reduce profits, is that this might turn out to be a cost worth paying for a secure operating environment. A "social development approach" would entail, for example, looking for ways of providing the local community with a shareholding in the venture. It would include using the industry's demand for infrastructure— such as power, water, waste disposal, and communications systems— to create an incentive for investment in larger systems meeting the needs of the wider community. A transformation approach might involve slowing down the pace of oil field development to match the build-up of the capacity of local people and businesses to service the industry, and allocating a proportion of the production to meeting local energy needs.

Recommendations

The conclusions outlined above lead to the following recommendations for oil companies, their contractors, and their financiers.

First, all these parties should take responsibility for conflict prevention by minimizing the risks of exacerbating tension or conflict related to operations, through the systematic application of high environmental and social standards. This action requires recognizing the risks of operations that could catalyze or exacerbate conflict and building this into risk and impact assessment; committing to risk prevention; minimizing negative local impact through the development and application of standards based on World Bank policies for impact assessment, land acquisition, compensation, consultation, and disclosure; and complying with the Voluntary Principles on Security and Human Rights. Within the industry, collaboration is necessary to develop standards, guidelines, and training in order to leverage the experience, strengths, and weaknesses of pioneering projects such as Chad-Cameroon and the BTC pipeline. Opportunities should also be sought out to include these standards in contracts with governments, concession partners, and contractors. The companies that understand the risks and have some tools to manage them should also seek to convince other companies, particularly the state oil companies and independents, of the urgency of applying higher standards.

Second, all parties should recognize the risks of conflict posed by oil revenue and seek to exercise influence in favor of transparency, effective macroeconomic management, and agreed-upon rules for revenue allocation. The best way to do this will vary according to company and country. Possible strategies include lobbying for concession agreements and revenue payments to become public-domain information worldwide; becoming involved in the EITI; participating in host-country economic planning processes, such as poverty-reduction strategies; sharing technical expertise; and taking steps to ensure the allocation of revenues to producing regions where a failure to do so could be a potent source of tension.

Third, companies should involve other organizations with an interest in conflict prevention as stakeholders in those projects that carry high risks of exacerbating conflict. One way to do this would be to structure projects so as to enable World Bank Group involvement.

Fourth, companies should consider contributing to peacebuilding in the specific case study countries as follows: In Angola, develop a country "code of practice" to govern the ethical, environmental, social, and human rights standards of the expanding industry as its footprint onshore increases; seek to agree—within the industry and with government—on a common framework for revenue reporting as the country moves toward greater transparency; and build an industry framework for aligning corporate social investment projects with postconflict reconstruction priorities alongside the donor-conference process.

In Azerbaijan, add corporate weight to efforts within the international relations community to secure greater attention by Western governments to the risk of renewed conflict in the Caucasus.

In Sudan, postpone new investment in the south until there is evidence of the North-South Peace Agreement being implemented, and meanwhile, volunteer support for the planned National Petroleum Commission in incorporating standards of transparency and environmental- and social-impact management into government management of the industry. No investments should be made in any other part of Sudan until cessation of violence in Darfur.

Finally, companies should go beyond risk management and seek to be catalysts for, and collaborators in, partnerships between host governments, international organizations, and companies to find ways of extracting oil resources in developing countries in a way that actively supports the countries' economic and social development. The large firms have the intellectual resources, global experience, networks, and prestige to take on this catalytic function. Making it happen depends on corporate leadership and the prior establishment of relationships of trust with governments and civil society.

In summary, oil exploration and production activities present a risk of catalyzing or exacerbating violent conflict. Risks derive largely from the revenues generated for governments, but also from the complex changes these activities set in motion, especially where developments are onshore, in regions with a distinct cultural identity or in areas without previous oil or gas projects. Businesses can contribute to conflict prevention by applying high standards of corporate social responsibility to their investments from the outset. In the absence of good governance, there are no guarantees of how effective this will be in limiting conflict risks. There are, however, strong arguments that not applying these standards increases risks of conflict and attendant risks to operations and to corporate reputation. It is important that businesses do what they can to contribute to conflict prevention, because violent conflict, once started, has a momentum that makes it difficult to stop.

Notes

1. Prime Minister Mari Alkatiri, quoted in AAP Finance, "Boundaries dispute leaves East Timor's riches in limbo," *Alexander's Oil and Gas Connections* 9, no. 14.

2. Government oil revenue projections are based on PFC Energy, "West Africa Petroleum Sector: Oil Value Forecast and Distribution" (unpublished paper prepared for the Centre for Strategic and International Studies Task Force on Rising U.S. Energy Stakes in Africa), www.csis.org/africa/index.htm. The task force report, "Promoting Transparency in the African Oil Sector," March 2004, can be found on www.CSIS.org/africa/risingoil/publications. These estimates were based on an oil price averaging $22.50 throughout the period. If the trend of substantially higher oil prices (averaging almost $40 barrel in 2004, and $50 in 2005) continues, then Angola's oil revenues will be substantially higher. Average income for 2003 is based on World Bank, "Angola Country Brief," http://web.worldbank.org/WBSITE/EXTERNAL/COUNTRIES/AFRICAEXT/ANGOLAEXTN/0,,menuPK:322500~pagePK:141132~piPK:141107~theSitePK:322490,00.html (accessed April 22, 2006).

3. The Millennium Challenge Account is designed to provide substantial aid through multiyear compacts so that it becomes the largest or second largest donor to those countries that rule justly, invest in their people, and encourage economic freedom. These criteria are evaluated using publicly available information, and the scores and standards against which countries are measured are published on the MCA Web site. See www.mca.gov.

4. International Crisis Group, "Crisiswatch," February 2006, http://www.crisisgroup.org/home/index.cfm?id=3929&l=1 (accessed April 22, 2006).

5. BP, "Statistical Review of World Energy," June 2006, www.bp.com.

6. Ibid.

7. U.S. Energy Information Administration, "Saudi Arabia Country Brief," August 2005, http://www.eia.doe.gov/emeu/cabs/saudi.html (accessed April 22, 2006). The Energy Information Administration (EIA) publishes online analyses of energy and power supply and demand, policies, and information sources for many countries and regions of the world. A listing of reports can be found at http://www.eia.doe.gov/emeu/cabs/contents.html (accessed April 22, 2006).

8. *BBC Newsnight,* television program, January 25, 2006. The estimated rents paid to the Government of Nigeria are based on Shell Petroleum Development Company of Nigeria Limited, "Annual Report 2004," 7, www.shell.com/static/nigeria/downloads/about_shell/2004_rpt.pdf.

9. Data on total oil and gas reserves must be treated with caution. There is no internationally accepted, standardized methodology for assessing reserves; moreover, what constitutes recoverable reserves is a function of technology and oil price and hence varies. "Proved" reserves are defined by BP as "those quantities that geological and engineering information indicates with reasonable certainty can be recovered in the future from known reserves under existing economic and operating conditions." Percent total shown exceeds 100 percent due to rounding. BP, "Statistical Review of World Energy," June 2006, 4, www.bp.com/statisticalreview.

10. Saudi Aramco produces 99 percent of Saudi Arabia's oil. Its output of crude oil in 2004—8.6 million barrels per day—was more than three times that of Exxon Mobil, the world's largest listed oil company, which averaged 2.6 million barrels per day in that same year. See ExxonMobil, "2004 Summary Annual Report," www.exxon mobil.com; and Saudi Aramco, "2004 Annual Review," www.saudiaramco.com.

11. There is some investment by international oil companies in Africa and in gas developments in Oman. In late 2003 the first contracts enabling international companies to invest in Saudi Arabia were made, for gas field development.

12. BP, "Statistical Review of World Energy."

13. For a list of all countries see BP, "Statistical Review of World Energy."

14. The EEZ is a zone under national jurisdiction (up to 200 nautical miles wide) outlined in the provisions of the 1982 UN Convention of the Law of the Sea, within which the coastal state has the right to explore and exploit, and the responsibility to conserve and manage, living and nonliving resources.

15. Barrows Company, "Listing of E&P Bid Evaluations," July 2004, www.barrows company.net/BBR.htm. The Barrows Company is a library and publisher that provides, on a commercial basis, an international reference library for oil, gas, and mineral laws. It publishes analyses and the complete text of laws and contracts.

16. Lukoil Oil Company, "Lukoil Discovered Major Field in Caspian Sea," press release, January 25, 2006, www.lukoil.com/press.asp?div_id=1&id=2485&year=2006.

17. U.S. Energy Information Administration, "Caspian Sea Country Analysis Brief," December 2004, www.eia.doe.gov/emeu/cabs/caspian.html.

18. BP, "Statistical Review of World Energy."

19. Ibid.

20. Ibid.

21. See the Web site of the China National Petroleum Corporation for information on its overseas oil and gas operations, www.cnpc.com.cn/english/inter/Exploration.htm.

22. BP, "Statistical Review of World Energy."

23. Ibid.

24. James T. Jensen, *The Development of a Global LNG Market* (Oxford: Oxford Institute for Energy Studies, 2004), 7.

25. Ibid., 75.

26. International Energy Agency / Organization for Economic Co-operation and Development, *Natural Gas Information 2005* (Paris: IEA/OECD, 2005), 1.3.

27. A fourth set of companies is the small-scale domestic producers. These play a minor role in the case study countries and are not considered further in this study.

28. Simon Briscoe, "Corporate Fortunes," *Financial Times,* June 11, 2005.

29. C. Hoyos, J. Chung, C. Hams, and S. Tucker, "Shell Chairman Forced Out as Investor Pressure Grows," *Financial Times,* March 4, 2004.

30. The World Bank Group announced in 2000 that it would conduct a comprehensive review of its activities in the extractive industries sector—the Extractive Industries Review—in response to concerns expressed by environmental and human rights organizations. In August 2004 the World Bank's management said that it would continue investments in oil, gas, and mining projects but would increase its efforts to see that projects meet high environmental, social, and governance standards and that government revenue from the projects be used transparently and effectively. See the official EIR Website, www.ifc.org/eir.

31. Robert Arnott, "Exploration and Production" (presentation, Oxford Institute of Energy Studies, Oxford, UK, February 22, 2005), www.oxfordenergy.org/presentations/exploration_production.pdf.

32. Premier Oil Web site, www.premieroil.com/render.aspx?siteID=1&navIDs=19,20,29.

33. The closest equivalents are mining and mobile telephony, both of which often involve companies "buying" exclusive rights from government.

34. Arnott, "Exploration and Production."

35. "Transitional" refers to the former Soviet Union and other countries changing from a planned to a market economy.

36. Also referred to as "production-sharing contracts."

37. Total, "Total Updates Block B Contractual Terms in Sudan in View of Possibly Resuming Operations once Peace Returns," Total press release, December 21, 2004, www.total.com.

38. See www.bp.com/caspian. This is a BP Web site containing information on the BP-operated oil and gas fields in the Caspian and the Baku-Tbilisi-Ceyhan and Southern Caucasus Pipeline.

39. BP, "Economic, Social and Environmental Overview of the Southern Caspian Oil and Gas Projects," February 2003, www.bp.com/caspian. This is a report published by BP, providing financial, operational, environmental, and social information about the BP-operated oil and gas fields in the Caspian Sea, and the export pipelines from these fields.

40. Total, "Sudan: History and New," Nov 17, 2005, www.total.com/en/group/corporate_social_responsibility/ethics_governance/ethics/history_sudan_7581.htm.

41. U.S. Energy Information Administration, "Angola Country Analysis Brief," January 2006, www.eia.doe.gov/emeu/cabs/Angola/Oil.html.

42. BP "Statistical Review of World Energy"; U.S. Energy Information Administration Country Briefs, "Angola," January 2006, "Azerbaijan," June 2005, "Sudan," March 2005, www.eia-doe.gov.

43. See, for example, Michael Klare, *Resource Wars: The New Landscape of Global Conflict,* 1st ed. (New York: Henry Holt, 2001).

44. Paul Collier and Anke Hoeffler, "Greed and Grievance in Civil War," *Oxford Economic Papers* 56 (2004): 563–95.

45. See *Journal of Peace Research* 41, no. 3 (2004) for a set of relevant papers.

46. Paul Collier et al., *Breaking the Conflict Trap: Civil War and Development Policy* (Washington, DC: International Bank for Reconstruction and Development/World Bank, 2003). This book draws together the findings of the World Bank research program and includes a comprehensive bibliography.

47. See www.worldbank.org/topics/social/conflictpreventionandreconstruction.

48. Collier et al., *Breaking the Conflict Trap,* 4.

49. Ibid., x.

50. Ibid., 4.

51. Ibid., 175. See chapter 6, "An Agenda for International Action."

52. Collier and Hoeffler, "Greed and Grievance in Civil War," 2.

53. Recent studies on timber and conflict include J. Thomas and R. Kanaan, "Conflict Timber: Dimensions of the Problem in Asia and Africa," ARD/USAID, 2004. See www.ard-biofor.com/asiaconflict.htm for this study and links to other references.

54. The various civil war data sets cover different time periods and states, use different methods for counting conflicts interspersed with periods of peace (i.e., as one war or two), and use differing thresholds of annual fatalities to define "civil war."

55. Michael Ross, "How Do Natural Resources Influence Civil War? Evidence from Thirteen Cases," *International Organization* 58, no. 1 (2004): 35–67.

56. Philippe Le Billon (2001), Michael Ross (2003a), Collier and Hoeffler (2002b), cited in Michael Ross, "What Do We Know about Natural Resources and Civil War?" *Journal of Peace Research* 3 (2004): 310.

57. Ross, "How Do Natural Resources Influence Civil War?"

58. Juan Pablo Pérez Alfonso, *Hundiéndonos en el excremento del diablo* (Caracas: Editorial Lisbona, 1976).

59. Government revenues from gas are generally lower on a unit-to-unit comparison than those from oil because the unit costs of producing and transporting gas are generally higher than those of oil. Thus, gas transportation (including the construction of gas liquification plants) accounts for most of the price of delivered gas. However, the growth of gas transportation infrastructure currently underway (that could, for example, see global LNG capacity grow from 151 million tons/year to 477 million tons/year if all planned projects are executed) is expected to reduce unit costs. See Michelle Michot Foss and Bala M. Wunti, "Brass LNG Shows Impact of Marketing Supply, Demand," *Oil and Gas Journal* 104, no. 4 (January 23, 2006); and OECD/IEA, *Natural Gas Information* (Paris: International Energy Agency, 2005), 1.9.

60. "The government share, averaged over the lifetime of a field, typically falls in the range of 45–50 percent at the lower end, to 80–89 percent at the higher end." See World Bank, "Management of Oil Revenues," *Oil Gas and Energy Law Intelligence* (*OGEL*) 1, no. 2 (2003), www.gasandoil.com/ogel.

61. Estimates for 2004, based on data in IMF Country Reports, www.imf.org. For Angola, see Report no. 05/228, July 2005; for Azerbaijan, see Report no. 05/19, January 2005; for Sudan, see Report no. 05/180, June 2005.

62. For a survey of the economics literature, see Paul Stevens, "Resource Impact—Curse or Blessing? A Literature Survey," *CEPMLP Internet Journal* 13 (2003), Article no. 14, www.dundee.ac.uk/cepmlp/journal/html/vol13/vol13-14.html. The seminal text focusing on governance issues is Terry Lynn Karl, *The Paradox of Plenty: Oil Booms and Petro-States* (Berkeley and Los Angeles: University of California Press, 1997). A short paper that considers the economic options in the case of Azerbaijan is John Wakerman-Linn et al., *Managing Oil Wealth: The Case of Azerbaijan* (Washington, DC: International Monetary Fund, 2004).

63. Oil revenue can also provide incentives for interstate disputes, such as the various boundary disputes linked to oil rights in the Gulf of Guinea.

64. "Junta Declared in Sao Tome," *BBC News,* July 16, 2003, http://news.bbc.co.uk/2/hi/africa/3070355.stm.

65. "Equatorial Guinea: Ripe for a Coup," *BBC News,* March 11, 2004, http://news.bbc.co.uk/2/hi/africa/3500832.stm.

66. Angus Macleod, "Mandarins Hid Scots' Oil Wealth," *The Times,* January 31, 2006. Official papers released in 2006 show that in 1974 UK government officials feared that if people in Scotland learned of the true wealth of the North Sea oil reserves that had been recently been discovered, it would increase pressures for full independence. One official is quoted as predicting, "It is concernable that income per head in Scotland could be 25 per cent or 30 per cent higher than that prevailing in England during the 1980s given independence."

67. Rotimi T. Suberu, *Federalism and Ethnic Conflict in Nigeria* (Washington, DC: United States Institute of Peace, 2001), 17. Besides revenue allocation, the other three issues identified are state and local reorganizations, intersegmental (including interreligious) representation, and population enumeration.

68. Ibid., 11.

69. Ibid., 11–12.

70. For information about MASSOB, see www.nigeriamasterweb.com/nmwpgl massobarrest.html and coverage in www.allafrica.com.

71. UN Integrated Regional Information Networks, "Oil-Rich Niger Delta Faces 'Shocking' New Wave of Violence," January 27, 2006, www.irinnews.org/report.asp?ReportID=51397&SelectRegion=West_Africa.

72. His Excellency President Olusegun Obansanjo, "Let Us Rebuild Nigeria Together," radio speech marking the forty-fourth anniversary of the Federal Republic of Nigeria, October 2004, www.dawodu.com/obas22.htm. Dawodu.com is a Web site covering sociopolitical issues in Nigeria, run from Virginia, USA. See also the Web site of the government of Nigeria, www.nigeria.gov.ng.

73. Paul Ibe, "National Conference: S/South, Northern Delegates Meet," *This Day* (Lagos), July 8, 2005.

74. Australia, Botswana, Canada, Chile, Norway, and the United States are widely cited as examples.

75. Jeffrey D. Sachs and Andrew M. Warner, "The Curse of Natural Resources," *European Economic Review* 45 (2001): 827–38.

76. See, for example, J. Clark Leith, "Botswana—A Case Study of Economic Policy Prudence and Growth," World Bank Working Paper, Washington, DC, August 1999. Before the diamond industry developed, Botswana was one of the twenty-five poorest countries in the world; it is now ranked by the World Bank as a "lower middle income country" despite the substantial setback resulting from its HIV/Aids epidemic.

77. David Goldwyn and J. Stephen Morrison, *Promoting Transparency in the African Oil Sector* (Washington, DC: Center for Strategic and International Studies, March 2004), 3. Available online at www.csis.org/component/option,com_csis_pubs/task,view/id,34.

78. Carlos Leite and Jens Weidmann, "Does Mother Nature Corrupt? Natural Resources, Corruption, and Economic Growth," International Monetary Fund Working Paper, Washington, DC, 1999, www.imf.org/external/pubind.htm.

79. See Peter Eigen, "Corruption Is Rampant in 60 Countries and the Public Sector Is Plagued by Bribery," speech by Peter Eigen, Chairman of Transparency International, at the launch of the TI Corruption Perceptions Index 2004, www.transparency.org/cpi/2004.

80. The Petroleum Revenue Management Law in Chad is discussed at the World Bank Chad-Cameroon Project Web site, http://web.worldbank.org/external/projects/main? pagePK=64283627&piPK=73230&theSitePK=40941&menuPK=228424&Projectid=P044305.

81. See, for example, International Monetary Fund, Guide on Resource Revenue Transparency (Washington, DC: International Monetary Fund, 2005). This follows the launch of the NGO campaign Publish What You Pay and the government/extractive industry Extractive Industries Transparency Initiative, discussed in chapter 4.

82. See, for example, Ritva Reinkka and Jakob Svenson, "Local Capture and the Political Economy of School Financing," Centre for Economic Policy Research (CEPR) and Institute for International Economic Studies (IIES) policy paper, April 2002, 1–3, www.cepr.org/meets/wkcn/3/3508/papers/svensson.pdf.

83. "Framework Agreement on Wealth Sharing between the Government of the Sudan (GOS) and the Sudan People's Liberation Movement/Sudan People's Liberation Army (SPLM/A)," July 1, 2004. Text of this and other components of the peace agreement can be found at the online peace agreements collection of the United States Institute of Peace library, www.usip.org.

84. Ehtisan Ahmad and Eric A. Mottu, "Oil Revenue Assignments: Country Experiences and Issues," International Monetary Fund Working Paper no. 02/203, Washington, DC, 2002.

85. The proportion of royalties going into the fund is one-fourth for fields leased before 1979, and one-half for fields leased after that date.

86. Alaska Permanent Fund Corporation, "Alaska and Permanent Fund History," www.apfc.org.

87. Ralph Klein, "An Open Letter to Albertans," press release, not dated, www.gov.ab.ca/premier/surplus.cfm.

88. Xavier Sala-i-Marta and Arvind Subramanian, "Addressing the Natural Resource Curse: An Illustration from Nigeria," IMF Working Paper no. 03/139,

25, Washington, DC, 2003. See also Nancy Birdsall and Arvind Subramanian, "Oil Spoils: Iraq and the Post Westphalian World," *Foreign Affairs* 83, no. 4 (2004).

89. Vernon Smith, "The Iraqi People's Fund," *Wall Street Journal,* December 23, 2003.

90. Helen Hughes, "From Riches to Rags: What Are Nauru's Options and How Can Australia Help?" Centre for Independent Studies, Issue Analysis no. 50, St. Leonards, Australia, 2004, www.cis.org.au.

91. Sea Island Summit Documents, "Fighting Corruption and Improving Transparency," June 10, 2004, www.g8.utoronto.ca/summit/2004seaisland/index.html.

92. Svetlana Tsalik, *Caspian Oil Windfalls: Who Will Benefit?* (New York: Open Society Institute, 2003), 107–27.

93. International Monetary Fund, "Delay in the Completion of the Fourth Review of the Azerbaijan Republic's PRGF Arrangement," IMF Statement, April 2004, www.imf.org/external/country/aze/index.htm.

94. International Monetary Fund, "Guide on Resource Revenue Transparency," 2005, www.imf.org/external/pubs/ft/grrt/eng/060705.htm.

95. World Bank, "World Bank Suspends Disbursements to Chad," News Release no. 2006/232/AFR, January 6, 2006, http://web.worldbank.org/WBSITE/EXTERNAL/NEWS/0,,contentMDK:20778928~pagePK:64257043~piPK:437376~theSitePK:4607,00.html.

96. Daniel Yergin, *The Prize: The Epic Quest for Oil, Money and Power* (New York: Free Press, 1992), 31.

97. Ibid.

98. Karin Barber, "Popular Reactions to the Petro-naira," *Journal of Modern African Studies* 20, no. 3 (1982): 434–35.

99. Yergin, *The Prize,* 234–35.

100. Ibid., 674–76.

101. World Bank Group, *Striking a Better Balance: The Extractive Industries Review* 3, annex 4 (2003): 64, www.worldbank.org/ogmc/eirreports.htm. The Extractive Industries Review (EIR) was a consultative research process sponsored by the World Bank to assess how World Bank Group involvement in extractive industry policies and projects, through its technical assistance and project financing, could best promote environmentally sustainable economic development.

102. These cases also illustrate how the sense of ethnic identity (as distinct from other categories of identity) can escalate into a basis for political organization and territorial demands. See Don Handelman, "The Organization of Ethnicity," *Ethnic Groups* 1 (1977): 187–200. In his seminal paper, Handelman identifies varying degrees of ethnic incorporation: "ethnic categories," where ethnicity is one of several identifiers for individuals or groups; "ethnic networks," which can be used for getting jobs and undertaking transactions in conditions of corruption; "ethnic associations," which can apply pressure for political representation within multiethnic states; and "ethnic communities," for which control of territories is key.

103. Barbara F. Walter, "Does Conflict Beget Conflict? Exploring Recurrent Civil War," *Journal of Peace Research* 41, no. 3 (2004): 371–88.

104. If employee volunteer release programs, sponsorships, and cause-related marketing are included, the corporate philanthropic total would increase to $40–$50 billion. See Susan Raymond, "Taking the Measure of Corporate Giving," online report, October 2003), www.onphilanthropy.com/tren_comm/tc2003-10-10b.html.

105. Illustrated in one case by the corporate executives' being asked to explain to socially responsible fund managers the company policies on human rights, and in a second by business's setting up one of the early joint ventures in post-Soviet Russia, in which employees went on strike because their children's summer camp was not paid for. This had not surfaced in negotiations—it was a "given" for the Russians and far outside the negotiating frame of the European company involved.

106. Some expressions of social responsibility from the late nineteenth century bear a strong resemblance to CSR initiatives of the late twentieth and early twenty-first centuries, for example, sugar sold on the London markets as "slave free." See Adam Hochschild, *Bury the Chains: Prophets and Rebels in the Fight to Free an Empire's Slaves* (Boston: Houghton Mifflin, 2005). The Sullivan Principles were developed by civil rights activist Reverend Leon H. Sullivan, the first African-American to serve on the board of a major corporation, when he was on the board of directors of General Motors. Sullivan developed the Principles to set a standard for businesses operating in apartheid South Africa. The Principles required that black and white employers share eating and work facilities and have fair and equal job opportunities, and that companies increase the number of nonwhites in supervising roles and work to improve the quality of employees' lives outside the workplace. Over time the Principles were expanded: in 1984, when apartheid remained in force, a seventh principle was added stating that apartheid had to be abolished within two years. In 1987 Sullivan called on U.S. companies to divest their businesses in South Africa, and on the U.S. government to enact an economic embargo. The eight Global Sullivan Principles build on this foundation to apply to all companies, in all countries, and commit signatory companies to develop and implement policies and actions in support of universal human rights; equality of opportunity; freedom of association; fair compensation; health, safety, and environmental protection; fair competition and ethical behavior; and community engagement. See www.thesullivan foundation.org.

107. This dichotomy of views was clearly illustrated in the debates around the June 2005 G8 meeting, with its focus on poverty in Africa. See, for example, BBC,

"African Business in Push for Trade," July 5, 2005, http://news.bbc.co.uk/1/hi/
business/4653149.stm; and the Make Poverty History campaign, "Make Laws that
Stop Big Business Profiting at the Expense of People and the Environment," www.
makepovertyhistory.org/whatwewant/index.shtml.

108. In a context where regulations were rapidly becoming more stringent
worldwide, and where, in the United States, the so-called Superfund legislation made
businesses liable for environmental damage caused in the past, corporations started to
develop proactive environmental management systems, voluntary standards, and audit
procedures to minimize regulatory and financial risk.

109. See www.wbcsd.org.

110. See www.globalcompact.org.

111. Interview with Adam Greece, vice president of Labor Affairs and Corporate
Responsibility, New York, December 2003. In some corporations a team holds this
responsibility; note also that the titles of CSR managers vary widely.

112. Companies choose whether to apply for inclusion; the FTSE4Good Index
regularly extends the criteria for listing—for example, in 2004 adding human rights
criteria—and delists companies that have not met the criteria. Few of the international
oil companies are included. See www.ftse4good.com/ftse4good/index.jsp.

113. The Dow Jones Sustainability Index identifies the top 10 percent of the
largest 2,500 companies in the Dow Jones World Index in terms of "sustainability"
and is compiled on the basis of responses to questionnaires completed annually
by companies, as well as published data and direct contact between analysts and
companies. Criteria cover economic, environmental, and social factors and aim to
identify the leading "sustainability" performers in each sector, including in oil and gas.
See www.sustainability-indexes.com/htmle/djsi_world/members.html.

114. The 2002 Sarbanes Oxley Law, passed following the Enron scandal, imposed
stringent requirements on financial reporting by corporations.

115. Jim Lobe, "Tentative Settlement Reached in Landmark Unocal-Burma
Case," *One World,* December 12, 2004, http://peaceandjustice.org/article.php?story=
20041221172907310&mode=print0.

116. The Extractive Industries Review (EIR) was commissioned in 2001 by the
World Bank Group to discuss with concerned stakeholders WBG's future role in
the extractive industries. The aim of this independent review was to produce a set
of recommendations that would guide the WBG's involvement in the oil, gas, and
mining sectors in the context of WBG's overall mission of poverty reduction and
the promotion of sustainable development. The EIR Final Report, "Striking a Better
Balance," and records of the consultation and documentation collected during the
process can be found on the World Bank's Web site, www.worldbank.org/ogmc/
eirreports.htm.

117. Amanda Blakely et al., "Corporate Social Responsibility, Public Policy and the Oil Industry in Angola" (World Bank Summary Report, 2003), 11, http://siteresources. worldbank.org/INTPSD/Resources/Angola/Angola_Petroleum_CSRsurvey.pdf.

118. See www.business-humanrights.org/Categories/Companypolicysteps. The set includes four of the five super majors, other majors, and four independents, each of which has been explicitly targeted by human rights NGOs because of investments in Sudan, Myanmar, or Bolivia.

119. See, for example, ExxonMobil, "Corporate Citizenship Report," www.exxon mobil.com; BP, "Sustainability Report," www.bp.com; Shell, "The Shell Report," www.shell.com; Chevron, "Corporate Responsibility Report," www.chevron.com; and Total, "Corporate Social Responsibility Report," www.total.com.

120. For example, Shell International has produced a series of guidance notes for its staff on managing social performance covering different aspects of "assessing impacts," "limiting adverse impacts," "stakeholder engagement," and "delivering benefits."

121. Goldman Sachs, "Introducing the Goldman Sachs Energy Environmental and Social Index" (report for United Nations Environment Programme Finance Initiative, 2004), www.unepfi.org/fileadmin/documents/materiality1/eesi_goldman_ sachs_2004.pdf.

122. Ibid., 14, 63. According to the 2004 study by Goldman Sachs that examined the environmental, social, and human rights records of twenty-three oil companies on behalf of the UN Environment Program, "Social investments typically involve spending within local communities in countries in which the companies are producing oil and gas. Examples of the infrastructure and services provided include schools and education, hospitals and heath services, roads, water, heating, and electricity." The study also notes of this spending, "Although the sums may seem large in absolute terms, they are small relative to capex (capital expenditure) levels overall, with no company spending more than 1 percent of its 2002 capex budget on social investments."

123. Paul Watchman, "Beyond the Equator," *Environmental Finance,* online newsletter, June 2005, www.environmental-finance.com/2005/0506jun/equator.htm. See Equator Principles Web site, www.equator-principles.com.

124. See, for example, Catholic Relief Services, "Bottom of the Barrel: Africa's Oil Boom and the Poor," CRS report, Washington, DC, 2003. This report argues the case for a "big push" to change the incentive structures surrounding the management of Africa's oil wealth to a sustained, coordinated, and coherent effort among all relevant actors (national governments of oil exporters, international oil companies, the United States and other northern hemisphere governments, the World Bank, the IMF, export credit agencies, the United Nations, and civil society) to increase the benefits and minimize the harm from oil development, particularly on transparency and protection of human rights. See also Daniel L. Goldwyn and J. Stephen Morrison, "Promoting

Transparency in the African Oil Sector: A Report of the CSIS Task Force on Rising U.S. Energy Stakes in Africa," Center for Strategic and International Studies report, Washington, DC, 2004. This latter report argues that the U.S. government should pursue sustained, high-level engagement, bilaterally and multilaterally, to promote transparency and reform in all African oil-producing nations, and that a special adviser to the U.S. president and secretary of state for African energy diplomacy, with ambassadorial rank, be designated to lead interagency policy.

125. Catholic Relief Services, "Bottom of the Barrel."

126. For example, the Shell Foundation Empowerment through Energy Fund, www.shellfoundation.org/index.php?menuID=3&smenuID=14&bmenuID=19.

127. International Business Leaders Forum, "Business Impact on Development: 10 Practical Actions to Support Africa's Development," online report, 2005, www.iblf.org.

128. The standards often referred to as "international standards" are those developed by the International Finance Corporation, the private-sector arm of the World Bank. See the IFC Web site, www.ifc.org.

129. See the IFC Web site for full details of the revised policies.

130. The text of the Principles and participant governments, companies, and NGOs can be found on the official Web site, www.voluntaryprinciples.org.

131. The EITI Web site is at www.eitransparency.org.

132. See, for example, joint work by International Alert and the International Institute for Sustainable Development on "Conflict Sensitive Business Practices," www.international-alert.org/our_work/themes/business.php; Jane Nelson, *The Business of Peace* (London: Prince of Wales Business Leaders Forum; International Alert, Council on Economic Priorities, 2000); Anton Wenger and Daniel Möckli, *Conflict Prevention: The Untapped Potential of the Business Sector* (Boulder, CO: Lynne Rienner, 2003).

133. Nelson, *Business of Peace,* 5.

134. Wenger and Möckli, *Conflict Prevention.*

135. International Alert, "Conflict Sensitive Business Practices: Guidance for Extractive Industries" (published as set of documents and available online, London, 2005), www.international-alert.org/our_work/themes/business.php.

136. Massiano Guidolin and Eliana La Ferrara, "Diamonds Are Forever, Wars Are Not: Is Conflict Bad for Private Firms?" Centre for Economic Policy Research (CEPR), Discussion Paper no. 4668, October 2004, http://papers.ssrn.com/sol3/papers.cfm?abstract_id=631608.

137. Statoil, "Conviction Politics," *Statoil* magazine, January 26, 2004, www.statoil.com/StatoilCom/svg00990.nsf?opendatabase&lang=en&artid=F339A511DE36C94B412568 2D0050E669.

138. BP, "Promoting Human Rights in Colombia," case study on company Web site, www.bp.com/extendedsectiongenericarticle.do?categoryId=9002406&contentId= 7005336.

139. Chevron, "$50 Million 'Angola Partnership Initiative' Launched to Support Education, Training and Small Business Development," press release, November 25, 2002, www.chevron.com/news/press/2002/2002%2D11%2D25.asp.

140. Extensive documentation and discussion can be found on the Web sites of the World Bank, www.worldbank.org/afr/ccproj/; ExxonMobil, www.essochad.com/ Chad/Chad_HomePage.asp; NGOs opposing or monitoring the project, such as the Bank Information Centre, www.bicusa.org/bicusa/issues/africa/index.php; and Catholic Relief Services, www.crs.org/our_work/where_we_work/overseas/africa/ cameroon/pipeline.cfm; and in teaching materials such as those developed by Dr. J. Paul Martin, SIPA, and the Center for New Media Teaching and Learning for Columbia University, www.columbia.edu/itc/sipa/martin/chad-cam/index.html.

141. The compensation system illustrates the approach to managing local impacts. According to ExxonMobil, "Compensation for the project's use of land and for other project impacts follows a four-step, consultation-based process. Although the details of the steps vary depending on the specific compensation program, the most common situation is compensation to individual land users in a village. For example, the first visit to a village provides preliminary information on the compensation program, explaining and posting in the village such details as the standard rates of compensation and the lands likely to be affected. A second visit gathers feedback from local residents as they react to the information provided in the first visit. Discussion takes place to arrive at solutions to local issues. On the third visit, project representatives post proposed payments for all to see, in a completely transparent process. That way everyone in the village can know that everyone is being treated equally and fairly. Finally, a team visits the village to complete the process with payments, again made in public at a village gathering so all can witness the process and see that each landowner has been treated equally. By mid-2002 the Project had paid over 5.6 billion CFA ($8.6 million) in cash and in-kind compensation to individual land users." In one of the first documented efforts to measure whether projects designed to limit damage and create local benefits are doing so, research by anthropologists commissioned by ExxonMobil found that villages affected by the project, where compensation was paid (and other social projects implemented) had better housing and diets and more extensive use of mosquito nets for malaria prevention than the control villages surveyed. See www.essochad.com.

142. World Bank Group, "Government of Chad and World Bank Group Joint Statement," press release, April 6, 2006, http://web.worldbank.org/WBSITE/EXTERNAL/ NEWS/0,,contentMDK:20879805~pagePK:34370~piPK:34424~theSitePK: 4607,00.html (accessed April 22, 2006).

143. American Petroleum Institute, "Building a Better Future through Partnerships and Oil and Gas Industry Guidelines on Voluntary Sustainability Reporting," Washington, DC, 2005, http://api-ec.api.org/environ/.

144. For analysis of the tension between voluntary agreements as actions to provide collective goods or collaboration to avoid legislation, see Virginia Haufler et al., *Private Authority and International Affairs* (Albany, NY: SUNY Press, 1999). For insight into potential regulatory systems to address revenue transparency and business impacts on human rights, see www.publishwhatyoupay.org; for discussion of work on United Nations human rights standards for business, see www.business-humanrights.org.

145. For example, Talisman Energy and Lundin Petroleum, both criticized for operating in Sudan and based in Canada and Sweden respectively, are independents with CSR policies, as are Cairn Energy and Tullow Oil, both fast-growing, large independents with portfolios based in developing countries. Statoil, the Norwegian state oil company, is active in CSR, while both Petronas and China National Oil Company are starting to become involved.

146. Map from the CIA World Fact Book, Azerbaijan. See http://www.cia.gov/cia/publications/factbook/geos/aj.html.

147. Thomas de Waal, *Black Garden: Armenia and Azerbaijan through Peace and War* (New York and London: New York University Press, 2003), 137.

148. Ibid., 285.

149. In his study of Eurasia's separatist states, Dov Lynch makes the important point that since the cease-fire, much work has been carried out *within* Nagorno-Karabakh to establish state structures, including armed forces, police, border guards, a constitution, and elections, and that any settlement will have to take this into account. See Dov Lynch, *Engaging Eurasia's Separatist States* (Washington, DC: United States Institute of Peace, 2004).

150. Emil Danielyan, "Armenia, Azerbaijan Appear to Edge Closer to Karabakh Peace," *Eurasianet,* May 20, 2005, www.Eurasianet.org/departments/insight/articles/eav052005.shtml.

151. Evgeny Polyakov, "Changing Trade Patterns after Conflict Resolution in South Caucasus," World Bank Policy Research Working Paper, 2000, 41, http://lnweb18.worldbank.org/eca/eca.nsf/0/23ac8865ee0dc520852568fc005ba9.

152. Armenian Center for National and International Studies, "Armenia's Thirteen-Year-Old Independence and Sovereignty: Opinion Poll," press release, Yerevan, October 8, 2004, www.acnis.am/pr/independence.htm.

153. Liz Fuller, "Armenian, Azerbaijani Foreign Minister Meet with Minsk Group Cochairmen…Who Express Concern over Cease-Fire Violations," Radio Free Europe/Radio Liberty, May 18, 2005, www.rferl.org/newsline/2005/04/2-tca/tca-280405.asp.

154. Patricia Carley, "Nagorno-Karabakh, Searching for a Solution," United States Institute of Peace, Peaceworks report, 1998, www.usip.org/pubs/peaceworks/pwks36.pdf.

155. De Waal, *Black Garden,* 3.

156. Mir-Yusif Mir-Babayev, "Azerbaijan's Oil History: A Chronology Leading Up to the Soviet Era," *Azerbaijan International* 10, no. 2 (2002); and "Azerbaijan's Oil History: A Chronology since 1920," *Azerbaijan International* 11, no. 2 (2003), www.azer.com.

157. Exploration activity on the Araz-Alov-Sharg block was halted in 2001 when Iranian gunboats attacked survey ships, claiming that Azerbaijan did not have the right to let PSAs for that area.

158. BP, "Statistical Review of World Energy," June 2006, www.bp.com/statistical review.

159. John Wakeman-Linn and others, *Managing Oil Wealth: The Case of Azerbaijan* (Washington, DC: International Monetary Fund, 2004), 1.

160. International companies with shares in the consortia:

The AIOC consortium (oil) (ACG PSA 1994)	BTC oil pipeline	The Shah Deniz consortium (gas) (Shah Deniz PSA, 1996)
BP	BP	BP
Unocal	SOCAR	Statoil
SOCAR	Chevron	SOCAR
Inpex	Statoil	LukAgip
Statoil	TPAO	NICO
Exxon/Mobil	ENI	Total
TPAO	Total	TPAO
Devon Energy	Itochu	
Itochu	Inpex	
Delta/Hess	Conoco Phillips	
	Amerada Hess	

161. International Monetary Fund, "Azerbaijan: Selected Issues and Statistical Appendix" (International Monetary Fund, Country Report no. 03/105, Washington, DC, May 2003), 23.

162. De Waal, *Black Garden,* 278.

163. Svante Cornell et al., "Regional Security in the South Caucasus: The Role of NATO," Central Asia–Caucasus Institute, Policy Paper, Washington, DC, 2004, 8, www.silkroadstudies.org/docs/publications/2004/nato.pdf.

164. Azerbaijan News Service, "Changes to State Budget Discussed in Milli Majlis," news report, June 21, 2006, www.ans.az/archivetest.php?y=2005&m=06&d=21&th enews=2739. ANS is a Baku-based news service. The ANS group also runs television and radio stations and a publishing house.

165. Justin Burke, "Azeri President Says 2003 to Be Better than 2002," *Eurasianet,* December 12, 2002, www.Eurasianet.org/resource/azerbaijan/hypermail/ 200301/0000.shtml.

166. Justin Burke, "Azerbaijan President Rules Out Karabakh War," *Eurasianet,* March 2, 2004, www.Eurasianet.org/resource/azerbaijan/hypermail/200403/0003. shtml.

167. President Ilham Aliyev, "Speech by the President of Azerbaijan," June 25, 2005, www.azertag.com. Azertag.com is the Web site of the state news agency.

168. Nick Killick, International Alert, interview with author, London, October 2003.

169. State Oil Fund of Azerbaijan, "2003 Revenue and Expenditure Statement," January 28, 2004, www.oilfund.az/inside.php?nID=30.

170. See assessment and data in IMF Country Reports, e.g., International Monetary Fund, "Azerbaijan Republic: Poverty Reduction Strategy Paper Progress Report," IMF Country Report no. 04/9, Washington, DC, January 2004. The Consumer Price Index shows increases of 1.3 percent, 3.3 percent, and 2.5 percent (estimated/forecast) for 2001, 2002, and 2003–05, respectively. GDP growth (at constant prices) was 9.9 percent in 2001, 10.6 percent in 2002, 10.3 percent in 2003, and 10.2 percent in 2004. The growth rate has been faster in the nonoil sector than in the oil sector, although this changed drastically starting in 2005, when new oil fields came onstream. See also "IMF Executive Board Concludes 2005 Article IV Consultation with the Republic of Azerbaijan," Public Information Notice 06/44, April 25, 2005, www. imf.org/external/np/sec/pn/2006/pn0644.htm.

171. See www.oilfund.az, the official State Oil Fund of Azerbaijan Web site, where revenue reports and statistics are published and the legal framework set out; and www. eiti-az.org, the Web site of the Azerbaijan NGO coalition participating in the EITI process.

172. See www.bp.com/caspian. This is a BP Web site containing information on the BP-operated oil and gas fields in the Caspian, and the Baku-Tbilisi-Ceyhan and Southern Caucasus Pipeline.

173. International Monetary Fund, "On the Delay in the Completion of the Fourth Review of Azerbaijan Republic's PRGF Arrangement," IMF press release, April 2004, www.imf.org/external/np/sec/pr/2004/pr0469.htm; and International Monetary Fund, "IMF Executive Board Completes Fourth Review under Azerbaijan

Republic's PRGF Arrangement and Approves US$19.7 Million Disbursement," IMF press release, December 2004, www.imf.org/external/np/sec/pr/2004/pr04276.htm.

174. Svetlana Tsalik, *Caspian Oil Windfalls: Who Will Benefit?* (New York: Open Society Institute, 2003), 165.

175. See www.transparency.org, the Web site of Transparency International, where the annual Corruption Perceptions Index can be found.

176. See www.transparency-az.org, the official Web site of TI Azerbaijan.

177. See, for example, Freedom House rankings, www.freedomhouse.org.

178. Organization for Security and Co-operation in Europe, "Elections in Azerbaijan Did Not Meet International Standards Despite Some Improvement," OSCE press release, November 7, 2005, www.osce.org/item/16887.html.

179. BP, "Regional Review: Economic, Social and Environmental Overview of the Southern Caspian Oil and Gas Projects," February 2003, 175–82, www.bp.com/caspian.

180. BP, "Response to Caspian Development Advisory Panel, Interim Report," August 2003, 1, www.caspsea.com.

181. See www.bp.com/caspian for the texts and documents referred to.

182. The ESAP monitoring reports and CDAP reports are available on www.bp.com/caspian; and reports by national NGO monitoring groups supported by the Open Society Institute, Azerbaijan, are available at www.osi-az.org/btcmonitoring.shtml.

183. Press coverage of the opening of the BTC pipeline in May 2005 noted, "International leaders and executives used the opening to express concern about the upcoming elections, saying a fair vote was needed to ensure future political and social stability." See Shahin Abbasov and Khadija Ismailova, "Pipeline Opening Helps Spur Political Opposition in Azerbaijan," *Eurasianet*, June 16, 2005, www.Eurasianet.org/departments/insight/articles/eav060605.shtml.

184. Thomas de Waal, "Make a Bitter Task Better in the Caucasus," *Wall Street Journal*, May 11, 2004.

185. CIA World Factbook: Angola, http://www.cia.gov/cia/publications/factbook/geos/ao.html.

186. A succinct history and a comprehensive bibliography are found in David Birmingham, "Angola," in *A History of Postcolonial Lusophone Africa,* ed. Patrick Chabal et al. (London: Hurst, 2002), 137–84.

187. Countries cited as supporting one or more of the liberation movements include China, France, Israel, North Korea, Romania, Senegal, South Africa, Tanzania, Uganda, the United States, West Germany, Zaire, and Zambia (FNLA, UNITA); and Cuba, the Scandinavian countries, and the Soviet Union and Eastern European countries (MPLA). See Gerald J. Bender, "Angola: A Story of Stupidity," *New York*

Review of Books 25, no. 20 (December 21, 1997). Bender reviews John A. Marcum's *The Angolan Revolution,* vol. 1, and John Stockwell's *In Search of Enemies: A CIA Story* (New York: Norton, 1978).

188. Paul Hare, *Angola's Last Best Chance for Peace: An Insider's Account of the Peace Process* (Washington, DC: United States Institute of Peace, 1988), 5.

189. Ibid.,5–8.

190. Donald Rothchild, *Managing Ethnic Conflict in Africa* (Washington, DC: Brookings Institution Press, 1997), 131.

191. Hare, *Angola's Last Best Chance,* xvii.

192. Inge Brinkman, "War and Identity in Angola: Two Case Studies," *Lusotopie,* (2003): 218. The quotation is from a thirty-eight-year-old woman living in southern Angola, interviewed in 1996. See also, for example, Tony Hodges, *Angola: Anatomy of an Oil State,* 2nd ed. (Bloomington: Indiana University Press, 2004).

193. Margaret Anstee, special representative of the UN secretary-general, as quoted in Rothchild, *Managing Ethnic Conflict in Africa,* 134.

194. Patrick Chabal, "The Limits of Nationhood," in *History of Postcolonial Lusophone Africa,* ed. Chabal et al., 121.

195. See, for example, Tony Hodges, *Angola from Afro-Stalinism to Petro-Diamond Capitalism* (Oxford: James Curry, 2001), 17.

196. World Bank, "Transitional Support Strategy for Angola," March 2003, www.worldbank.org.

197. Angola Ministry of Planning, *Estratégia de Combate à Pobreza (ECP),* February 2004 (published in full, in Portuguese, on the Angolan government Web site), www.angola.org/relief/index.htm. The ECP is Angola's equivalent of a Poverty Reduction Strategy Paper (PRSP) that the World Bank and IMF require countries to prepare as a basis for assistance.

198. Government information sources cite a population of 100,000. See www.angola.org/referenc/provinces.html. Sources associated with secession politics cite 300,000. See, for example, Web site of the Unrepresented Nations and Peoples Organization, www.unpo.org.

199. Human Rights Watch, "Angola: Between War and Peace in Cabinda," online report, 2004, www.hrw.org/backgrounder/africa/angola/2004/1204/.

200. Guus Meijer, ed., *From Military Peace to Social Justice? The Angolan Peace Process* (London: Conciliation Resources, 2004), 94.

201. See, for example, Ad Hoc Commission for Human Rights in Cabinda, "Cabinda 2003, a Year of Pain," www.conectasur.org/files/AngolaCabindaHRreport03.pdf; and U.S. State Department, "Country Reports on Human Rights Practices, 2003: Angola," www.state.gov/g/drl/rls/hrrpt/2003/27711.htm.

202. Jean-Michel Mabeko-Tali, "La question de Cabinda," *Lusotopie,* 2001, 49–62.

203. Jean-Michel Mabeko-Tali, "Cabinda between 'No Peace' and 'No War,'" in Meijer, *From Military Peace to Social Justice?,* 39.

204. Unrepresented Nations and Peoples Organization, "Cabinda: Chairs Stay Empty around the Negotiating Table," March 15, 2006, http://www.unpo.org/news_detail.php?arg=13&par=4009.

205. There are regular reports of new finds. See, for example, BBC News, "Angola Discovers New Oil Deposit," April 22, 2004, http://news.bbc.co.uk/1/hi/business/3646653.stm.

206. Roc Oil, "ROC Formally Agrees to Trigger Production-Sharing Agreement for Cabinda South Block, Onshore Angola," press release, October 2004, www.rocoil.com.au.

207. The Sonangol Web site gives information on the blocks and concessionaires. See http://www.sonangol.com/sonangolEP/concessions_en.shtml.

208. U.S. Energy Information Administration, "Imports of Crude Oil and Petroleum Products into the United States by Country of Origin" (2005 estimate based on data for January to April 2005), www.eia.doe.gov/oil_gas/petroleum/info_glance/importexport.html.

209. BP, "Statistical Review of World Energy," June 2006, www.bp.com/statistical review.

210. U.S. Energy Information Administration, "Angola Country Analysis Brief," January 2006, www.eia.doe.gov/emeu/cabs/Angola/Oil.html.

211. U.S.-Angola Chamber of Commerce, "Angola Earns Nearly Nine Bln. Dollars through Oil, Diamonds, Granite," press release, December 2004, www.us-angola.org/press.

212. Author interview, Washington, DC, 2004.

213. The importance of maintaining the flow of oil income was illustrated when Gulf Oil suspended production from Cabinda in November 1975 at the request of the United States. According to Piero Gleijeses, the suspension prompted the MPLA to consider seizing the Gulf holdings. Initial approaches were made to Romania (with its long oil industry history) to see if it would be willing to operate the fields, but the Cubans succeeded in persuading President Neto to keep pressure on Gulf Oil to resume, and six months later "the Ford administration had finally acceded to Gulf's repeated requests to resume operations." Piero Gleijeses, *Conflicting Missions* (Chapel Hill, NC: University of North Carolina Press, 2002), 312, 343.

214. Ibid., 312.

215. Eugene Smith, "The New Condottieri and US Policy: The Privatization of Conflict and Its Implications," *Parameters* 32, no. 4 (Winter 2002–03): 104–95.

216. "In December 2000 the French authorities arrested a Franco-Brazilian businessman, Pierre Falcone, and Jean-Christophe Mitterand, the son of the former French president, on charges of arms trafficking related to an arms-for-oil deal with Angola in 1993. The charges were later dismissed on legal technicalities, but 'Angolagate,' as the affair came to be known, helped create an aura of suspicion about the opaque world of Angolan oil-guaranteed loans, trade finance, and arms contracts." See Hodges, *Angola: Anatomy of an Oil State,* 165.

217. Jean-Michel Mabeko-Tali, "Cabinda between 'No Peace' and 'No War,'" 37.

218. Rothchild, *Managing Ethnic Conflict in Africa,* 131.

219. U.S. Energy Information Administration, "Angola Country Analysis Brief," July 2000, www.eia.doe.gov/emeu/cabs/Angola/Oil.html (accessed July 2004).

220. See, for example, Hodges, *Angola from Afro-Stalinism to Petro-Diamond Capitalism,* 173.

221. Gleijeses, *Conflicting Missions,* 262.

222. Ibid.

223. Jean-Michel Mabeko-Tali, "La question de Cabinda," 50. Mabeko-Tali notes that in the 1960s MPLA was allied with some independence activists in Cabinda. In the 1970s the view that Cabinda should be totally included within a unitary state took hold, and according to later interviews with certain leaders from that time, this change was driven by the belief that oil companies presented the nucleus for a potential "Rhodesian" model for a unilateral declaration of independence in Cabinda.

224. Pedro de Morais Jr., "Promoting Accountability and Transparency in Africa's Oil Sector: Reform Efforts in Nigeria, Angola, and São Tomé and Príncipe" (speech at CSIS conference, Washington, DC, March 2004).

225. BBC News, "IMF: Angola's 'Missing Millions,'" October 18, 2002, http://news.bbc.co.uk/1/hi/world/africa/2338669.stm.

226. Human Rights Watch, "Some Transparency, No Accountability: The Use of Oil Revenues in Angola and the Impact on Human Rights" (Report A1601, 2004), www.hrw.org/reports/2004/angola0104/.

227. Angola Ministry of Finance (statement on the Human Rights Watch report, January 13, 2003), www.angola.org.uk/press_release_human_rghts.htm.

228. PFC Energy, "West African Petroleum Sector: Oil Value Forecast and Distribution" (paper prepared for the Center for Strategic and International Studies project, Reforming Africa's Oil Sector, December 2003), www.csis.org/africa/index.htm.

229. See the "Data and Statistics" page at the World Bank's Web site, www.worldbank.org.

230. Author interview, Washington, DC, January 2004.

231. World Bank, "Transitional Support Strategy for the Republic of Angola," March 2003, www.wds.worldbank.org/servlet/WDS_IBank_Servlet?pcont=details& eid=000094946_03031304013163.

232. IRIN News, "Angola: Economic Reforms Bring Donor Conference Closer," May 19, 2004, www.irinnews.org/report.asp?ReportID=41148&SelectRegion= Southern_Africa&SelectCountry=ANGOLA. In November 2004 news services reported that agreement had been reached on a donor commitment conference in 2006. See also "Donors Will Give Angola the Benefit of the Doubt and Hold a Pledging Conference Next Year," *Africa Confidential* 45, no. 22 (November 5, 2004).

233. KPMG, "Assessment of the Angolan Petroleum Sector, Final Report," Angola Ministry of Finance report, March 2004, www.angola.org/referenc/reports/ oildiagnostic/index.html.

234. IRIN News, "Angola: Donor Conference Likely in 2005, Says World Bank," November 19, 2004, www.irinnews.org/report.asp?ReportID=44228&SelectRegion= Southern_Africa&SelectCountry=ANGOLA.

235. US-Angola Chamber of Commerce, "Angola's Donor Conference to Follow IMF Deal," press release, December 15, 2004, www.us_angola.org/press.

236. IMF, "IMF Executive Board Concludes 2004 Article IV Consultation with Angola," Public Information Notice no. 05/85, July 6, 2005, www.imf.org/external/ np/sec/pn/2005/pn0585.htm.

237. See www.sonangol.co.ao/sonangolEP/concessionsBidSubmission_en.shtml and links to PDF files.

238. Augusto Alfredo, ed., "ENI oferece USD 902 milhões pelo Bloco 15," *Jornal de Angola,* April 10, 2006. The ENI bid of $902 million was for an operating share of parts of offshore Block 15 not included in the existing Block 15 concession.

239. Alexander's Gas and Oil Connections, "Angola Seeks Increase of Oil Transparency," online news report, December 9, 2004, www.gasandoil.com/goc/news/ nta44984.htm.

240. IRIN News, "IMF Told to Keep Its Money, but Help Needed with Old Debts," November 8, 2005, www.irinnews.org/report.asp?ReportID=49986&SelectRegion= Southern_Africa&SelectCountry=ANGOLA.

241. The oil sector audit report published by the Ministry of Finance in March 2004 states, "The consultants do not view the current system of regional payments as being completely transparent (and) The Ministry has no control over these payments or how they are used by the provincial governments." KPMG, "Assessment of the Angolan Petroleum Sector," 16.

242. IRIN News, "Angola: Economic Recovery Plan Fails to Appease Cabindans," June 3, 2004, www.irinnews.org/Advsearch.asp?RecordJump=120&QuickSearch=

&SelectRegion=any&SelectCountry=ANGOLA&SelectTheme=any&LookFor=
AND&StartDate=3/19/2005&EndDate=6/3/2004.

243. Brinkman, "War and Identity in Angola," 210.

244. "Post Postponed: Lengthy Preparations for National Elections Mean No Vote This Year," *Africa Confidential* 17, no. 2 (January 20, 2006): 7. The delay in holding elections in Angola compares poorly with the position in neighboring Democratic Republic of Congo, where, despite continuing conflict from militias in the east of the country, a successful constitutional referendum was held in December 2005, and parliamentary elections are scheduled for 2006.

245. Transparency International, "Corruption Perceptions Index, 2005," www.transparency.org/policy_and_research/surveys_indices/cpi.

246. BBC News, "Oil Firms Funding Angolan Conflict," December 5, 1999, http://news.bbc.co.uk/1/hi/world/africa/550686.stm.

247. Human Rights Watch, "Some Transparency, No Accountability," 39–42.

248. Barrows Company, "Angola: Model Production-Sharing Agreement of 1999" (taken from the Basic Oil Laws and Concession Contracts (BOLCC) database, available on subscription from Barrows Company), www.barrowscompany.com.

249. Ibid.

250. Human Rights Watch, "Some Transparency, No Accountability," 55.

251. Author interview, Washington, DC, December 2004.

252. Chevron, "ChevronTexaco Awarded Extension to Block 0 Concession in Angola," www.chevrontexaco.com/news/press/2004/2004-05-13.asp; and Roc Oil, "Angola Cabinda South," www.rocoil.com.au/Pages/World_Map/Angola/angola.html.

253. With the exception of oil spills in Cabinda, for which Chevron Texaco was fined $2 million for environmental damage that dirtied beaches and damaged the local fishing industry. See BBC News, "Angola Fines Chevron for Pollution," July 1, 2002, http://news.bbc.co.uk/1/low/business/2077836.stm.

254. Interview with Angolan oil industry executive, Washington, DC, 2003.

255. Decree-Law no. 5/95 sets limits on the employment of expatriates by companies based in Angola. For text, see Alexander Blakely, *CSR in the Oil Sector in Angola* (Washington, DC: World Bank, 2003). Ministry of Petroleum Order 127/03 establishes local content requirements for oil companies. See Miranda Law Office, "New Local Content Law for Oil Companies," February 2004, www.mirandalawfirm.com/articles (subscription service).

256. See, for example, BP, "Angola Location Report," online report, http://www.bp.com/subsection.do?categoryId=723&contentId=2004008.

257. Nicholas Shaxson, "Move that Could Weaken IMF Leverage," *Financial Times*, April 21, 2004. "Angola's non-oil sector is a treacherous place to do business because of tight whimsical control by an oil-rich clique around President Eduardo dos Santos." Evidence of the problems in implementing local content strategies is provided by international comparisons of the "business climate." Although above the regional average in terms of GDP, Angola scores substantially worse on measures such as the ease of starting a business and the complexity of registering a property. See World Bank, "Doing Business: Benchmarking Business Regulations Database," online database, http://rru.worldbank.org/DoingBusiness/.

258. Human Rights Watch, "Some Transparency, No Accountability," 7; and author interview, Washington, DC, January 2004.

259. See, for example, IRIN News reports, "Monitoring Pressure for Early Election Date," June 11, 2004, www.irinnews.org/report.asp?ReportID=41640&Sel ectRegion=Southern_Africa&SelectCountry=ANGOLA; and "Survival Top Priority Rather than Up-Coming Elections," June 14, 2004, www.irinnews.org/report. asp?ReportID=41663&SelectRegion=Southern_Africa&SelectCountry=ANGOLA.

260. Angola Ministry of Planning, *Estratégia de Combate à Pobreza.*

261. Interview with government official, Washington, DC, January 2004.

262. David Birmingham, "Angola," 137–84.

263. www.cabinda.net.is the Web site of one of the succession groups in Cabinda. The content of the Web site changes; in February 2006 it states, "The American oil company Chevron is participating alongside the invaders in raping and murdering the Cabindan people. We live in misery because of the greed of an American oil company."

264. Jane's Information Group, *Jane's Security Sentinel Assessments, Angola,* London: August 2004, http://sentinel.janes.com (subscription online service).

265. The "main outlines of Sudan's borders were set by 1903." See Douglas H. Johnson, *The Root Causes of Sudan's Civil Wars* (Bloomington: Indiana University Press, 2003), 10; and J. Millard Burr and Robert O. Collins, *Africa's Thirty Years War: Libya, Chad and the Sudan, 1963–1993* (Boulder, CO: Westview, 1999), 14: "The boundaries between Chad and Sudan were demarcated under a treaty between Britain and France in 1899 and delineated in detail in 1924."

266. Framework Agreement on Wealth Sharing Between the Government of the Sudan (GOS) and the Sudan People's Liberation Movement / Sudan People's Liberation Army (SPLM/A), July 7, 2004, widely referred to as the wealth-sharing agreement (WSA). This forms part of the Comprehensive Peace Agreement (CPA) signed by the parties on January 9, 2005. Full texts of the CPA can be found in the United States Institute of Peace Jeanette Rankin Library Peace Agreements Digital Collection, www. usip.org/library/pa/sudan/pa_sudan.html (accessed March 17, 2006).

267. CIA World Factbook, Sudan. See http://www.cia.gov/cia/publications/ factbook/geos/su.html.

268. Anne Mosely Lesch, "Ethnic Conflict in the Sudan," in *Encyclopedia of Modern Ethnic Conflicts* (Westport, CT: Greenwood, 2003), 235–42.

269. See, for example, Johnson, *Root Causes of Sudan's Civil Wars,* 3: "Thus, prior to the establishment of Muslim states from the fourteenth century A.D. onwards, pagan and Christian kingdoms were active in the organized raiding of their peripheries, and part of the impetus of that raiding came from external trade relations. Muslim rulers later continued a tradition already established by their pagan and Christian predecessors."

270. The condominium was described by Lord Cromer, then British agent and consul general in Egypt, as a "hybrid form of government." Theoretically, there was joint Anglo-Egyptian sovereignty over the Sudan, although the British-nominated governor-general was empowered to rule by decree. See P. M. Holt and M. W. Daly, *A History of the Sudan,* 5th ed. (Harlow, UK: Longman, 2000), 102.

271. Donald Rothchild, *Managing Ethnic Conflict in Africa* (Washington, DC: Brookings Institution Press, 1997), 216.

272. Johnson, *Root Causes of Sudan's Civil Wars,* 18, 32–33, 51–55.

273. Ibid., 27.

274. Lesch, "Ethnic Conflict in the Sudan," 237.

275. See Johnson, *Root Causes of Sudan's Civil Wars,* 30: "The Sudanese gained independence with a temporary constitution drafted for them by a British academic constitutional expert. Two issues arose which were to prevent agreement on a permanent constitution: whether the Sudan should be a federal or a unitary state, and whether it should have a secular or an Islamic constitution."

276. Francis M. Deng, *War of Visions, Conflict of Identities in the Sudan* (Washington, DC: Brookings Institution Press, 1995), 11.

277. World Bank, "Sudan: Stabilization and Reconstruction," Country Economic Memorandum, June 2003, 1:5.

278. See, for example, Abdel Salam Sidahmed, *Politics and Islam in Contemporary Sudan* (New York: St Martin's, 1996), 56–59; and Peter Woodward, "Parties and Parliaments," in *Sudan since Independence,* ed. Muddathir Abd Al-Rahim (Brookfield, VT: Gower, 1986), 53–64.

279. See, for example, Burr and Collins, *Africa's Thirty Years War.*

280. Holt and Daly, *History of the Sudan,* 170.

281. The text of the agreement (comprising the Draft Organic Law to Organize Regional Self Government in the Southern Provinces of the Democratic Republic of Sudan; the Agreement on the Cease Fire in the Sudan Region, and the Protocols on Interim Arrangements) can be found in *The Southern Sudan and the Problems of National Integration,* ed. Dunstan M. Wim (London: Frank Cass, 1973), Appendix VII, 221–44.

282. Ann Mosely Lesch, *The Sudan: Contested National Identities* (Bloomington: Indiana University Press, 1998), 47.

283. Rothchild, *Managing Ethnic Conflict in Africa,* 237.

284. Douglas Johnson makes the strong case in *Root Causes of Sudan's Civil Wars* that from the 1980s the overall civil war was composed of many interlocking struggles: "Not only are Muslims fighting Muslims, but 'Africans' are fighting 'Africans'" (xiii).

285. Rothchild, *Managing Ethnic Conflict in Africa,* 237.

286. Johnson, *Root Causes of Sudan's Civil Wars,* 58; and Harold D. Nelson, *Sudan: A Country Study,* Area Handbook Series (Washington, DC: U.S. Government Printing Office, 1982), 256, http://countrystudies.us/sudan/ (accessed March 17, 2006): "Shipments of United States–made military equipment and participation of Sudanese forces in United States military exercises gave Sudan's antagonists a visible demonstration of United States support for Nimeiri."

287. Holt and Daly, *History of the Sudan,* 178.

288. Jemera Rone, *Sudan, Oil and Human Rights* (New York: Human Rights Watch, 2003), 129.

289. Johnson, *Root Causes of Sudan's Civil Wars,* 45–46.

290. Sharon Hutchinson, *Nuer Dilemmas, Coping with Money, War and the State* (Berkeley: University of California Press, 1996), 5. After completing fieldwork in 1983, Hutchinson writes, "By late 1984 I had learned that my principal field sites in both eastern and western Nuerland had been destroyed. Tharlual had been overrun and razed by a band of northern Baggara (Misseriya) Arabs that had been armed with automatic weapons and ammunition by the government and instructed to clear the oil-rich lands of the western upper Nile of its Nilotic inhabitants" (5).

291. Ibid., 9.

292. Johnson, *Root Causes of Sudan's Civil Wars,* 127.

293. Lesch, "Ethnic Conflict in the Sudan," 240.

294. Ibid., 241.

295. U.S. House of Representatives Act H.R.5531, Sudan Peace Act (October 2002). See the State Department Fact Sheet, www.state.gov/r/pa/prs/ps/2002/14531. htm (accessed March 17, 2006).

296. World Bank, *Sudan: Stabilization and Reconstruction,* 7.

297. Framework Agreement on Wealth Sharing Between the Government of Sudan (GOS) and the Sudan People's Liberation Movement/Sudan People's Liberation Army (SPLM/A), January 7, 2004, www.usip.org/library/pa/sudan/wealth_sharing_01072004.pdf (accessed March 17, 2006).

298. Agreements cover power sharing; resolution of the Abeyei conflict; resolution of conflict in south Kordofan, Nuba Mountains, and Blue Nile states; distribution of wealth; security arrangements; and structures of government. See www.usip.org/

library/pa/sudan/pa_sudan.html (accessed March 17, 2006) for the complete texts of the peace agreements.

299. Colin Powell's judgment that the events in Darfur constituted genocide are reported in Michael E. Ranneberger (principal deputy assistant secretary for African affairs), "Sudan: Prospects for Peace" (speech made at the Providence Committee on Foreign Relations, Washington, DC, December 2004), http://www.state.gov/p/af/rls/rm/39751.htm (accessed March 17, 2006).

300. Mike Jobbins and Harold Wolpe, "A Director's Forum with H. E. Salva Kiir Mayardit" (online report of the forum at the Woodrow Wilson Center for Scholars, Washington, DC, November 2005), www.wilsoncenter.org/index.cfm.

301. BP, "Statistical Review of World Energy," June 2006, www.bp.com/statistical review.

302. A detailed analysis undertaken in 2002 on concessions in south and south-central Sudan is cautious. It argues that in the Red Sea area as a whole exploration has resulted more often in finds of gas than of oil and that historically only small reserves have been found in the central area of the country. Michael Rogers, "Sudan: Projected Oil Production and Revenues" (unpublished working paper, PFC Strategic Studies, August 2002). However, an industry newsletter published in early 2005 argues, "In the long run companies will be primarily interested in the northwest of Sudan. Composed of two giant concessions, block 12 (Darfur) and block 14 (north), the region remains entirely unexplored and lies alongside two potentially oil-rich basins." See "Sudan to Draw the Crowd in 2005," *Africa Energy Intelligence,* January 5, 2005, www.africaintelligence.com.

303. The blocks are areas of territory in which the concession holder is entitled to carry out exploration activities.

304. In a speech presented on April 9, 1985, John Garang, leader of the SPLM/A, said, "We assure the generals that oil will not flow; water will not flow in the Jonglei canal; vehicles will not move in War Zone No.1; the air will continue to be dangerous for air transport." See John Garang, *John Garang Speaks* (London: KPI, 1987), 46.

305. SPLM/A refers to the joint political and military organizations of the Sudan People's Liberation Movement and the Sudan People's Liberation Army.

306. Economist Intelligence Unit, *Sudan Country Report,* quarterly newsletter, London, December 2005, 24.

307. "White Nile May Be a Watershed," *London Evening Standard,* March 10, 2005. A deal being negotiated by politicians from south Sudan and the White Nile Company replaced the conventional government share of production with a 50 percent share in company equity.

308. "Sudan to Draw the Crowd in 2005."

309. Since 1997 U.S. sanctions have prevented any investment by U.S. companies.

310. Benaiah Yongo-Bure, "Prospects for Socio-economic Development in the South," in *The Search for Peace and Unity in the Sudan,* ed. Deng and Gifford (Washington, DC: Wilson Center Press, 1987), 44.

311. World Bank, *Sudan: Stabilization and Reconstruction,* 25.

312. International Monetary Fund, Country Report no. 03/390, December 2003; and International Monetary Fund, Country Report no. 05/185, June 2005, www.imf .org/external/country/SDN/index.htm (accessed March 17, 2006).

313. World Bank, *Sudan: Stabilization and Reconstruction,* 50, 71.

314. Michael Rogers, "Sudan's Oil Sector, Background Briefing," August 2002. Douglas Johnson quotes a figure of $2.2 billion as the government share of "these first export revenues" following opening of the pipeline in mid-1999. See Johnson, *Root Causes of Sudan's Civil Wars,* 162.

315. U.S. State Department, "Sudan Peace Act," fact sheet, www.state.gov/r/pa/ prs/ps/2002/14531.htm. Denying government access to oil revenues is one of four sanctions.

316. International Monetary Fund, Country Report no. 05/180, (26), www.imf. org/external/pubs/ft/scr/2005/cr05180.pdf.

317. World Bank, *Sudan: Stabilization and Reconstruction,* 66.

318. Dunstan M. Wai, ed., *The Southern Sudan: The Problem of National Integration* (London: Cass, c. 1973), 229–32.

319. See www.usinternet.com/users/helpssudan/SudanPeaceAgreement.htm (accessed March 17, 2006) for full text of this agreement.

320. Christine Batruch, "Oil and Conflict: Lundin Petroleum's Experience in Sudan," in *Business and Security: Public-Private Sector Relationships in a New Security Environment,* ed. Alyson J. K. Bailes and Isabel Frommelt (Oxford: Oxford University Press, 2004).

321. Ibid., paras. 5.0–5.8.

322. Protocol between the Government of Sudan (GOS) and the Sudan People's Liberation Movement/Army (SPLM/A) on the resolution of the Abeyei conflict, May 2004, www.usip.org/library/pa/sudan/abyei_05262004.pdf (accessed March 17, 2006).

323. Protocol between GOS and SPLM/A on the resolution of the conflict in southern Kardofan / Nuba Mountains and Blue Nile States, May 2004, para. 8.3, www.usip.org/library/pa/sudan/nuba_bnile_05262004.pdf (accessed March 17, 2006).

324. Traci D. Cook and Thomas O. Melia, *On the Threshold of Peace: Perspectives from the People of New Sudan,* National Democratic Institute for International Affairs, online report, 2004, www.ndi.org/ndi/library/1781_su_focus_122004.txt (accessed March 17, 2006).

325. The Implementation Modalities of the Wealth Sharing Agreement, Naivasha, December 31, 2004, www.usip.org/library/pa/sudan/cpa01092005/cpa_toc.html (accessed March 17, 2006).

326. Dana Esposito and Bathsheba Crocker, *To Guarantee the Peace: An Action Strategy for a Post-Conflict Sudan* (Washington, DC: Center for Strategic and International Studies, 2004), 10. Initial reports of new concession contracts being negotiated without open tendering conditions or disclosure on terms add weight to these concerns.

327. Framework Agreement on Wealth Sharing, Section B.

328. United Nations Mission in Sudan, *CPA Monitor,* online monthly report, February 2006, 18–19, www.unmis.org/english/cpaMonitor.htm (accessed March 17, 2006).

329. Lundin Petroleum sold these rights in 2003 but still holds rights in block 5B, where, in January 2005, work was suspended for security reasons.

330. Author interview, Washington, DC, December 2004.

331. According to Human Rights Watch, this was the government's intention: "The Khartoum Peace Agreement of 1997 was what the government needed to show foreign investors. It supposedly put an end to the war that had driven Chevron away; it provided 'African ex-rebel leaders' to meet with and assure oil investors that Chevron's bad experience would not be repeated; and it supplied ex-rebel forces with arms and ammunition to brush away rebel 'remnants' who might venture too close to the oilfields." See Rone, *Sudan, Oil and Human Rights,* 71.

332. Author interview, Washington, DC, December 2004.

333. Philip Ngunjiri, "White Nile to Prospect in Disputed Block Ba," *The East African* (Nairobi), February 7, 2006.

334. Author interview, Washington, DC, 2004.

335. Rone, *Sudan, Oil and Human Rights,* 260–78, 377–82, 223–36.

336. Ibid., 185–86.

337. Holt and Daly, *History of the Sudan,* 151.

338. Johnson, *Root Causes of Sudan's Civil Wars,* 130–35.

339. Ibid., 134.

340. John Harker, *Human Security in Sudan: The Report of a Canadian Assessment Mission* (Ottawa: Ministry of Foreign Affairs, 2000). John Harker led a Canadian government fact-finding mission to Sudan in 1999 to examine allegations of human rights abuses and the link between oil development and human rights violations, particularly in the forced removal of populations from areas around oil fields and oil-related development.

341. *Sudan, Oil and Human Rights.* Rone consolidates and extends information from a large number of previous reports issued by the organization. See also United

Nations, "Interim Report of the Special Rapporteur of the Commission on Human Rights," UN General Assembly Report A/57/326, August 2002, paras. 34–41, www.unhchr.ch/Huridocda/Huridoca.nsf/0/bfd92a8b2481e657c1256c5d003360c5/ $FILE/N0253192.pdf (accessed March 17, 2006).

342. Johnson, *Root Causes of Sudan's Civil Wars,* 164.

343. Harker, *Human Security in Sudan,* 11.

344. U.S. Department of State, "Country Report on Human Rights Practices: Sudan," February 2004, www.state.gov/g/drl/rls/hrrpt/2004/index.htm (accessed March 17, 2006). The following year's report noted, "Unlike in the previous year, there were no reports that the government had razed squatter and IDP dwellings in the oil-producing regions or that government and allied militia pursued a scorched-earth policy aimed at removing populations from the areas of oil pipelines and oil production." See U.S. Department of State, "Country Report on Human Rights Practices: Sudan," February 2005, www.state.gov/g/drl/rls/hrrpt/2005/61594.htm (accessed March 17, 2006).

345. Author interview, Washington, DC, December 2003.

346. Barrows Company, "World Petroleum Arrangements" (report prepared by a commercial online information service), www.barrowscompany.com. "No exploration expenditures of any kind shall be burden for cost recovery excepting exploration expenditures in the same development area of the Existing Oil Fields."

347. Author interviews, 2003–04.

348. Harker, *Human Security in Sudan,* 11–16.

349. The International Code of Ethics for Canadian Business was launched in 1997 for Canadian businesses operating abroad. It sets out a vision and discusses beliefs, values, and principles on community participation and environmental protection, human rights, business conduct, employee rights, and health and safety. Signatory companies commit to implement the code through the development of operational policies and practices consistent with the code. See www.cdp-hrc.uottawa.ca/globalization/busethics/codeint.html (accessed March 17, 2006).

350. See Talisman Energy's Web site for current and previous reports referred to here and below, www.talisman-energy.com/corporate_responsibility/cr_report.html (accessed March 17, 2006).

351. Talisman Energy, "2001 Corporate Social Responsibility Report," 14, www.talisman-energy.com/corporate_responsibility/cr_report.html.

352. Ibid., 17.

353. Ibid., 18.

354. See Talisman Energy, "2004 Corporate Social responsibility report," www.talisman-energy.com/corporate_responsibility/cr_report.html.

355. Talisman Energy, "2003 Corporate Social Responsibility Report," www.talisman-energy.com/corporate_responsibility/cr_report.html.

356. Rick Westhead, "Dangerous Liaisons," *Toronto Star,* February 20, 2006, www.thestar.com/NASApp/cs/ContentServer?pagename=thestar/Layout/Article_Type1&call_pageid=971358637177&c=Article&cid=1140304233434 (accessed March 17, 2006).

357. Author interview, December 2004.

358. Batruch, "Oil and Conflict."

359. The code of conduct can be found at Lundin Energy's Web site, www.lundin-petroleum.com/eng/code_of_conduct.php.

360. See http://www.lundin-petroleum.com/eng/operation_sudan.php (accessed March 17, 2006).

361. Batruch, "Oil and Conflict."

362. Rone, *Sudan, Oil and Human Rights,* 686–700.

363. Total, "Total Updates Block B Contractual Terms in Sudan in View of Possibly Resuming Operations Once Peace Restored," press release, December 2004, www.total.com/en/press/press_releases/pr_2004/041221_Sudan_block_b_5769.htm (accessed March 17, 2006).

364. Author interview, Washington, DC, December 2004.

365. Author interview, Washington, DC, December 2004.

366. For example, the Crisis Watch database maintained by the International Crisis Group, www.icg.org.

367. Barrows Company, "Listing of E&P Bid Evaluations," July 2004, www.barrowscompany.net/BBR.htm. Other "conflict areas" inviting bids at this time were Nepal, Afghanistan, Colombia, and the North Caucasus region of Russia.

368. Based on BP "Statistical Review of World Energy," June 2006, energy charting tool, www.bp.com/statisticalreview. Statistics for Europe refer to the European Union's fifteen members as of 2003. Note that data for Germany included in the totals refers to West Germany in 1970, and the unified Germany in 2003.

369. BP "Statistical Review of World Energy." Note that China is not yet a significant consumer of natural gas, although this is set to change as China secures contracts to import gas on a large scale from Russia and Asia-Pacific suppliers.

370. Energy Information Association, "International Energy Outlook," July 2005, www.eia.doe.gov/oiaf/ieo/highlights.html (accessed March 13, 2006).

371. An example is the leasing of a share of the Upper Zakhum oil field in Abu Dhabi to ExxonMobil in 2004. See U.S. Energy Information Administration, "Country Analysis Brief: United Arab Emirates," April 2005, www.eia.doe.gov/emeu/cabs/uae.html (accessed March 13, 2006).

372. Joseph E. Stiglitz, "The Resource Curse Revisited," *Jakarta Post*, August 12, 2004.

373. The term "Dutch disease" originated in the Netherlands in the 1970s after the discovery of North Sea gas.

374. Fradique de Menezes, "Creating a Stable Base for Transparency in São Tomé's Oil Sector" (speech made at Center for Strategic and International Studies conference, "Promoting Accountability and Transparency in Africa's Oil Sector," Washington, DC, March 30, 2004). For the English text of the Revenue Management Law (unofficial translation), see the Web site of the Earth Institute's São Tomé e Príncipe Advisory Project, Columbia University, www.earthinstitute.columbia.edu/cgsd/STP/index_oillaw.htm (accessed March 13, 2006).

375. Nancy Birdsall and Arvind Subramanian, "Saving Iraq from Its Oil," *Foreign Affairs* 83, no.4 (July–August 2004): 77–89; and Xavier Sala-Martin and Arvind Subramanian, "Addressing the Natural Resource Curse: An Illustration from Nigeria," IMF Research Department Working Papers, no. 03/39, July 2003.

376. The text of the World Bank's Governance and Economic Management Assistance Program for Liberia (GEMAP) can be found on http://siteresources.worldbank.org/LIBERIAEXTN/Resources/GEMAP.pdf (accessed March 13, 2006).

377. See the Earth Institute Web site for a description of the National Forum, www.earthinstitute.columbia.edu/cgsd/STP/index_forum.htm.

378. See the Revenue Watch Web site for links to reports on activities in Azerbaijan and other countries and regions, www.revenuewatch.org.

379. See the EITI Web site, www.eitransparency.org.

380. World Bank, "World Bank Group Board Agrees Way Forward on Extractive Industries Review," press release, no. 2005/50.IFC, August 3, 2004, http://web.world bank.org/WBSITE/EXTERNAL/NEWS/0,,contentMDK:20237406~menu PK:34463~pagePK:34370~piPK:34424~theSitePK:4607,00.html (accessed March 13, 2006).

381. International Monetary Fund, "Angola: 2003 Article IV Consultation—Staff Report," IMF Country Report no. 03/291, September 2003, www.imf.org/external/pubs/ft/scr/2003/cr03291.pdf (accessed March 13, 2006).

382. See, for example, U.S. Department of State, "U.S., G8 Building Partnerships to Fight Corruption," Fact Sheet, June 10, 2004, http://usinfo.state.gov/xarchives/display.html?p=washfile-english&y=2004&m=June&x=20040610171543liameruoy0.5136835&t=livefeeds/wf-latest.html (accessed March 13, 2006).

383. See the Web site of the Millennium Challenge Corporation, which oversees the Millenium Challenge Account, www.mca.gov.

384. Author interview, January 2003.

385. Author interview, January 2003.

386. Author interview, June 2003.

387. The approach is documented on the Web site of the Voluntary Principles of Security and Human Rights, www.voluntaryprinciples.org/news/index.php (accessed March 13, 2006).

388. Arguably there remains greater scope for companies to set the terms of their involvement in gas projects, especially those producing liquefied natural gas for export, because of high capital costs and complex technologies involved, leading to governments finding fewer companies in a position to compete for this business.

389. ChevronTexaco, "ChevronTexaco Awarded Extension to Block 0 Concession in Angola," press release, May 13, 2004, www.chevron.com/news/press/2004/2004-05-13.asp (accessed March 13, 2006).

Appendix
List of Acronyms

ACG	Azeri-Chirag-Guneshli
AIOC	Azerbaijan International Operating Company
ATCA	Alien Tort Claims Act
BBC	British Broadcasting Corporation
BOLCC	Basic Oil Laws and Concession Contracts
BTC	Baku-Tbilisi-Ceyhan
CDAP	Caspian Development Advisory Panel
CEPMLP	Centre for Energy, Petroleum and Mineral Law and Policy
CEPR	Centre for Economic Policy Research
CFA	Communauté Financiaire Africaine (currency of Chad)
CIA	Central Intelligence Agency
CNOOC	China National Overseas Oil Corporation
CNPC	China National Petroleum Corporation
CPA	Comprehensive Peace Agreement
CPI	Corruption Perceptions Index
CSR	Corporate Social Responsibility
EBRD	European Bank for Reconstruction and Development
EEZ	Exclusive Economic Zone
EIA	Energy Information Administration
EIR	Extractive Industries Review
EITI	Extractive Industries Transparency Initiative
EO	Executive Outcomes

ESAP	Environmental and Social Action Plans
ESIA	Environmental and Social Impact Assessment
Exim Bank	U.S. Export-Import Bank
FLEC	Front for the Liberation of the State of Cabinda
FLNA	National Liberation Front of Angola
FPSO	Floating Production, Storage, and Offloading vessel
FSU	Former Soviet Union
GDP	Gross Domestic Product
GEMAP	Governance and Economic Management Assistance Program
GNPOC	Greater Nile Petroleum Operating Company
GOS	Government of Sudan
GOSS	Government of Southern Sudan
HGA	Host Government Agreement
IEA	International Energy Administration
IFC	International Finance Corporation
IGAD	Intergovernmental Authority on Development
IIES	Institute for International Economic Studies
IMF	International Monetary Fund
IRIN News	Integrated Regional Information Networks
KUFPEC	Kuwait Foreign Petroleum Exploration Company
LNG	Liquefied Natural Gas
MASSOB	Movement for the Actualization of the Sovereign State of Biafra
MCA	Millennium Challenge Account
MEND	Movement for the Emancipation of the Niger Delta
MPLA	People's Movement for the Liberation of Angola
NATO	North Atlantic Treaty Organization
NGO	Nongovernmental Organization
NIOC	National Iranian Oil Company
NPC	National Petroleum Commission
OECD	Organisation for Economic Co-operation and Development
OGEL	Oil Gas and Energy Law
OPEC	Organization of the Petroleum Exporting Countries
OPIC	Overseas Private Investment Corporation
OSA	Oil Savings Account
OSCE	Organization for Security and Cooperation in Europe
PRGF	Poverty Reduction and Growth Facility
PRSP	Poverty Reduction Strategy Paper
PSA	Production-Sharing Agreement
PSP	Premier & Shell Pakistan

SOCAR	State Oil Company of Azerbaijan
SPLM	Sudan People's Liberation Movement
SPLM/A	Sudan People's Liberation Movement/Sudan People's Liberation Army
SPPRD	State Program on Poverty Reduction and Economic Development
SWAPO	South-West Africa People's Organization
TI	Transparency International
TPAO	National Oil and Natural Gas Company of Turkey
TSS	Transitional Support Strategy
UKCS	United Kingdom Continental Shelf
UN	United Nations
UNDP	United Nations Development Program
UNITA	National Union for the Total Independence of Angola
UNMIS	United Nations Mission in Sudan
USAID	United States Agency for International Development
USIP	United States Institute of Peace
WBCSD	World Business Council for Sustainable Development
WBG	World Bank Group
WSA	Wealth-sharing agreement

Bibliography

Ahmad, Ehtisan, and Eric A Mottu. *Oil Revenue Assignments: Country Experiences and Issues.* Washington, DC: International Monetary Fund Working Paper no. 02/203, 2002.

Alfonso, Juan Pablo Pérez. *Hundiéndonos en el excremento del Diablo.* Caracas: Editorial Lisbona, 1976.

Bailes, Alyson J. K., and Isabel Frommelt. *Business and Security: Public-Private Sector Relationships in a New Security Environment.* Oxford: Oxford University Press, 2004.

Barber, Karin. "Popular Reactions to the Petro-naira." *Journal of Modern African Studies* 20, no. 3 (1982).

BP. *Statistical Review of World Energy.* June 2006, www.bp.com.

Brinkman, Inge. *War and Identity in Angola: Two Case Studies.* Bordeaux, France: Lusotopie, 2003.

Burr, Millard J., and Robert O. Collins. *Africa's Thirty Years War: Libya, Chad and the Sudan, 1963–1993.* Boulder, CO: Westview, 1999.

Carley, Patricia. *Nagorno-Karabakh, Searching for a Solution.* A Peaceworks report. Washington, DC: United States Institute of Peace, 1998.

Catholic Relief Services. *Bottom of the Barrel: Africa's Oil Boom and the Poor.* Washington, DC: CRS, 2003.

Chabal, Patrick, et al. *A History of Postcolonial Lusophone Africa.* London: Hurst, 2002.

Collier, Paul, and Anke Hoeffler. "Greed and Grievance in Civil War." *Oxford Economic Papers* 56 (2004).

Collier, Paul, et al. *Breaking the Conflict Trap: Civil War and Development Policy.* Washington, DC: International Bank for Reconstruction and Development/World Bank, 2003.

De Waal, Thomas. *Black Garden: Armenia and Azerbaijan through Peace and War.* New York and London: New York University Press, 2003.

Deng, Francis M. *War of Visions, Conflict of Identities in the Sudan.* Washington, DC: Brookings Institution Press, 1995.

Esposito, Dana, and Bathsheba Crocker. *To Guarantee the Peace: An Action Strategy for a Post-Conflict Sudan.* Washington, DC: Center for Strategic and International Studies, 2004.

Gleijeses, Piero. *Conflicting Missions.* Chapel Hill, NC: University of North Carolina Press, 2002.

Guidolin, Massiano, and Eliana La Ferrara. *Diamonds Are Forever, Wars Are Not: Is Conflict Bad for Private Firms?* Centre for Economic Policy Research (CEPR), Discussion Paper no. 4668, October 2004, http://papers.ssrn.com/sol3/papers.cfm?abstract_id=631608.

Handelman, Don. "The Organization of Ethnicity." *Ethnic Groups* 1, 1977.

Hare, Paul. *Angola's Last Best Chance for Peace: An Insider's Account of the Peace Process.* Washington, DC: United States Institute of Peace, 1988.

Haufler, Virginia, et al. *Private Authority and International Affairs.* Albany: SUNY Press, 1999.

Hodges, Tony. *Angola from Afro-Stalinism to Petro-Diamond Capitalism.* Oxford: James Curry, 2001.

Holt, P. M., and M. W. Daly. *A History of the Sudan.* 5th ed. Harlow, UK: Longman, 2000.

Hughes, Helen. *From Riches to Rags: What Are Nauru's Options and How Can Australia Help?* St. Leonards, Australia: Centre for Independent Studies, Issue Analysis no. 50, 2004. Available at www.cis.org.au.

Hutchinson, Sharon. *Nuer Dilemmas, Coping with Money, War and the State.* Berkeley: University of California Press, 1996.

International Energy Agency / Organization for Economic Co-operation and Development. *Natural Gas Information 2005.* Paris, IEA/OECD, 2005.

Jensen, James T. *The Development of a Global LNG Market.* Oxford: Oxford Institute for Energy Studies, 2004.

Johnson, Douglas H. *The Root Causes of Sudan's Civil Wars.* Bloomington: Indiana University Press, 2003.

Karl, Terry Lynn. *The Paradox of Plenty: Oil Booms and Petro-States.* Berkeley and Los Angeles: University of California Press, 1997.

Klare, Michael. *Resource Wars: The New Landscape of Global Conflict.* 1st ed. New York: Henry Holt, 2001.

Leite, Carlos, and Jens Weidmann. *Does Mother Nature Corrupt? Natural Resources, Corruption, and Economic Growth.* Washington, DC: International Monetary Fund Working Paper, 1999. Available at www.imf.org/external/pubind.htm.

Leith, J. Clark. *Botswana—A Case Study of Economic Policy Prudence and Growth.* Washington, DC: World Bank Working Paper, August 1999.

Lesch, Ann Mosely. *The Sudan: Contested National Identities.* Bloomington: Indiana University Press, 1998.

Lesch, Ann Mosely. "Ethnic Conflict in the Sudan." *Encyclopedia of Modern Ethnic Conflicts.* Westport, CT: Greenwood, 2003.

Lynch, Dov. *Engaging Eurasia's Separatist States.* Washington, DC: United States Institute of Peace, 2004.

Mabeko-Tali, Jean-Michel. "La question de Cabinda." *Lusotopie,* 2001.

Meijer, Guus, ed. *From Military Peace to Social Justice? The Angolan Peace Process.* London: Conciliation Resources, 2004.

Nelson, Jane. *The Business of Peace.* London: Prince of Wales Business Leaders Forum; International Alert, Council on Economic Priorities, 2000.

Reinkka, Ritva, and Jakob Svenson. *Local Capture and the Political Economy of School Financing.* Centre for Economic Policy Research (CEPR); Institute for International Economic Studies (IIES), Policy Paper, April 2002. www.cepr.org/meets/wkcn/3/3508/papers/svensson.pdf.

Rone, Jemera. *Sudan, Oil and Human Rights.* New York: Human Rights Watch, 2003.

Ross, Michael. "How Do Natural Resources Influence Civil War? Evidence from Thirteen Cases." *International Organization* 58, no. 1 (2004).

Rothchild, Donald. *Managing Ethnic Conflict in Africa.* Washington, DC: Brookings Institution Press, 1997.

Sachs, Jeffrey D., and Andrew M. Warner. "The Curse of Natural Resources." *European Economic Review* 45 (2001).

Sala-i-Marta, Xavier, and Arvind Subramanian. *Addressing the Natural Resource Curse: An Illustration from Nigeria.* Washington, DC: IMF Working Paper no. 03/139, 25, 2003. See also Nancy Birdsall and Arvind Subramanian. "Oil Spoils: Iraq and the Post-Westphalian World." *Foreign Affairs* 83, no. 4 (2004).

Sidahmed, Abdel Salam. *Politics and Islam in Contemporary Sudan.* New York: St Martin's, 1996.

Smith, Eugene. "The New Condottieri and US Policy: The Privatization of Conflict and Its Implications." *Parameters* 32, no. 4 (Winter 2002–03).

Suberu, Rotimi T. *Federalism and Ethnic Conflict in Nigeria.* Washington, DC: United States Institute of Peace, 2001.

Tsalik, Svetlana. *Caspian Oil Windfalls: Who Will Benefit?* New York: Open Society Institute, 2003.

Wakeman-Linn, John, et al. *Managing Oil Wealth: The Case of Azerbaijan.* Washington, DC: International Monetary Fund, 2004.

Walter, Barbara F. "Does Conflict Beget Conflict? Exploring Recurrent Civil War." *Journal of Peace Research* 41, no. 3 (2004).

Wenger, Anton, and Daniel Möckli. *Conflict Prevention: The Untapped Potential of the Business Sector.* Boulder, CO: Lynne Rienner, 2003.

Wim, Dunstan M., ed. *The Southern Sudan and the Problems of National Integration.* London: Frank Cass, 1973.

Yergin, Daniel. *The Prize: The Epic Quest for Oil, Money and Power.* New York: Free Press, 1992.

Yongo-Bure, Benaiah. "Prospects for Socio-economic Development in the South." In *The Search for Peace and Unity in the Sudan.* Edited by Francis Deng and Prosser Gifford. Washington, DC: Wilson Center Press, 1987.

Index

A

Abuja Conferences
    revenue sharing and, 127
ACG project. *See* Azeri-Chirag-Guneshli project
Addis Ababa Agreement on the Problem of South Sudan
    ending of the first civil war, 119
    oil wealth distribution and, 120, 126
    Southern Regional People's Assembly, 126
    text, 188 *n*281
Africa. *See also specific countries and regions*
    international oil industry investment in, 15–16, 166 *n*11
    major African oil and gas producers (table), 16
    U.S. Department of State examination of the impact of oil wealth, 44
Ahmad, Ehtisan
    sub-national revenue sharing, 46, 171 *n*84
Alaska
    Alaska Permanent Fund, 46, 171 *n*85
    long-term contracts for oil companies, 27
    oil fund, 45
Alberta, Canada
    direct distribution of oil revenue, 46–47
    oil fund, 45
Algeria
    oil and gas production, 16
Aliev, Pres. Heydar
    Nagorno-Karabakh War and, 83

---

n preceding number indicates note

E

East Timor
    offshore exploration and, 18, 33
    oil resources, 3
EBRD. *See* European Bank for Reconstruction and Development
Ecuador
    alleged human rights abuses in, 59
EEZs. *See* Exclusive economic zones
Egypt
    oil and gas production, 16
    Sudan colonization and governance, 115, 117, 188 *n*270
EIR. *See* Extractive Industries Review
EITI. *See* Extractive Industries Transparency Initiative
Elf oil company
    support for the Front for the Liberation of Cabinda, 102
Enron scandal
    focus on corporate governance and corruption and, 57
Environmental and Social Action Plans
    monitoring of environmental and social impact in Azerbaijan, 89, 90, 181 *n*182
Environmental and social impact statements
    aim of, 63
    Azerbaijan and, 86–90
    description, 62–63, 155–156
    Equator Principles and, 60–61
    Sudan and, 135
EO. *See* Executive Outcomes
Equator Principles
    adoption by major financial institutions, 61
    financing process, 61
    social and environmental impact statements and, 60–61, 62
Equatorial Guinea
    international oil industry investment in, 15
    oil and gas production, 16, 143
    oil revenue as an incentive for conflict over control of the state, 42
Eritrea
    exclusive economic zone concessions, 145
ESAPs. *See* Environmental and Social Action Plans
Escuela Judicial
    Statoil support for, 68
ESIAs. *See* Environmental and social impact statements
European Bank for Reconstruction and Development
    Azerbaijan oil project financing, 88
    exploration and production financing, 26
Exclusive economic zones
    Angolan oil fields, 99

O

P

About the Author

Jill Shankleman is a sociologist by training, with a long-standing interest in the interaction of economic growth, rural communities, and conflict. She works as a consultant to corporations, international organizations, and nongovernmental organizations, focusing on the social and environmental impacts of large-scale investments in developing countries. During 2003–04 she was a senior fellow at the United States Institute of Peace. Jill Shankleman is based in Oxford, England, but likes to spend as much time as she can in Washington, D.C., and in remote communities seeking to come to terms with the welcome and unwelcome consequences of having oil-and-gas-industry neighbors.

Oil, Profits, and Peace:
Does Business Have a Role in Peacemaking?

This book is set in Adobe Garamond; the display type is Eurostile. The Creative Studio designed the book's cover. EEI Communications, Inc., made up the pages and prepared the index. The text was copyedited by Michael Carr and proofread by EEI.